A STUDENTS'
SURVIVAL
MANUAL

A STUDENTS'
SURVIVAL
MANUAL
or how to get an education
DESPITE IT ALL

Alan N. Schoonmaker

HARPER & ROW, PUBLISHERS
New York, Evanston, San Francisco, London

To my grandparents, Walter and Amy Wittemann
and my children, Erica and David

CONTENTS

14. A FINAL WORD   318

PREFACE

*The system is miserable, but there are better reactions
to it than passive compliance, sullen withdrawal, and
blind revolt.*

As an undergraduate and graduate student I became appalled at the
inefficiency and waste of the American higher educational system.
When I became a professor and had a chance to observe the system
from another perspective, I became even more disturbed. Obviously, it is not functioning very well, nor are students getting the
education they deserve.

Many other professors have come to the same conclusion and
have tried to change the system. They have written hundreds of
articles and books, conducted research, and served on countless
committees—but their efforts have had little effect.

For years, I was one of the reformers. I wrote articles and
letters to the editor, sent memos to the faculty, and worked on
various committees, but succeeded only in irritating the establishment. Finally, one of my memos struck a very sensitive nerve—
military influence on university policy—and I was fired *20 minutes*

after a powerful professor publicly objected to my criticism.[1]

I realized then what countless professors had realized before me—that the system cannot change very rapidly, that the men who control it run it for their own benefit and will violently resist any change. As a professor I can therefore best fulfill my responsibilities to students by helping them individually.

Most professors who come to this conclusion stop trying to change the system and concentrate on teaching their classes and advising individual students. This book is part of that tradition. It will not change the system, but it should help some students get more out of their college years.

It should help you to understand and to cope with the system, and it will focus on the problems *you* feel are important—such as studying for exams, finding competent professors (and avoiding incompetents), getting into graduate school, interviewing for jobs, living with parents, considering drugs, and dealing with sexual problems.

It will go beyond the trivia of the college guides (number of books in the library, year in which degrees were first granted, etc.) and provide some of the information you really need: how grading systems really work, how professors exploit students, why bureaucrats run the universities, how graduate schools select students, how the campus recruiters operate, and so on.

You have a right to this information, but you probably cannot get it now. High-school guidance counselors are so incompetent that commercial organizations can now charge huge fees to do their jobs. Student advisors in most universities are too busy, ill-informed, or uninterested to help their students.

Another, more ominous, factor prevents you from obtaining the information you need and deserve: the people who have the information—the professors and administrators—are not supposed to give it to students. We are allowed to write scholarly critiques or

---

[1]The professor in question had taken tens of thousands of dollars from the Navy. The formal decision on my contract was made a few weeks later, but immediately after the professor objected the acting dean told me it "probably" would not be renewed. This incident reveals an obvious fact that professors choose to ignore: politics and greed are as much a part of the universities as the corporations; powerful men can violate fundamental principles (such as academic freedom), and institutions will ignore morality to protect their finances.

even to offer utopian reform proposals, but they must be written for other professors. Writing or even speaking to students about the system is generally regarded as "unethical" or "unprofessional."

All groups have similar "ethical codes" to protect members from out-siders: doctors refuse to testify against each other in malpractice suits; the Mafia executes informers; the military courtmartials critics. Academia, which talks so much about "intellectual freedom," couldn't use such crude techniques, but it does use its own kinds of pressures to suppress dissent. In fact, academic censorship of certain kinds of ideas is much greater than the censorship exerted by executives—even though professors generally regard executives as reactionaries who demand conformity.

Deans and professors warned me not to write *A Students' Survival Manual*; they made it very clear that doing so would harm or destroy my career. After months of deliberation I decided to leave academia so that I could write this book. All censorship is abhorrent, but academic censorship is inexcusable.

I am particularly appalled by attempts to suppress this book because the American Management Association, which most professors regard as reactionary, has published two volumes of "an executives' survival manual." And The American Chamber of Commerce has published excerpts in its journal, *Nations' Business.* The actual titles were *Anxiety and the Executive* and *Executive Career Strategy,* but their purposes and approach were the same as this book's: they analyzed the system, showed how it affected executives, and told them how to cope with it. When confronted by the fact that the "reactionaries" have published the same sort of book that the "liberals" have tried to suppress, I must ask the obvious question: who really believes in intellectual freedom?

The freedom to criticize does not, however, guarantee that a book will be useful, and my basic purpose is not to criticize or even to describe the system; *it is to help students to solve their problems.* Description and criticism are means to that end, not ends in themselves. You have to understand the system so that you can get the most out of your college years. If you understand it, you can use the system to help you solve your problems, especially the crucial ones of learning who you are and where you are going.

These problems have never been easy, but because our society has changed so rapidly, they are especially difficult today. You know how hard they are. You can recall the endless bull sessions, the lonely hours you have lain in bed wondering, the causes you have espoused and then rejected. You know that you must come to terms with an irrational educational system and prepare to enter an even more irrational society. You must resist pressures your parents cannot understand and make decisions on issues they do not even recognize.

Most important of all, you must develop a style of living which is uniquely your own, which expresses your individuality without alienating you from other people. It is not easy to be a student today, and it is very hard to develop that style, but I hope this book provides some help.[2]

ACKNOWLEDGMENTS

I would like to thank Professors Vroom and Aiken for criticizing portions of the manuscript; Mrs. Khan, Mrs. Van Aerschot, and Miss Neesen for typing the manuscript; and my wife for her moral support.

Alan N. Schoonmaker
Louvain, Belgium
January 1971

[2]Black students may be disappointed because this book does not discuss their special problems. The reason for this omission is not motivation, but ignorance. I am sympathetic, but, having worked in lily white schools, I don't know anything. Since enough ignorant people (both black and white) are giving you advice, I shall keep quiet.

A STUDENTS'
SURVIVAL
MANUAL

YOU'RE STUCK
WITH THE SYSTEM

"The more things change, the more they
remain the same."

French folk saying

The system[1] is archaic, inefficient, and inhuman, but you're stuck with it. Professors will write scholarly critiques; editors will demand reforms; students will demonstrate; and militants will even kidnap a few deans; but, when the noise dies down, the system will remain intact —and it will still be archaic, inefficient, and inhuman.

There may be a few token changes—a few black faces, occasional meetings between students and administrators, or a slightly revised curriculum—but the system itself will continue. It will continue because all the forces which created it are still operating, and many of them are becoming even more powerful. Critiques, editorials, and demonstrations may make people feel righteous and important, but they have not changed the system in the past and will not change it in the future because they do not affect these controlling forces. You

---

[1]The purpose of this chapter is to help you realize that you must cope with the system *as it is*. If you already agree that the system will not change very rapidly or are uninterested in changing it, you may want to skip this chapter.

1

are going to live in the system for a few years and should understand why it will not change very much.[2]

SOCIAL INERTIA

The most basic force preventing change is plain old social inertia. People and institutions have always resisted change, and social systems have always changed very slowly. For example, lectures became obsolete with the invention of the printing press 500 years ago, but they are still the core of nearly every educational system. Inertia operates in all social systems, regardless of their purpose or form of organization. The American South is still segregated more than 100 years after the Civil War and more than 15 years after the Supreme Court Decision. The Russians still encounter massive resistance to collectivized agriculture more than 50 years after the Communist Revolution and nearly 40 years after they liquidated the Kulaks. Every corporation has outdated departments and procedures, and the United States Government even has an office for Yellow Fever Control—50 years after the disease was conquered.

Academia has changed more slowly than most social systems because it is extremely traditional, and tradition is the most powerful form of social inertia. Most of our policies and rituals are justified not on logical grounds but on the grounds that we have always done things that way. We wear caps and gowns and go through the yearly graduation ritual because it is part of our tradition. We ignore the knowledge explosion and label a man as "educated" after four years and 120 odd credits because these are the traditional requirements for a Bachelor's Degree. We have Departments, Deans, credits, transcripts, exams, textbooks, etc., because they are part of our tradition, and we are unwilling to examine their value or relevance.

THE IRON LAW OF OLIGARCHY

Passive social inertia is not the only or the most powerful force resisting change. Professors make pious speeches about modernizing educa-

---

[2]Exceptions can be cited to each of the principles discussed here, but they are quite rare. Furthermore, even if one finds a few exceptions, he cannot change the system very much because the status quo is maintained by the combined weight of *all* these forces.

tion, but they *want* to preserve the present system, and they have done everything they can to prevent change. They have done so because they care more about their pay, power, and privileges than your education. They have therefore organized the universities not to improve education but to protect their own interests. Most students feel that they and the faculty are on the same side, fighting against reactionary administrators, but the professors are the major conservative force.

> When there is a movement toward reforming in a college, it is the collective faculty who usually seem to be dragging their feet. . . . Faculties have fostered an in-group spirit, built up the tradition of faculty prerogatives, and installed the machinery of campus democracy. These are the very things that now make change very difficult. . . . Faculties sometimes go so far in protecting their professional status or in using their professional status to satisfy their desires for security and advancement of their own interests that they neglect the legitimate needs and aspirations of the society.[3]

That is not nearly so severe an indictment as it appears to be. In an abstract, ethical sense this kind of behavior is, of course, inexcusable. Professors and administrators (to a lesser extent) have violated their trust. But a student of history compares men not to some ideal but to other men, and it is painfully clear that *all* organizations are run for the benefit of the people who control them.

Michels, a very famous social scientist, called this principle "The Iron Law of Oligarchy." If we translate it into simple, nonacademic English, the law states that the people who control organizations are primarily concerned with retaining their control and privileges and will sacrifice the purposes of the organization to do so. The law applies to every kind of organization—educational, military, political, charitable, even religious. Armies spend billions on expensive military toys, officers' clubs, golf courses, PXs, and other things which are unrelated to the national defense. The Brazilian army even suspended the constitution so that they could punish a congressman who asked young ladies to snub officers until democracy was restored. The heads of the Russian Communist Party have repeatedly shown that they are more

[3]Nevitt Sanford, "Higher education as a social problem," in Nevitt Sanford (ed.), *College and Character*. New York: Wiley, 1964, p. 10–12.

interested in their own power than in world revolution or the economic development of other Communist nations. Managers of publicly owned corporations pay themselves lavish salaries and fly around in company jets (which are usually unmarked so that stockholders will not know where their money is going). Congressmen use the taxpayers' money to get reelected. Popes have fought wars, impoverished their people, and violated church doctrine to increase their wealth and power. The March of Dimes was threatened with extinction when the polio vaccines were developed, but the leaders preserved the organization (and their salaries, power, and privileges) by completely changing the purpose of the organization (to birth defects). Inasmuch as leaders of all other organizations use their power for their own interests, it is naive to expect academicians to act differently.

THE IRRESISTIBLE BUREAUCRATS

Even if demonstrations or other pressures should force changes at the top, the universities still would not change very much or very rapidly. The bureaucrats—the registrars, administrative assistants, controllers, etc.—would still control day-to-day operations, and all bureaucrats are notoriously resistant to change.

Bureaucrats, regardless of where they work, care very little about the overall purposes of their organizations. They want to preserve their little empires and run their operations with a minimum of disruption. Any change—regardless of how good it may be for the organization or the people it should serve—is perceived as a threat, and they will undercut policies, conceal information, and mislead their superiors to protect themselves and their positions.

Our State Department bureaucracy has resisted several Secretaries of State and frustrated countless Congressional and Presidential investigations. "In Weimar, Germany the Social Democratic Party, which held majority power from 1918 to 1920, was not able to make fundamental changes in the power and economic structures. . . . the bureaucrats played a major role in obstructing changes." George Lansbury, a leader of the British Labor Party, noted: "All through the life of the late [1929–1931 Labor] government Treasury officials obstructed and hindered the Ministers in their work." The radical government of Saskatchewan was undercut by its conservative civil servants who continued the reactionary procedures, changed the intent of new laws and regulations through administrative procedures, and influenced cabinet ministers to adopt policies which would "maintain the stability of their departments and their own positions."[4]

The bureaucrats can maintain their policies and positions because they are the only people who know how the organization operates, and they remain in office despite changes at the top. Ministers, Congressmen, Professors, and College Presidents come and go; they have only the vaguest idea of how things are done; and they really don't care about procedures. The bureaucrats, however, care very much about them, and they will resist any policies which require changes in these procedures, or in their own habits and positions. Inasmuch as Presidents, Cabinet Ministers, and the Congress, who are relatively permanent and possess legitimate authority, cannot overcome bureaucratic resistance, it is foolish to believe that students and other critics, who have neither legitimacy nor permanence, can materially change the universities.

THE ECONOMICS OF MEDIOCRITY

You get a poor education from American universities for exactly the same reason you get poor cars from GM, Ford, and Chrysler—quality costs money that the organizations don't want to spend. And they don't want to spend it because people won't pay for quality. To provide a quality education professors would have to spend a great deal of time with individual students, time that they could use to build their reputations by doing research, time the universities must pay for. Universities and professors therefore prefer to march 40, or 100, or 1000 students into a room to hear a lecture.

Lectures are almost completely useless, but they are very profitable. At Columbia, for example, some lecture courses gross well over $50,000 per semester, but they cost the same amount of professorial time as a reading course or seminar that would bring in only a few hundred. Because nearly every school has serious financial problems, lectures are a very attractive source of revenue. They are especially attractive because universities lose money on most other classes. Tui-

[4]R.K. Merton *et al.* (eds.), *Reader in Bureaucracy.* New York: Free Press.

tion covers one-third to one-half the total cost of instruction (an indication of the public's unwillingness to pay for education).

Research, on the other hand, makes a profit. Research grants pay professors' salaries (especially their summer salaries), and universities make a very nice profit by adding on an "overhead" charge which can be more than 50% of their direct costs. Research also builds prestige which brings in gifts, endowment funds, support from the legislatures, and good students who will contribute to the university after they become wealthy.

Inasmuch as research yields prestige and profits, while teaching —especially good teaching—loses money without providing prestige, it is not very surprising that research is emphasized and teaching is downgraded.

Both the universities and the automobile companies can, however, make a very reasonable defense for their policies. They do not provide quality because people will not buy quality. The foundations, corporations, military, and legislatures are willing to pay for research, but very few people would pay the price of quality education. Since you and your parents do not value quality education highly enough to pay for it, you must accept some of the responsibility for the present situation. You cannot expect a Rolls-Royce for the price of a Chevrolet.

THE ACADEMIC REWARD SYSTEM

The academic salary and prestige system is closely related to these economic factors, and it clearly indicates that teaching is not valued very highly. This evaluation is a very powerful obstacle to reform. Most research schools pay higher salaries (about $14,000 for 12 months) to beginning professors than the small liberal arts colleges pay to their *department heads.* Big-name researchers can earn well over $50,000 per year from salary, consulting, and other sources, but the median salary for all professors is well below $10,000 per year (and for nonresearchers it is probably around $8,000). At the nonresearch schools, the faculty, in effect, subsidizes the students' education by working for very low salaries.

Research is also much more prestigious than teaching; in fact, it is the primary source of professorial prestige. No one but the students (who have no power) knows how well we teach, but everyone can read our research reports. Publications earn the respect of our colleagues, higher salaries, opportunities to speak, to consult, and to travel, as well as offers from other institutions. Teaching earns nothing at all except the fleeting gratitude of the students and a sense of contribution.

Perhaps that should be enough for us. Perhaps we should be above caring about money and prestige, but we are not. No principle of human behavior is more firmly supported than that people take actions that lead to rewards. In a materialistic, status-conscious society such as ours, money and prestige are very powerful rewards, and it is naive to expect us to ignore them.

THE UNBRIDGEABLE GAP

Despite all these pressures, many professors sincerely want to help you become educated—but very few succeed. Good intentions are not enough, and we fail because we simply do not understand you. We do not know what you want and need, nor do we know how to communicate with you.

Part of our problem is simply the generation gap. Your parents don't understand you either, and most of us belong, chronologically or psychologically, to your parents' generation. But there is an even more basic problem: we are basically different from you, your parents, and most other Americans. *Americans are doers; we are thinkers.* We want to understand things—not because understanding will help us to do anything, but because we get our primary satisfaction from understanding. Theory is not irrelevant to us; it is the center of our lives and careers. We do not regard history, footnotes, and precise definitions as trivial; they are important because they help us to analyze ideas and events and to place them into a larger perspective. We feel uncomfortable with isolated and concrete examples, and we constantly strive to abstract general principles and to relate events to larger trends.[5]

We became professors because we had these habits and tastes. We enjoyed studying and liked professors who had us wrestle with abstract ideas. When we became professors, we simply assumed that you

---

[5]The professorial desire to look for general principles is even evident in this nonscholarly book. Instead of dealing with universities in isolation, I have used principles discovered in other organizations to support my arguments.

wanted what we had wanted when we were students. We therefore copy the approaches of our favorite professors, assign the books we enjoyed reading, and discuss the topics we find interesting.

Unfortunately, these topics and books seem dull, impractical, and irrelevant to you. Most of you are doers, not thinkers. You regard understanding as a means to an end, not an end in itself. You want facts, not theories; guides to action, not rules for abstract analysis; solutions to practical problems, not a historical perspective or a sense of abstract relatedness. And we cannot give you these things because we don't understand or care about them.

The gap between us has always troubled me, but two recent experiences showed me how large this gap really is. One of my colleagues, who owns a very successful marketing company, was invited to my entrepreneurship class to discuss the marketing problems the students would face when they began their own companies. He did not, however, analyze their problems or discuss the general principles of marketing in small businesses; he simply told one story after another of the successes and failures of his firm. After several unsuccessful attempts to get him to abstract some general principles from his experiences, I sat back, angry and rather bored. But then I noticed that the students were fascinated! As a professor I had felt that his presentation was inadequate—but there the students were, leaning forward, listening to every word, and obviously learning much more from him than they did from me.

The second incident was even more upsetting. A group of professors worked very hard on our reading list for an undergraduate course, selecting articles we thought were well-written, interesting, and important. We deliberately selected material which we felt was *not* overly academic. However, the course evaluation forms indicated that the students felt that most of the readings were poorly written, dull, and irrelevant.

Incidents like this are so unpleasant that many professors stop listening to their students. They come to feel that nothing will satisfy the students, and they simply ignore student's complaints. As one professor put it: "When the students start complaining, I turn my hearing aid off."

Some professors are so threatened by these complaints that they justify their indifference by regarding all student complaints as juvenile emotionalism or by rationalizing that "students don't know what is good for them." A few professors go a step further and say that we *should not* try to understand or to respond to these complaints and needs because our job is to "raise the student to our level." This attitude is summarized by the very common remark that the professor who speaks to the students in their own language about the problems they find important is "selling out to the students."

THE AMERICAN CULTURE

Not all of the obstacles to change are within the universities; some are part of the surrounding culture. Americans—despite constant references to our revolutionary heritage—are a profoundly conservative people. We like things pretty much the way they are and are afraid to make changes, especially rapid and radical changes.

The student activists are condemned by most Americans not because they have analyzed the educational system, but because they dislike anyone who rocks the boat. This attitude is, of course, rather immoral, but whether they are right or wrong, ignorant or informed, cowardly or courageous, the conservatives have virtually all of the power in this country. We have never had a radical President; there are virtually no radical Congressmen; and there is no possibility whatsoever of seeing a shift away from conservatism in the near future.

In addition to being conservative, America is also very anti-intellectual. Relatively few Americans *ever* read a serious book after they leave school; college alumni rarely even remember, much less discuss, the books and topics they studied in college; *The New York News* has twice the circulation of any other newspaper; professors, writers, and journalists have less influence in the United States than in almost any other country; very few political leaders are well educated; and in the 1968 Presidential elections George Wallace won millions of votes with his attacks on "pointy-headed intellectuals."

Although Americans don't like or trust intellectuals they want their children to go to college—not to get an education, but to get a degree so they can move up in the world. We are therefore inundated with millions of students. The overcrowding problem is increased by society's demands that we perform a baby-sitting function. The shortage of jobs for teenagers has forced the colleges to become the modern equivalent of the WPA and CCC, a place to keep young people off the streets and out of the labor market.

Overcrowding prevents educational reform in many ways. Classes *have* to be large; there is simply no way to provide reading courses and personal contact to 7 million students. Newer, larger facilities must be built, tightening the money squeeze. Administrations have to be bureaucratic because they cannot deal with all these people on an individual basis. Professors become more powerful and irresponsible because they have a sellers' market; if pressure is placed upon them to teach or to do anything they don't want to do, they simply move to another institution.

Another characteristic of Americans, their insistence on tangible benefits, is a serious obstacle to educational improvements. By its very nature education is intangible; no one can measure the quality of an education, or even be sure that he "has" one. Students may learn more from free reading and informal conversations than they do in class, but classes and credits are much more tangible, and any fool can understand the formulae that dominate American education: 45 hours in class = 3 credits; 128 credits = 1 degree.

This need for tangibility also reduces communication between students and faculty. The things we have to offer—a sense of history, a larger perspective, an understanding of the world and one's place in it—don't have much market value. But anyone can count the number of dollars college graduates earn, and it is easy to see how much better they live. Professor Harold Burstyn once found how powerful this emphasis upon tangibility really is. He asked a group of high-school honor students: "Would you rather have college tuition or a car and other goods which cost the same amount?" Everyone preferred the tuition, an apparently encouraging sign. But further questioning revealed that they weren't interested in an education, but in the cash value of a college degree: "We would rather go to college because then we can make more money and get even more goods."

THE HIGH-SCHOOL

This attitude is, of course, related to the most obvious and most frequently discussed obstacle to reform at the higher educational levels —the high-schools. The high-schools are so utterly inadequate that we cannot accomplish very much at the college level. We must spend countless hours on basic skills and knowledge the students did not learn in high-school, and we must struggle with the attitudes they did learn.

The skill problems are more easily recognized. *Most* college freshmen are semiliterates who can hardly read or write. (They are also semiliterates when they graduate, but that is another problem.) They have only the vaguest conception of English grammar and cannot construct an adequate sentence, paragraph, or essay. Furthermore, they usually don't want to learn how to write. Some professors try to teach writing by correcting English and stylistic errors on term papers, but many students feel that doing so is illegitimate, that only their "ideas" should be considered, because "content is more important than style or grammar."

Even more shocking, most college students literally do not know how to read. They have learned how to pick up facts which they can regurgitate on examinations, but they usually do not grasp an author's purpose or the methods he used to achieve that purpose. They also do not know how to read rapidly, an absolutely essential skill.

Because so many students are unprepared for college-level work, we spend an enormous amount of time on high-school subjects—basic English, introductory foreign languages, surveys of history, economics, political science, etc. This time is, of course, taken out of the 128 hours that "equal an education," leaving us little time for college-level studies.

Students do, however, learn something in high-school. They learn that education is a bore which one tolerates to increase his earning potential, that the system is based on coercion, that their role is essentially passive and dependent, that they should regurgitate facts instead of thinking, and that their major problem is to "psyche out" the teacher. These attitudes and the expectations related to them are a serious obstacle to change. Students do not like the system, but they have learned to live with one set of rules and usually object if a professor tries to change them.

Most professors have experimented with different teaching methods—such as reading courses, group projects, seminars, video tapes, programmed instruction and pass or fail grades. Surprisingly, the students usually react negatively. Perhaps the new methods will help them to learn more, but they do not know what to expect or how grades will be assigned or how long papers should be. Therefore, they become anxious and exert pressures for more structure and certainty.

When this happens, we usually feel hurt or angry. We have tried to respond to student complaints and demands, but the students have rejected us. After a few attempts most of us stop trying new methods and do the easiest, most "natural" thing—lecture and get our satisfactions from our research and the few students who come to us on their own.

THE UNCLEAR MANDATE

A somewhat different set of pressures deserves separate analysis. Not all the cultural forces are conservative. Some Americans do want changes in the educational system, but their demands are incompatible with each other. We live in a pluralistic society, with many power blocks; and each block wants different things from the educational system. Some want a more practical education, others a more "liberal" one. Some want a more "modern" and "relevant" system, others a reemphasis on the classics. Some feel that technical subjects are the wave of the future; others that a man should learn these subjects after he graduates. Some want to return to the old virtues: religion, restraint, conventionality; others want us to help students to "do their own thing."

In other words, the conflicts and questions that face this nation are reflected in its demands on the educational system. These demands push us in so many directions that we do not know what to do. How can the educators get in step with a country that does not know where it is going?

In this situation inaction is inevitable. When people face incompatible demands, the simplest, safest, and most natural decision is to do nothing. And that is essentially what the educators have done.

THE CASE AGAINST VIOLENT DEMONSTRATIONS

All of the forces mentioned thus far will limit the effectiveness of any student demonstrations, but there are even more powerful arguments against *violent* demonstrations. These arguments are pragmatic, not moralistic. The system certainly should be changed, and the frustrations which produce violence are certainly understandable. But violent demonstrations just have not done any good, and they have often led to greater repression and rigidity.

Student militants, like militants everywhere, have overlooked one of the most basic principles of history: real revolutions rarely occur. Most violent revolutions are crushed; the ones that succeed result only in a change of autocrats and bureaucrats. One power elite is deposed, but a new one takes over—and the people's situation remains the same. The Russians threw out the Czars, but got Lenin and then Stalin. The French deposed the Bourbons, but lived through a reign of terror and turned to Napoleon. The Cubans revolted against Batista, only to suffer under Castro. The Berkeley students helped remove Clark Kerr, but got Dr. Hitch, a former bureaucrat with the Rand Corporation, a subsidiary of the Air Force. At San Francisco State the students forced out a nonentity (even his name escapes me) only to get Hayakawa, academia's answer to Mayor Daley.

Violent demonstrations are an attempt to increase student power and force changes, but they frighten other power centers and cause them to act repressively. Since these other centers have much more power than the students, there is no doubt at all who will win in a face-to-face confrontation. Many Californians, including some regents, wanted to replace Clark Kerr with a *general,* and the name Curtis Lemay, was commonly mentioned. (Can you imagine the military running loose in a university?—bombing the student-held administration building, breaking up SDS meetings, censoring classes, and forcibly shaving students?) Millions of Americans saw Daley's policemen go wild, but polls showed that three out of every four felt that he had acted properly. And let us not forget that George Wallace, who was helped immeasurably by the reaction against student demonstrations, almost gained the balance of power in this country.

We are repelled by Daley, Wallace, Lemay, and the people who support them, but they have the power. And, when we get beneath the surface, they are not much worse than some militant leaders—the Cleavers, Savios, and Haydens. They all advocate violent repression of those who disagree with them, and they all use their followers to satisfy their own desires for power. I would hate to be in a country or a university run by George Wallace, but it would not be worse than one run by Eldridge Cleaver.

The simple, obvious fact is that freedom can exist only in a stable, essentially bourgeois society. When stability is threatened, dictators take over, and it does not matter very much whether they are from the right or the left. They immediately wipe out freedom, both academic and personal, and people are worse off than they had been. Mussolini and Hitler wiped out the intellectuals and supressed academic freedom; Lenin, Stalin, Mao, and Castro did the same thing, and the students lost everything the American students are demanding—personal freedom, participation in decisions, a chance to explore ideas, etc.

We professors are no bargain. We are unaware of your needs, unable to respond to them, and more than a little incompetent. But we are *infinitely* better than the men who would replace us after a violent revolution—whether this revolution "succeeds" or "fails." It may be boring and wasteful to listen to our lectures and to read our books, but it is much more rewarding than listening to a steelworker's recitation of the thoughts of Mao, or reading the biography and philosophy of George Corley Wallace.

I therefore suggest that you play it cool. Demand your rights, protest injustice, even picket—but don't take over the administration building and kidnap the deans, don't sacrifice your cause to your emotions. Your complaints are legitimate; your cause is just; and militant methods may even be justified. But violent demonstrations just increase the forces of repression. The next time you feel like grabbing a building or a dean, remember the public support for Mayor Daley, the 10 million people who voted for Wallace, and the 30 million people who put Nixon and Agnew into office. The militants helped these men, and America now stands on the verge of an era of savage repression. Therefore, if you really want to change the system, recognize that any change will be slow and small; understand the forces which resist change and take the actions which will be most effective, not the ones that make you feel most heroic.

This has not been a very inspiring chapter. It has dealt with harsh realities, not noble sentiments; described an undesirable system, but said that you can't change it very much; and argued that some student heroes are no better than the men they seek to depose. These are not very uplifting ideas; it is much more exciting to demand immediate changes and to "man the barricades." But the barricades don't solve the problems. In the final analysis my job as an educator is to communicate to you my beliefs about the truth, and your job as a student is to cast aside the emotional habits of your youth, to separate my opinions from my facts, and to develop the brains and courage to face the truth about yourself and the world you live in. Doing so is an essential part of growing up—and growing up is, of course, your primary task during your college years.

A STRATEGY
FOR SURVIVAL

If the system will not change, and violent demonstrations are harmful, what should you do? Conform passively? Ignore the system and get your satisfaction from football, sex, or drugs? Concentrate on getting a degree? Drop out and find a job?

Although you have more than enough provocation to take any of these actions, none of them will solve your problem. They will frustrate your basic need to grow, and they will deprive you of an education (such as it is). You must therefore find or develop a better strategy, one which solves *all* your problems. It must allow you to enjoy your college years, provide the training and academic degree that you need to make a living, and help you to grow and to develop all of your potentialities. And, since the system will not change and you have no place else to go, your strategy must do all of these things *within* the constraints imposed by the system.

DEPENDENCE, COUNTERDEPENDENCE, AND INDEPENDENCE

Your strategy must help you to become independent of the system, and able to act freely and intelligently within the academic system and the rest of the world you live in. Many people never become independent. They respond to external pressures instead of controlling their own lives. They take the easy way out by letting other people and the system make their decisions.

Their professors tell them what to read; their friends tell them what to wear; everyone tells them what to believe and what to think. They are "well-adjusted." They fit in. They get good grades, are popular with other people, and are sought by the corporations.

But there is no core to them; they are hollow, empty, and meaningless. They have copped-out, given up their humanity for the fleeting security of fitting in. They have escaped uncertainty and aloneness by allowing other people to make their decisions, but they have created the far greater uncertainty and aloneness of losing themselves.

Other people are so frightened of losing themselves, of being dominated by other people or the system, that they spend most of their time and energy proving their "independence." They rebel. They wear beards, argue with professors, advocate or even practice revolution.

Doing these things "proves" they are free—but the proof is illusory, and the freedom is a fraud. They are no freer than the man who conforms passively to the system. They are not free to choose, to obey some rules and to break others; they must prove their independence by breaking *all* the rules. The system, therefore, dominates them just as much as it dominates the conformist.

True independence does not depend on what you wear or how often you bathe or shave. A man can be as free or as dominated in a Brooks Brothers suit as in a dirty sweat shirt and sandals. The important thing is not what you wear, but who you are and what you do.

The independent person makes his own decisions and controls his own life. He understands the world he lives in and knows what he wants from it. He can distinguish between important and trivial issues, and does not squander his time or energy on meaningless, self-destructive protests about trivialities. But, when the chips are down, when the issues are important, he is courageous enough to take a position and smart enough to do so without destroying himself.

It is obviously much easier to be dependent or counterdependent than it is to be independent. You simply yield to your impulses and conform or rebel against the system. Some people even do both at different times. Independence requires much more thought, work, and courage.

You must resist your impulses to yield passively or to revolt blindly; you must analyze yourself and the world, decide what is really important to you, and take positions on the important issues. It is not easy, but if you can do it, you are your own man, controlling your own life, rather than responding to external pressures.

Many students have told me that they cannot act independently because the pressures against them are too great. They feel that they have to work so hard to survive that they have no time left to pursue their own interests or to make their own decisions. Or they are afraid that trying to act independently will result in lower grades. But that is a cop-out.

You do have some choices, and, for your own sense of selfhood, you have to make them. If you let the system make all your decisions, you will not get much from college, and you will prepare yourself for a life of bland mediocrity. Pressures are a fact of life, and they will grow *more* severe as you grow older. If you cannot assert your independence now, what will you do when you have a wife, three children, and a mortgage, and your boss tells you to do something you abhor? What will you do if your girlfriend or her mother start arranging a wedding that you don't want?

These pressures are greater than the ones you face in college. In fact, college is a relatively low-cost, low-pressure environment (even if you don't think so now). You can make mistakes without paying excessive penalties. If you take the wrong course or irritate a professor, the cost might be a poor grade or some wasted time, a rather trivial penalty. Because mistakes are relatively inexpensive, you can try out new roles and strategies. You can try to define yourself by putting yourself in a different situation. You can learn *how* to assert your independence by making decisions.

If you do not learn *how* to act independently in college you will probably never learn, and other people will make your decisions for the rest of your life. Some girl or boy will decide whom you will marry. The placement office will decide which companies you interview. Advertising will decide what you buy. Your bosses will decide what you do and where you live.

Then, someday when you are 35 or 40 you will lie in bed wondering: "How in the world did I ever end up here?" Then it will hit you: you will feel the blind panic of the trapped rat and look desperately for ways to escape. But it will be too late.

TAKE AN ACTIVE ROLE

To get the most from your college years, you must invest much more than your money and time. You must commit yourself and take an active role in your own education. The system will demand its due, and you will have to do a lot of Mickey Mouse work, but you do have much more freedom than you think.

Most students do not use this freedom. They respond passively to the system and then complain that it dehumanizes them. They try to get an education the way a baby gets its milk—by demanding to be fed. But demands don't work because no one can give you an education. You have to get it for yourself.

The last paragraph is rather unfair. It blames you for something which is primarily our fault. You would probably accept this responsibility and take a more active role if you knew how to do so, but we haven't taught you. In fact, we have taught you to be passive. For years we have been coercing and manipulating you; you have had to respond to so many pressures that you may not know how to act on your own.

A major purpose of this book is to help you to overcome the habits that the system has already developed in you, to help you to assert your natural desire to be more active by showing you *how* you can act more independently. The remainder of this chapter outlines several general principles which will be developed much more fully in later chapters.

Analyze Yourself

The very first thing you must do to act independently is to analyze yourself. You must find out who you are and what you want before you can go out and get it. Self-analysis has never been easy, and it is especially difficult today. You must adjust to so many conflicting pressures and present so many different images that you may have trouble separating your self from your roles, the core of your personality from the masks you wear.

The next chapter *("Who are You?")* focuses directly on this issue, and many other chapters show you how to learn more about yourself when you make critical decisions—such as deciding whether to go to graduate school, or getting your first job.

Analyze the System

You should also analyze the system. It contains many more constraints and opportunities than most students realize, and, if you understand them, you can work around the constraints and take advantage of the opportunities.

The professors are, of course, the greatest resource and, at times, the greatest constraint. We can be a guide, information source, model, and mentor—if you know how to approach us. If you do not, we become just another obstacle in your path, another set of pressures you must adjust to.

Administrators are bureaucratic, but there are ways to get faster, more effective action from them. Librarians are fuss-budgets, but they are also superb sources of information and guidance. Diversity within each school and between different schools presents enormous opportunities, but most students never take advantage of them. They are in a gigantic cafeteria, with hundreds of options, but, because they don't know how to act, they end up eating tasteless left-overs.

Understanding the system is so important that Chapter 4 is devoted to general background material, and system analysis is a recurrent theme throughout the rest of the book.

TAKE WHAT WE CAN OFFER

It is much more intelligent to take what we can offer than it is to insist that we offer something else. Perhaps that something else is better, perhaps we should be more relevant, practical, and down to earth, but we are not. Like all other men we have our limitations, and we can offer only what we have within ourselves.

Furthermore, what we offer is not that bad. We don't offer it very well, because we don't really know how to teach, but the "product" is much more valuable than you think it is. Detachment, objectivity, perspective, a sense of history, and a sensitivity to relatedness may not be so attractive as practical skills or social involvement, but they are far from worthless. They can help you to make sense of the world and to relate yourself to it.

You can castigate us for "irrelevance" because we do not focus on current events or practical problems, but we can help you to realize that these "new" problems and ideas are not new at all. The threat of nuclear destruction is overwhelming, but total wars have been the rule, not the exception, through most of history: Carthage was destroyed more completely than Hiroshima. Poverty amidst plenty is immoral and outrageous, but America has a more equitable distribution of wealth than any great power has ever had (including the USSR).[1] The "new left" may be new to you, but men have been saying the same things for decades.

When you realize that these ideas and problems are not new, when you can put them into perspective, they are not nearly so frightening—or seductive. You can retain your equilibrium and avoid the excessive anxieties and enthusiasm which comes from ignorance. You can challenge the prophets instead of following them blindly. You can avoid the inevitable disillusionment and self-reproach which comes from espousing a great "new" idea that has failed in the past and will fail in the future. You can understand what is really happening and act intelligently and independently.

We professors have also been criticized for being too abstract, for not getting down to concrete examples and practical skills. But this same abstractness can help you to see similarities and patterns in apparently dissimilar situations. In the changing world we live in, you desperately need this ability; without it, the world becomes unstable and unmanageable, and your precious skills soon become obsolete.

A broader, longer-term perspective also helps you to know who you are and where you are going. Many Americans are lost, alienated from themselves and the world, and they strive frantically to find

[1] Some students have countered that assertion with comparisons with Sweden, Switzerland, and Denmark but they are hardly great powers. Perhaps powers should be more humane than small nations, but they never have been.

themselves. They work at jobs they abhor for money they don't need to buy things they don't enjoy to impress people they don't like because they hope to find or to prove themselves. Others try to ease the pain of aloneness by drinking too much or having one affair after another. But these things provide very temporary relief, and the doubts and the pain soon return.

An educated man has a much better solution to that problem of aloneness. Knowing who he is, and understanding the world he lives in, he can relate himself to it in a productive, satisfying way.[2]

HELP US TO HELP YOU

Unfortunately, because we do not really know how to teach, you will have to work very hard to understand what is inside of us. Our nit-picking examinations and pedantic approaches may hide the underlying messages. The countless terms may blind you to the beautiful logic and structure of the biological classification system. The dates and details may obscure the flow and meaning of history.

A few gifted teachers can communicate the importance, logic, and meaning of their subjects, but most of us cannot. We know what they are; they are what got us excited and committed to our fields. We can communicate them to each other because we share the excitement and have a common language, but we cannot always communicate them to you. We think you can't understand until you learn the vocabulary and some of the basic facts, so that is what we teach. But that turns you off and takes up all the time we have. By the time you learn the vocabulary and facts, the course is over, and you never get the underlying message.

The message is worth having, and you should help us to communicate it to you. You should help us to go beyond the details, beyond the nonsense you give back on exams. You must keep us focused on the important things and not let us bog you down with details and trivia.

Unfortunately, you are no more competent at helping us than we

[2]These remarks do not mean that you need *only* what we have. They just mean that you can get from us only what we have and will have to go elsewhere to get the things that we can not offer you. The remainder of this book lists several of these alternative sources.

are at helping you. We have frustrated you, and you pass your frustration back to us. We have used force against you, and you use force against us. We have used grades to dominate you, and you want to use grades to dominate us. We have criticized, pressured, and manipulated you, and you do the same things to us.

Most student-faculty dialogues remind me of two children calling each other names: the professors say: *"Hey, stupid,* can't you understand a few simple ideas? Since you can't, or are too lazy to try, I'll have to use examinations, quizzes, term papers, grades, and every other type of force to teach you what is *really* important!"*

The students reply: *"Hey, stupid,* can't you learn how to teach? Don't you know what is important? Since you are so stupid and incompetent, I'll have to use grades, picketing, sit-ins, and every other type of force to teach you what is *really* important!"*

But that kind of behavior will not solve your problems. Telling a professor that he is "lousy" will not make him improve. Grading a course as a "D" will not make it a better course, nor will it help the professor to improve. This kind of information just puts us on the defensive, stifles our natural desire to improve our teaching, and breaks down communication between us.

The only way to improve the situation is to develop better relationships with us. You may feel that we, as the worst offenders, should make the first move, but that is a childish argument, the equivalent of: "Mommy, he hit me first." We did hit you first; we are the guiltier party; but accusations and demands don't solve your problem. Since we are not big enough to make the first move, and since the system punishes the occasional professor who does move toward you, you have to come to us.

In other words, despite my sympathy for your grievances, I suggest that you act realistically and pragmatically. Complaints, grades for professors, strikes, demonstrations, etc., have not solved your problem in the past, nor will they solve them in the future. Therefore, if you sincerely want to improve our teaching and your education, if you want us to become more responsive to your needs, you must apply a few psychological principles.

    1. People usually do not correct their mistakes or change their behavior when they are on the defensive.

2. Criticism, especially public criticism, creates defensiveness.
3. General evaluations (such as: "You are a poor teacher") are the least helpful information of all. They create defensiveness without providing any information that the person can use to change himself.
4. People need *specific, nonthreatening* information to change themselves.
5. *Every* person, even your professors, has a basic desire to grow and to improve.

If these principles are correct (and considerable research indicates that they are), you can improve teaching and you can certainly learn more during your college years by relating to us in noncoercive, helpful ways. Believe it or not, we do want to be good teachers, and we need your help to improve ourselves.

We are also human, as human as you are, and we dislike the impersonality and emphasis on grades. If you approach us properly, you will find us very receptive on both the intellectual and the human levels. We enjoy our work, and we are usually eager to discuss our subjects with interested students. We are also interested in discussing a broader range of topics, if they are discussed in an intelligent, objective way.

Students rarely offer us that kind of conversation. Most students never come to us except to talk about grades, exams, credits, and gripes about the system. These topics turn us off, and we do our best to avoid that sort of conversation. But the same professor who brushed you off when you tried to talk about grades is probably willing to spend a great deal of time with you discussing books about his subject or research projects in his area or the applications of his field to contemporary problems. We feel comfortable in that sort of conversation, and we like people with whom we can discuss these topics. Therefore, if you want to learn more and to reduce the impersonality of the system, approach us in the right way.

SELECT YOUR ENVIRONMENT

The general principle of taking what we can offer should also be applied to your choice of institutions, courses, and instructors. Different ones offer different things, and it is much more reasonable to select ones which offer what you want than to make poor choices and then demand that the institution or instructor change to fit your needs.[3]

Unfortunately, many students follow exactly the opposite pattern. They go to Berkeley, Columbia, and other universities which are famous for poor teaching and inhuman administration and then demonstrate for better teaching and less impersonal administration. Such a policy is useless and self-destructive. The nature and organization of these institutions guarantee that they will *never* provide even minimally adequate instruction or administration. Therefore, if you want good teaching, the moral is quite clear: don't go to Berkeley, Columbia, Harvard, or any other research factory; go to a school which really cares about teaching. Even in this research-dominated world there are such schools. Some of them have outstanding faculty and reputations (e.g., Dartmouth, Swarthmore, Princeton, and Reed), and many small local schools provide much better teaching than the prestige universities. My undergraduate degree was from Monmouth College, a small, unknown school, but teaching there was much better than I've seen at Berkeley, UCLA, Carnegie-Mellon, or Pitt.

The same principle applies to selecting courses and instructors. Since every course or professor cannot satisfy your needs, you must make a decision. You must decide what you want to learn and then take the professors and courses which can help you.

These decisions are not easy. You have to analyze yourself and the system—analyses which are difficult, time-consuming, and anxiety-provoking. It is much easier to leave the decisions to the system and then protest you have been treated unfairly. But that won't solve your problem.

Your problem is complicated by a lack of information. Universities, which talk loftily about "the rule of reason," do their best to deceive students about what they really offer.[4] Catalogues all say the same things; course descriptions are meaningless; there is no official or reliable information about instructors' competence or style. Some

---

[3]The same general principle should be applied to many other decisions. Instead of taking a poor job and complaining about it, analyze your opportunities beforehand. Instead of marrying an unsuitable person and then trying to change that individual, pick someone who matches your needs.

[4]Doing so is hypocritical because reason can operate only when one is adequately informed.

schools even withhold instructor's names or assign students randomly to courses or sections to keep class sizes equal and their less adequate professors occupied.

You are not, however, completely helpless. You do have some freedom of choice, and you can get useful information. A major purpose of this book is to help you exercise this freedom by providing the information you need to make these choices.

MAKE REAL DECISIONS

Most students do not make real decisions. They act impulsively, or drift, or take what the system or other people offer them. They go to the most prestigious school which accepts them, or experiment with LSD, or marry a girl who attracts them without really analyzing the consequences of their decision.

Even people who are trained to analyze professional problems fail to apply the same principles to personal decisions. Engineers, scientists, and accountants learn excellent analytic procedures, but they don't use them for personal decisions. In fact, they act about as impetuously and foolishly as everyone else.

A major purpose of this book is to help you to apply the analytic methods and decision strategies which you will learn in physics, engineering, and economic courses. They have helped us to put men on the moon and to build a fantastically powerful economy, and they can help you to select a school or a spouse, to understand yourself, to solve sexual problems, or to relate to your parents.

Unfortunately, many people have a strong, irrational bias against using these methods for personal decisions. The same nation which worships rationality in economics and science rejects it in personal affairs. We believe that a man should analyze alternatives carefully before investing his money, but that one should not think rationally about the consequences before choosing a school or a wife. Doing so is regarded as being too cold-blooded. Young people therefore rely on emotions and intuition when they make their most important decisions.

The results are predictable and disastrous. We have one of the highest divorce rates in the world, and students are so dissatisfied that they are tearing down their schools. Since poor decisions have much more serious consequences, I suggest that you discard the romantic dependence upon emotions and use the analytic procedures described in later chapters to make your decisions.

WORK ON THE CRUCIAL SKILLS[5]

Thus far the emphasis has been entirely on education, on understanding and self-development. There are, however, certain skills which can best be learned during your college years. Most skills can be learned elsewhere; in fact, your company will teach you most of the skills you need to do your job. But a few skills must be learned during your college years, or they will probably never be learned at all.

You will probably have to learn these skills on your own. Facts can be learned from a book; understanding can even be developed from passive reading; but you can learn skills only by *doing* things and getting feedback on your performance. Since the system presents opportunities to practice these skills, but does not emphasize them or routinely provide useful feedback, you must do most of the work yourself.

Professors know that the communication skills—reading, writing, and speaking—are extremely important, but we don't teach them properly. If we and your high-school teachers had done our jobs, you could now read at least 1000 words per minute with a high degree of comprehension. Highly skilled readers can read several times that fast. Since this skill is not taught at most colleges, you will have to get it elsewhere. Fortunately, many commercial organizations offer courses which can dramatically improve your reading. You should take such a course as soon as possible because it will help you with your school work, reduce the time you spend studying, and increase your freedom to pursue your other interests.

Writing is America's lost art. Even professors have not mastered it; our articles and books are almost always poorly written. We also do not help you to improve your writing, although we constantly complain about it. You must therefore study the principles of writing, outline everything you do, write several drafts, criticize each as severely as you can, and then get criticism from someone else. This

[5] These issues will be discussed in much greater detail in the chapter on learning.

criticism should come from your professors, but they usually give only grades. However, if you take the initiative and *ask* for criticism, many professors will provide it.

A few schools offer courses in which students receive genuine feedback about their writing, but most so-called writing courses focus on basic grammar and sentence construction, a very small part of writing. You should therefore discuss the course with the professor before committing yourself. If he is going to teach an "idiot English" course, save your time.[6] On the other hand, if he will assign several themes and provide real feedback on them, take the course, and as many similar courses as you can get and afford.

The same general principle applies to speaking, but it is often much easier to get feedback. Many campuses have Toastmasters' Clubs in which members make speeches and get criticisms from each other. Some formal courses are also useful here, but far too frequently the emphasis is on grades rather than *informative* feedback. You should therefore check out speaking courses in the same way as writing courses, and you might also join or start a Toastmasters' Club.

In addition to the communications skills, college should help you to develop your general analytic and problem-solving abilities. Formal course work can help you to develop your analytic abilities, but it does not have much effect on your problem-solving ability. In fact, my work in business schools suggests that business students are much better at performing abstract analyses than they are at using these analyses to solve problems.[7]

Courses in research methods, engineering, mathematics, statistics, and the sciences can develop your analytic abilities. Liberal arts courses are also useful if they are taught properly. Again you must take an active role and select the courses and professors in which the emphasis is upon analysis rather than examinations, memorizing, and trivia.

Developing your problem-solving ability is much more difficult. It can be developed only by solving problems, and we rarely let you do that. You must therefore seek out the rare professor who wants his

[6]Unless you don't know the basic principles of grammar.
[7]Countless executives would agree with that conclusion. Their most common complaint about universities and business schools is that graduates don't know how to solve problems.

students to solve problems, or who at least allows them to do so. If, for example, you take a course in political science, ask the professor for an assignment in which you are to solve some sort of political problem. You might ask him to allow you to write not on the history of the electoral system, but on a proposal for revising it. You should also ask him to criticize both the proposed revision and the steps which you suggest taking to implement it.

Ideal solutions are easy to propose, but it is much harder to propose a sequence of actions which will lead to the desired result. If you can find a professor who will let you try to solve problems and give you feedback on your proposals, you may develop the rarest and most valuable skill, the ability to solve problems.

SUMMARY AND PREVIEW

This chapter has outlined a general strategy for educating yourself and controlling your own life. This strategy is based on two very simple assumptions: you're stuck with the system; you're also stuck with yourself. You must therefore work out a relationship with the system that helps you to define yourself and to reach your goals.

The central elements of this strategy are independence, an active role, self- and system-analysis, taking what we can offer, helping us to help you, selecting your environment, making real decisions, and working on the crucial skills.

The remainder of the book applies this strategy to specific problems and issues. It provides information and procedures which can help you to understand yourself and the system, to learn more effectively, to find the right job, etc. These are not easy problems, and the book does not try to solve them for you. It simply shows you how to approach them more intelligently. The rest is up to you.

IDENTITY PROBLEMS: "WHO ARE YOU?"

Most people answer "Who are you?" by referring to roles and extrinsics, not to themselves. "I am Charley Jones, a sophomore at Dartmouth, 19 years old, Sigma Chi, a history major" and so on. If you probe a little deeper, you may get a little closer to the person; he may tell you something more about his thoughts, hopes, and dreams—but the answers will still be superficial. "I plan to go to graduate school in physics. I am hoping to study in France next year. I'm pinned to a girl, but I'm not sure we'll get engaged."

People don't give real answers to the question because they don't know the answer and because they are afraid to expose themselves. They are so used to wearing masks that they do not know what is underneath them, and they may even be afraid to find out—afraid that their real self is much less attractive than their ideal or pseudo-self.

If you are at all typical, you don't know who you are. Sometimes you want to know; sometimes you are afraid to find out; but you really don't know who you are, what you want, or where you are going. I can't answer those questions for you, but I can help you to understand why you are confused and outline a method for meaningful self-analysis. This chapter will simply outline that method; later chapters will show you how to use it.[1]

THE ELEMENTS OF IDENTITY

There are two elements to your identity: a continuity within yourself and a continuity in the self which you present to other people.

> The term identity . . . connotes both a persistent sameness within oneself . . . and a persistent sharing of some kind of central characteristic with others.[2]

Both elements are indispensable, but most people emphasize one or the other. Some people emphasize their images at the expense of their inner continuity; other people are so intent upon "doing their own thing" that they alienate others. Solving your identity problems therefore requires working on both elements: you must develop a style which expresses your inner individuality without alienating other people.

THE ROOTS OF THE PROBLEM

People from many other countries are often amazed at Americans' concern about identity problems. They know who they are and cannot understand why we are so confused.[3] They wonder whether some defect of the American character causes us to be so confused, and some people even doubt the genuineness of our confusion. It is seen as part of the great American charade.

[1]Decisions such as selecting a college, major, job, graduate school, or spouse can tell you a great deal about yourself, if you learn how to analyze your own motives and actions. This chapter will, therefore, describe that method and other chapters will contain questionnaires to guide your self-analysis.
[2]Erik Erikson, in M. Stein, A. Vidich, and D. White (eds.), *Identity and Anxiety.* New York: Free Press, 1960, p. 38.
[3]The more traditional and less industrialized a society is the clearer conception people have of their identities. Some Northern Europeans are almost as confused as we are.

But you know it is genuine. You know how many times you have asked: "Who am I?"—and you know how painful it is to be unable to answer that question. It is probably particularly painful right now. You have been confused before, and you will be confused again, but you will probably never suffer more deeply than you are suffering now. Everything is hitting you at the same time: you have to make a choice about your occupation and future schooling, change your relationship to your parents, develop intimate relations with the opposite sex, assume new social roles, and decide who you are. Identity crises are such a common part of American adolescence that many Americans feel that *all* adolescents suffer from them. But in some societies the transition from youth to adult is smooth and painless.

Since identity problems are more severe in the United States than in any other society, we should briefly examine some of the causal factors. Space limitations will make this analysis superficial; you should therefore read some of the suggested books.[4]

Conformity Pressures

Conformity pressures are the villian in many modern melodramas. Authors, social critics, and students deplore the modern pressures for conformity and long for the good old days when a man could be an individual. Unfortunately the good old days never existed.

Conformity pressures are a fact of life in *all* societies. Every society which has ever existed has demanded that its members conform to its standards. Modern conformity pressures are *not* greater than those of earlier eras or other countries; in fact, they are much weaker. You have much *more* freedom than your grandparents or adolescents in any other country.

You *seem* to have less freedom because the standards to which you must conform change so rapidly. Members of other societies can conform almost unconsciously because the standards are stable. But American standards change so rapidly for each group and are so

---

[4]The best known writer on identity problems is Erik Erikson; unfortunately, his books and articles are hard to read because he insists on using an excessive amount of psychoanalytic jargon. The most comprehensive source is *Identity and Anxiety*, edited by Morris Stein *et al.* but it is rather academic. The works of David Riesman, Erich Fromm, and Rollo May are readable and perceptive.

different between groups that you must constantly monitor and adjust your behavior. In other words, the conformity pressures you face are *not* more severe—they are just harder to live with.

Furthermore, the real problem is not that Americans do not have enough freedom, but that we are afraid of the freedom we already have. The freedom is there, but we try to escape from it because it makes us feel uncertain and anxious. Americans are conformists not because social pressures are so severe but because each individual is so afraid of being different. The real pressures come from *within*—from our own insecurities, from our inability to stand on our own two feet. We conform because *we want* to conform, not because we are forced to do so. The conformity problem in America is therefore not the social pressures for conformity, but the inner weaknesses and fears which make conformity so attractive. These fears and their consequences will be discussed more fully in the chapter on loneliness.

Pluralism

Ours is probably the most pluralistic society in history. Other societies have included more divergent groups, but in America these groups are mixed together by social and geographical mobility. Southern Baptists live in the same towns and go to the same schools as Sephardic Jews, second-generation Italians, and newly arrived Puerto Rican immigrants.

People in more homogeneous societies know where they fit, and they can assume their roles easily and naturally. You may not know where you fit, and you must choose your roles deliberately and explicitly. Furthermore, because you have been a part of so many different groups, you do not fit completely into any one of them. Your values, interests, needs, and talents have been created by so many disparate groups that you are somewhat marginal—neither fish nor fowl nor flesh, but a little of each.

Upward Mobility

This problem is greatly aggravated by the fact that most college students are upwardly mobile. Your parents were probably not so well educated as you will be, and getting a college degree may put you into a different socioeconomic class. Since the values, habits, etc., of this class will be new and strange to you, you must think and act in ways which are inappropriate for your new status or inconsistent with your old one.

Mobility, either upward or lateral, therefore weakens either one or both of the elements of identity: you must either act in ways which are inconsistent with your past, or clash with your present associates. Most Americans emphasize fitting-in with their present associates. Fitting-in is so important to them that they work hard to reject or to suppress their pasts. They show contempt for their parents and copy the style, dress, mannerisms, values, etc., of their new group.

Rejecting one's past is a major cause for identity problems and anxiety. If one rejects his past, he cuts himself off from one of the basic foundations of his psychological security, and there is *no* substitute for that foundation. Social status, money, power, etc., may relieve some of the anxiety caused by dissociating yourself from your past—but there will still be an unfillable void, a great gaping hole in your sense of selfhood.

Furthermore, no matter how hard you try, you cannot escape your past. The futility of trying to do so is illustrated by a Jewish story. A wealthy Episcopalian was bragging to a hunchback about his business, golf game, country club memberships, etc. The hunchback listened respectfully as the Episcopalian told him how he had become a pillar of the community. Finally, after more than an hour, the Episcopalian said: "You know, I used to be a Jew." The hunchback turned slightly to face him, twisted his malformed little neck, and said, "I know; I used to be a hunchback."

Since you have about as much chance of forgetting your past as he had of forgetting his hunchback, you may as well face up to the inevitable. No matter how high you go, or how well you dress, or how many clubs you join, you can never escape from your past. To reject your past or to try to bury it will only make you insecure and alienated. The *first* and most important rule for resolving identity problems is therefore: *remember where you came from.* Remember that beneath that uniform which says Miss or Mr. Middle Class is a farm boy from Iowa, a seamstress's daughter from Chicago, or a carpenter's son from Georgia.

The Marketing Orientation[5]

In contemporary American society, popularity, social acceptance, and "making friends and influencing people" are emphasized much more heavily than self-knowledge or self-development. You have been conditioned since birth to try to please, and "to develop skill in 'selling [your] personality' may appear far more important than to develop any personality worth selling, or indeed worth having."[6]

The pressures toward marketing yourself are everywhere—from toothpaste ads to popularity polls, to an obsessive concern with what is "in." You may spend so much time trying to be what other people want you to be that you never find out what you really are.

Success Worship

Closely related to the marketing orientation is America's obsession with success—an all-consuming goal that is usually defined in terms of economic and social mobility rather than personal development and satisfaction. Success is moving up; failure is staying at the same level or—the ultimate horror—moving down.

In addition to being an all-consuming goal, success is regarded as a *moral* obligation. It is your *duty* to become rich and successful, to climb the pyramid to reach the top. Not doing so—or, worse yet, not even trying—is a sign of moral weakness, of lack of character.

People in more traditional societies don't feel that sense of obligation, nor does remaining at the same level suggest a lack of character. In fact, one is expected to follow in his parent's footsteps. If your father was a barber, you would naturally become a barber, and no one would think less of you for doing so.

In success-worshipping America you cannot simply follow your parents. You are expected to go beyond them, to be more successful, to raise yourself in society. This emphasis upon success is a major cause for our fabulously successful economy. It is also a major cause for psychological insecurity, divorce, suicide, alcoholism, and homi-

---

[5]The term "marketing orientation" comes from Erich Fromm and is a central concept of his books.

[6]Christian Bay, "Toward a Social Theory of Intellectual Development," in Nevitt Sanford (ed.), *College and Character*. New York: Wiley, 1964, p. 263.

cide. The freedom to succeed includes the freedom to fail, and you must run hard to escape that fear.

You know that fear—it has been drummed into you since childhood. You have been graded on everything from speed of toilet training to social adjustment to academic performance. Thus far you have been rather successful; you may have had a few minor failures, but you are still in college—the great obstacle course which separates you from the upper-middle class. But you know very well that when you finish this race, you will just start another one—with higher obstacles and tougher competition.

An increasing number of students have tried to reject the success ethic, but very few people can really turn their backs on success and competition. They don't compete for grades, but they try to become the best bridge players, or the people with the longest hair, or the most militant radicals. The success ethic and the competitive approach are so much a part of your personality that you probably cannot escape them. Americans define themselves by competing with each other and by seeing where they stand in one or more races. Rejecting one form of competition usually leads to competing in a different race.

A fairly good case can even be made that the recent rejection of materialistic success as the primary criterion of individual worth has *increased* personal anxiety and identity problems. Men who have an all-consuming drive to reach the top of the economic pyramid do not have nearly so many problems in defining themselves as people who are almost as competitive, but unsure of *where* they want to compete.

I am certainly not advocating that you suppress all your other desires and become obsessed with materialistic success, but you should realize that the reduced interest in economic success (which is largely caused by our fantastic wealth) combined with the continued competitive atmosphere in American society makes your problem much more difficult. You have to make choices that your parents never even considered. When one grows up during a depression or war, he knows darned well what he wants to do with himself—but you have been inculcated with a spirit of competition which seems pointless in such a wealthy society.

Academic Pressures

Many of the pressures which have already been mentioned are exerted within both our society and academic institutions, but the institutions exert a specific set of pressures which hinder your self-understanding.

EXTERNAL DISCIPLINE   The emphasis upon *external* discipline is a serious obstacle to self-development, and it combines readily with the success ethic and the emphasis upon selling yourself. Weekly reading assignments, quizzes, regular examinations, term papers, and all the other disciplinary pressures prevent you from reading what you want, acting spontaneously or creatively, learning who you are, or developing the *internal* discipline you need to control your own life.

Students resent external discipline, but, because it prevents them from developing internal discipline, they become dependent upon it. They *need* someone to tell them what and when to read.

THE RIGHT ANSWERS   The same general process occurs with the content of courses and examinations. Students resent being forced to regurgitate what the professors tell them, but they feel profoundly uncomfortable when they have to think for themselves. They have been so conditioned to parroting the *right* answers (i.e., the ones the teacher wants) that they cannot or will not think for themselves.

IMPERSONALITY AND ABSTRACTNESS   This inability to enjoy freedom or to use it constructively is increased by the impersonal, abstract, pigeonholing academic methods. When people have *personal support* they are willing and able to accept freedom. For example, psychotherapists help people to drop their rigid, defensive ways of thinking by creating a supportive, understanding atmosphere.

This kind of atmosphere rarely exists in the universities. In fact, professors who attempt to create it are usually severely criticized because the academic norm is to be impersonal and abstract. We are expected to teach our subjects, not our students.

PIGEONHOLING   In addition to teaching our subjects impersonally and abstractly, we isolate them from each other. Economics, psychology, and sociology are not taught as parts of a unified body of knowledge, but as separate disciplines. Students are therefore unable to relate our courses and information either to themselves and their own needs or to the other courses they have taken.

> Apparently students tend first to segment information from the rest of their personality, and then to segment departments of information from each other. . . . Pigeonholed and temporarily forgotten, it is only to be drawn upon when the schoolroom bell rings for it again.[7]

Powerlessness

The size of our societies and institutions makes the individual powerless and dependent. You know that you will probably *never* be your own boss—that you will always be taking orders from someone.

Your education, both inside and outside of school, has been devoted almost entirely toward preparing you for a life of powerlessness and mediocrity. You are being trained to enter the bureaucracies, to become a cypher, another cog in a gigantic wheel over which you will exert no control.[8]

Some people say that modern universities fail to provide students with the skills they need to live in our society. I think these charges are utterly unjustified. We don't provide you with the skills you need to become an independent human being because the system teaches you to become exactly the sort of passive robot that the bureaucracies demand. We have, therefore, done a superb job of preparing you to live in a society in which nothing you do really matters.

The problem is that in preparing you for this life of cheerful mediocrity we undermine your ability to think independently and make it harder for you to find out who you really are.

Disillusionment

We professors increase your dependency and passivity with our exter-

---

[7]Joseph Katz and Nevitt Sanford, "Curriculum and Personality" in Sanford, *op. cit.*, p. 124.
[8]College prepares people for roles which require and allow more independence than those taken by less-educated people, but the emphasis is still on *fitting-in* rather than controlling your own life and career.

nal discipline, but we also undermine your security by stripping away your illusions about American society.[9] You were raised on myths, and the truth about the Puritans, Indians, American foreign policy, Lincoln's attitudes toward slavery, etc., can be profoundly disturbing —especially when it hits you so suddenly.

Some students are so shocked and so incapable of dealing with truth in its full complexity that they reject America completely, but accept all of the myths about America's enemies—because America's enemies are thought to be allies in their great struggle against the people who have failed them.

Complete rejection of your country has almost exactly the same effects as a naive acceptance of it. It divorces you from the truth, and weakens the foundations of your personal identity. Your task is, therefore, neither to accept America naively nor to reject it completely: it is to understand it in all of its complexity and to relate yourself to it *as it is.*

Unacceptable Role

Identity problems are aggravated by the fact that the role of *student* is not socially acceptable. A student is, by definition, a developing person—but that role is not a legitimate one in American society. Instead of giving young people the opportunity and support they need to develop themselves, we expect them to behave as miniature adults. For example, dating, which should be a developmental opportunity, usually degenerates into going steady—a miniature marriage. School work, which should provide an opportunity to experiment and to express oneself, is a junior edition of adult drudgery.

Since we have failed to create and to legitimatize the role of the developing person, you will have to assume that role on your own.

The arch-problem for the student is to know how to wait, how to tolerate ambiguity and the open questions about himself while he prepares for the future. The problem is not easy, for he is constantly tempted to take

[9]The illusions must be stripped away, but there are obviously better ways to do so. Dominating and manipulating students and then suddenly stripping away their illusions will inevitably create irrational reactions—violence is only the most visible reaction; earlier reactions, such as superpatriotism and apathy, were equally irrational.

short-cuts to maturity; neglecting the paths to full development by imitating adult behavior and prematurely fitting himself to adult roles.[10]

Conclusions

The major effects of the pressures listed in this chapter are insecurity, a separation of role and self, an emphasis upon extrinsics, and an ambivalent attitude toward freedom. America is such a pluralistic society and you are a member of so many different types of groups that you must wear many masks and you may be unable to separate the masks from the underlying personal reality. Your problem is complicated by the fact that most Americans emphasize self-presentation and minimize self-analysis.

Freedom is, therefore, very frightening. It is often seen not as an opportunity, but as a threat; not as a chance to express and to become yourself, but as a source of anxiety and uncertainty.

Because these tendencies are so pervasive and are reinforced by most of the groups to which you belong, finding yourself may be the most difficult task you ever attempt, but it is also the most important. You must therefore overcome these tendencies by increasing your personal freedom and using this freedom to understand yourself. Later I shall outline a strategy for accomplishing these tasks, but first let us look at some *in*effective approaches to them.

INEFFECTIVE APPROACHES

Because identity problems are so painful, most students look for quick and easy solutions. They join mass movements, use drugs, or conform slavishly. Many people think that this sort of behavior helps students to find themselves, but their optimism is not supported by the facts. Using defense mechanisms is also an ineffective approach, but there is no need to discuss these strategies because they are described in most psychology texts.

Activism

Activism is the most fashionable panacea. It is very "in" right now,

---

[10]Nevitt Sanford, "Freshman Personality: A Stage in Human Development," in Sanford, *op. cit.*, p. 89.

and people of all ages feel that students learn who they are by taking extreme political and social positions. The barricades are a modern form of psychoanalysis.

There is some truth to this position, but not very much. Actions can be valuable *if* they are accompanied by a serious, thoughtful analysis of your own motives and behavior, but this analysis is rarely encouraged—or even tolerated—by most activist groups. To question one's motives or actions is to raise the possibility that they are not perfect, and most activist groups will not tolerate this sort of wavering:

"Of course we're right."
"Of course they're wrong."
"They're bad, we're good."
"Our cause is right, true and just, and we will tolerate no backsliding or wavering."
"If you're not with us all the way, you're against us."

These attitudes are a common, even an indispensable, part of most activist movements, and they may prevent you from making the necessary analyses. If student activists did analyze themselves, they would find that their motives are not pure at all. They are protesting injustice and trying to correct various abuses, but they are also struggling for power and status,[11] having a lot of fun, satisfying their social needs, and acting out[12] their inner problems.

These remarks do not mean that activism has no *social* values. Any honest observer can detect a few reforms which have been caused by it. But its social value should not blind us to the fact that it has little value for defining yourself. In other words, if you want to understand yourself, spend less time acting and more time thinking.

Drugs

The other extreme is a drug-centered, passive, introspective way of life, but that kind of introspection rarely helps you to under-

[11]A reformer's desire for status and blindness to his own motives are portrayed brilliantly in Ibsen's *An Enemy of the People.* If you read it, you may recognize some of your friends (or yourself).

[12]The term "acting out" is used by psychologists to refer to behaviors which express one's inner needs, but which generally have undesirable side effects such as creating defensiveness or irritating other people.

stand yourself or to relate yourself to the world. It deals with the wrong levels and the wrong information, with sensory impressions and deeply repressed feelings, while you need to understand where you fit in the world, where you come from, and where you are going.

Some drug advocates claim that drugs can perform the tasks of psychotherapy, but do them faster and better. Instead of taking years to break down your defenses, drugs can dissolve them in a few minutes and bring you face to face with your repressed feelings and memories. These arguments are very seductive to people whose knowledge of psychology comes from movies and junk books, but they are utter nonsense. Fictional psychiatrists probe until they find the one traumatic experience which has caused all of the problems. Then, as in other fairy tales, everyone lives happily ever after.

Psychologists wish that therapy were that easy, but we all know that it is not. If all we had to do was to make you aware of your repressed memories, sodium pentothal and hypnosis would work as well as LSD—without its unpleasant and dangerous side effects. But sodium pentothal, hypnosis and dozens of other short-cuts have been tried and discarded because simply uncovering repressions does not do any lasting good, and if it is done too rapidly it can cause serious and permanent damage.[13]

The unpleasant fact is that there are no short-cuts, no quick and easy solutions to the problem of identity. Because the problem is so difficult and frightening, charlatans and demagogues can always find disciples to accept their extravagant claims—but they can't fulfill their promises. Since the evidence clearly shows that LSD therapy is generally ineffective as well as extremely dangerous,[14] I urge you to avoid LSD—with or without medical supervision (but especially without).

---

[13]Psychological tests are much more respectable and less dangerous short-cuts than drugs, but they don't help very much. They have great value for repetitious institutional decisions (such as hiring people or accepting students), but they cannot tell you who you are. They can tell you how intelligent you are and give you a crude picture of some poorly defined personality traits, but they cannot tell you what is really important to you. Furthermore, even if they could provide all the information you need to discover yourself, your habits and defenses would prevent you from accepting or using this information.

[14]Even when LSD is administered by a physician, prolonged psychotic reactions and anxiety states have occurred. This issue is discussed much more thoroughly in the chapter on drugs.

Drugs can't solve your problems, and they may well create more serious ones.

Negation

Many students try to discover or to affirm their identity by negation, by eliminating and degrading what they are not or what they do not want to be. "I am not a vicious racist—or a dirty imperialist—or a rotten communist." One inadequacy of this approach is that it deals with what you are not, rather than what you are. Since the list of things that you are not is nearly infinite, your chances of finding your identity by elimination are virtually nonexistent. You simply cannot eliminate all the negatives.

This approach also includes both self-deception and self-rejection. People recognize some undesirable quality in themselves, but they try to force this knowledge out of their awareness by attacking people who display it visibly. The extraordinarily Puritan attitude toward homosexuals is the most conspicuous example; as Kinsey and other investigators have found, many people have had homosexual experiences or feelings, but they try to beat them down by attacking "dirty queers."[15] Many of the criticisms of racists, profit-grubbers, lazy bums, etc., are based upon the same psychological dynamics.

Rejecting part of yourself or deceiving yourself about what you really are will not solve your problem. Your task is not to create a self which fits some impossible ideal, but to come to terms with yourself *as you are*, and the first step in accomplishing this task is to be honest with yourself.

Conformity

Conformity is the most common reaction to identity problems. People try to avoid the problem by being the same as everyone else, but conformity (or its mirror image, nonconformity) does not solve your problem. Whether you like it or not, you are an individual and must relate to the world as one. (This issue and the inadequacies of both conformity and nonconformity are discussed more thoroughly in the chapter on loneliness.)

[15]This issue is discussed more fully in the chapter on sex.

Inferiority Complex

"Inferiority complex" is a very popular phrase in our psychologically oriented age, but most people do not understand what it means. The term is from the writings of Alfred Adler, a prominent psychoanalyst who disagreed with Freud about the importance of sex. Adler felt that many psychological problems were caused by feelings of inferiority, and that these feelings often cause people to overcompensate for their weaknesses, either real or imaginary. An inferiority complex is an extreme degree of compensation: an individual concentrates most of his attention upon overcoming his weaknesses. For example, a person who is shy and introspective forces himself to become an aggressive salesman.

This sort of compensation is an intrinsic part of the American ethic. Americans are encouraged to minimize their weaknesses, to concentrate on overcoming them, to prove their character by overcoming biological defects. Occasionally, this compensation works: it results in some sort of outstanding achievement, but more frequently it results in mediocrity and lasting frustration.

It is far more reasonable *to understand and* to accept your weaknesses and to concentrate on your strengths. You can not be all things to all men, and trying to do so will probably lead to a life of mediocrity and frustration.

SOLVING THE PROBLEM

If the approaches used by millions of people don't work, how can you solve the problem? Chapter 2 listed some of the basic elements, and the following chapters will develop these ideas more fully—but now we can examine the basic approach more intensively.

The approach suggested here is essential because identity problems are different from most other problems. They can *never* be completely solved. Some day you may think that you have discovered who you really are, but then a new demand or opportunity will reveal unsuspected aspects of your personality. Solving identity problems is therefore a life-long task which requires developing both a realistic conception of who you are now and a way of responding to life and yourself which enables this self-conception to grow.

Take It Seriously

The first and most important step is to take the problem seriously. Finding out who you are is the *most* important thing you will ever do —you cannot do it casually or quickly. It takes time and effort, and it creates serious discomfort. You cannot find your real self without giving up some of your defenses, and giving them up invariably creates anxiety. Defenses are self-deceiving and self-defeating, but they do protect you. When you weaken or destroy them, you will feel the anxiety they existed to prevent.

This anxiety is so painful that most people are afraid to weaken their defenses. From time to time they lift their masks and try to look beneath them, but they immediately feel frightened and pull their masks down again.

Since your natural desire to avoid the pain of anxiety will make you want to avoid weakening your defenses, you must decide that finding yourself is important enough to justify the pain, time, and effort.

If you will not make that decision, if you refuse to pay the price, you will not solve the problem. And 30 years from now you will look back on your life and say: "I blew it." You may have satisfied all of your conscious needs and climbed to the top of the pyramid, but you will know that you are a failure.

Concentrate on Reality

It is banal to suggest that you concentrate on reality, but the suggestion is necessary because most people concentrate on presenting an image or changing themselves, not on discovering who they really are. Image-building has already been discussed, but a word on trying to change yourself seems necessary.

Changing oneself is an integral part of the American rhetoric. You are constantly bombarded with appeals to improve yourself. Best sellers, teachers, ministers, and parents say that "you can be anything you want to be, " that you should "think big" and "think positively". Books on these topics sell millions of copies, but they are self-defeating nonsense.

You can change a few superficial details, but no amount of will-power or determination can change your basic personality. You are stuck with yourself, and the sooner you accept that fact and concentrate on understanding and accepting yourself, the sooner you will be happy.

Surprisingly, when you stop trying to change yourself, when you accept yourself as you really are, change and growth occur easily and naturally.

> The curious paradox is that when I accept myself as I am, then I change. . . . We cannot change, we cannot move away from what we are, until we thoroughly *accept* what we are. Then change seems to come about almost unnoticed.[16]

Learn Where You Are

You cannot know *who* you are unless you know *where* you are. No matter how much you value your individualism, no matter how much you resent customs, traditions, and other social restraints, you are a product of our society and cannot find yourself without understanding it.

The blacks understand this principle. It is, in fact, their dominant reason for demanding black studies programs.[17] Unfortunately, most whites, whether they accept or reject the need for black studies programs, do not realize that their own needs are as great as the blacks! *Everyone* needs to understand his heritage and society, and failing to do so inevitably leads to identity confusion.

One way to learn where you are is to expose yourself to ideas which disagree with your own. Most people ignore people who disagree with them; they read only to get ideas and facts which support their own biases. Since no one can grow without challenging his biases, you should look for conflicting ideas. If you lean to the left, read *The National Review, The Conscience Of A Conservative, None Dare Call It Treason,* and other conservative publications; listen to "Lifeline" and "The Mannion Forum". If you are a conservative, try *The New*

---

[16]Dr. Carl Rogers, *On Becoming a Person.* Boston: Houghton Mifflin, 1962.

[17]While I have serious doubts about the way many black studies programs are conducted, it is obvious that *both* blacks and whites need a greater understanding of black history, sociology, etc.

Republic, The Arrogance of Power, The New York Post, etc. In addition to reading, try to get into genuine discussions with people with different opinions. These discussions often degenerate into debates in which each person is more concerned with scoring points than learning or listening, but, if you are at all open-minded, you will realize that the other side does have some facts. You must then either ignore these facts or try to fit them into your own philosophy. Since they probably will not fit in easily, your philosophy will stretch a little and become a little more congruent with the truth. This process is often disturbing, but it is an indispensable part of growth.

Look Hard at Yourself

Because self-analysis has been recommended several times, there is no need to belabor its importance. You simply cannot learn who you are without analyzing yourself carefully. This statement is so obvious that most people would agree with it, but very few people are able to analyze themselves. They try, but become frightened or discouraged, and soon retreat into their shell.

People fail because they do not know *how* to do it. They attempt this exceedingly difficult task without the vaguest idea of how to accomplish it. Earlier comments about taking it seriously, concentrating on reality, and talking with people who disagree with you will help, but you still need an orderly procedure and the time to use it. Many suggestions throughout the book concern ways to relieve external pressures. Going to low-pressure schools, taking a year off for a European trip, becoming an efficient learner, and so on may provide the pressure-free time you need to be able to understand yourself.

This time will be used most profitably if you follow an orderly analytic procedure. This procedure should break down that unanswerable question: "Who am I?" into smaller questions such as "Why do I want to go to a prestige college? Why do I enjoy physics more than history? Why do I want to join a fraternity? Why do I work so hard to get good grades? What kind of company do I want to work for?"

These questions are certainly not easy to answer, but they are infinitely easier than "Who am I?" If you develop the habit of asking yourself these questions, and if you pause regularly to relate the answers to each other and your own self-concept, you will slowly become surer about who you are. Many of the following chapters contain questionnaires to stimulate and to organize your analysis.

Counseling

While these questionnaires can be useful, they have very serious limitations. They can only stimulate and organize your self-analysis—and stimulation and organization may not be enough to overcome your defenses. Furthermore, you will not know the answers to many questions and, if you cannot accept your natural confusion or if you try to force the answers by using an excessively critical, cross-examining approach, these questionnaires may actually make you *more* defensive. You may find that systematic self-analysis is so frightening that you answer the questions superficially or ignore them completely.

Even if you recognize their limitations, the questionnaires are certainly no substitute for counseling. Counseling can do something that no questionnaire can accomplish: it can help you to drop your defenses so that you can really see yourself. Your defenses exist because they help you to cope with stress and anxiety, and you will not discard them as long as you need them. Counseling provides an environment in which you may feel safe enough to drop some of them. There are many kinds of counseling, but we shall discuss only the grossest distinction, individual versus group.[18]

INDIVIDUAL COUNSELING   If you see a counselor, he will do everything he can to understand you; this understanding and the knowledge that he is concerned with your growth and happiness will slowly make you feel secure enough to tell him the truth about yourself. Many of the things you tell him will surprise you because you had not known your true feelings; having a sympathetic listener helps you to express them. After you have expressed them and found that he accepts them, you will become more able to accept and to incorporate them into your self-conception.

You slowly become better acquainted with yourself and realize

[18]A much more complete discussion of different types of counseling can be found in Alan Schoonmaker, *Anxiety and the Executive.* New York: American Management Association, 1969, pp. 253–266.

that you are not so bad a person as you had feared. You stop comparing yourself unfavorably to an unrealistic ideal and learn to live with yourself *as you are.*

The great advantage of individual counseling is that it is much more supportive and tolerant than group counseling. Aside from "working with" the counselor, you have no responsibilities other than paying your bills and keeping your appointments. You can therefore do whatever you like, without fear of being rejected. If you have a strong fear of rejection, or if you feel that underneath your masks is a very bad person whom people would not like, individual counseling may be best.

The great disadvantage of individual counseling is its expense: private counselors generally cost from $15 to $35 per hour. Clinics are much cheaper (many charge no fees at all), but the counselors are usually students (with professional supervision), and the waiting lists may be long (six or more months).

Some clinics, particularly at universities, try to keep waiting lists down by severely limiting the number of visits per person. Each person, regardless of his problems, is allowed three, four, or five visits. This policy allows the clinic to "look good" by handling a lot of people, but it is inexcusably irresponsible. Some people are helped by a few visits, but many people lose some of their defenses, then feel rejected by the counselor,[19] and are left with neither a solution to their problems nor defenses against their anxiety. They would have been much better off if they had never started.

Therefore, before you go to a clinic, find out whether its counselors are students and whether you will be kicked out after a few sessions. Adequately supervised students can do a good job, but I recommend that you avoid any clinic which limits visits.

GROUP COUNSELING   Hundreds of campuses now offer various forms of group counseling, usually without calling it counseling or therapy. Courses such as "human relations," "supervisory skill development," and "group dynamics" are often thinly disguised therapy groups, and many campus organizations (such as the YMCA) offer

---

[19]The fact that clinic policy forces the termination of the counseling relationship does *not* keep people from feeling rejected.

weekend or evening "T-groups", "encounter groups", "self-development programs," and so on.

Regardless of what they are called, these programs have many common elements: meetings are unstructured; there is no agenda or task; and people's behavior is therefore determined primarily by their own needs and habits.

Interpersonal honesty is encouraged; remarks which would not normally be made or which would cause the speaker to be rejected are encouraged as legitimate. People say: "You really irritate me when you talk so much," or "I think you are insincere," or "I really wanted to hug you when you said that." This honesty helps people to learn how they affect people.

Analysis is encouraged. When people get angry with each other, or team-up against a third party, or feel affectionate, they are encouraged both to express and to analyze the reasons for their feelings. *Why* do they feel that way?

In addition to being much cheaper than individual counseling, groups offer three advantages. First, you can learn from your own behavior. Instead of just talking to a counselor, you are in a group with real people, and you can analyze the way you act toward them. Second, other people will tell you how they feel about you. You can therefore learn what sort of impression you make on people. Third, the group provides a low-cost environment in which you can try out new ways of relating to people. You can be more aggressive, or less talkative, and see how people react to you.

There are two major disadvantages of group programs: First, groups are much less supportive than an individual counselor. If the members don't like the way you behave, they will tell you, and they may reject you completely. Criticism and rejection are so disturbing to some people that they break down; they cry or become extremely depressed, and some breakdowns are so serious that the individual requires hospitalization.

Second, this possibility of breakdowns is greatly increased by the fact that many group leaders are utterly unqualified. Programs are often run by people with little or no formal training in psychology, and some of these people are so ignorant that they are dangerous. Men who work in business schools are particularly likely to be unqualified; human relations is so "in" these days, and there are so few qualified

men, that many business schools use unqualified group leaders. There-
fore, before entering a program, make sure that the trainer has a
Ph.D., *in psychology,* or certification from the National Training
Laboratories or a similar organization.

Develop Honest Personal Relations

Counseling encourages interpersonal honesty, but many people fail to
apply the principles in their everyday life. They learn to be open and
honest with a counselor or counseling group, but remain inhibited
with everyone else. Since learning who you are is a life-long task, you
should develop a few relationships in which you can really be yourself.
It is certainly not easy to develop this sort of relationship, but the
chapter on loneliness may help you.

Now that we have discussed the basic principles for discovering
yourself, let us turn our attention to the environment in which you
must work out your identity and other problems—the academic system.

THE SYSTEM

"The university and segments of industry
are becoming more and more alike."[1]

"The university is being called upon to
merge its activities with industry."[2]

The very first thing you must understand about American Universities is that they are *not* educational institutions.[3] They are factories—part of the military-industrial-university complex, grinding out products for sale to the highest bidder. Research is their most profitable and therefore their most valued product. At some schools football and basketball are the high-profit lines, and they are emphasized. You are

[1]Clark Kerr (former president of the University of California), *Uses of the University,* Cambridge, Mass., Harvard Univ. Press, 1963, p. 90.

[2]*Ibid.,* p. 86.

[3]This chapter will not attempt to provide a complete or objective picture of the academic system. Here I shall concentrate on a few important aspects of the system which are usually ignored. However, because this description is incomplete and biased, you should certainly read some of the standard books. *College and Character,* edited by Nevitt Sanford, (New York: Wiley), is probably the best place to start.

I should also admit that my own hands are far from clean. I was a member of the system, faced the same pressures as my colleagues, had the same weaknesses, and committed many of the same offences.

a much less important product. Your individuality, uniqueness, and basic humanity mean no more to the universities than a car means to General Motors or a hog means to Armour Star. You are simply a product to be processed and sold as cheaply as possible.

In fact, to keep their costs down and to satisfy their customers' needs for faceless, gutless organization men, the universities do everything they can to destroy your individuality. They force you to become a member of a faceless mob, passively listening to lectures. They demand absolute obedience to rigid, ridiculous regulations. They make you take courses you don't want from men who can't teach. Then, with the supreme arrogance of the omnipotent, they say: "If you don't like it, leave so someone else can get an education."

The factory atmosphere also dominates the professors. In an earlier era professors were free thinkers and broadly educated men. They read widely, made up their own minds, and wrote what they thought. Now they are narrow specialists, working on miniscule problems, parroting the words of the dominant figures in their fields. They have changed from individualists to organization men, from genuine scholars to business men. "The career-driven college professor does not differ in essentials from his industrial and business counterparts."[4] Frequently their primary motive is not to express what they think, but to publish in the right places. Since the men who control the journals will publish only articles which follow some party line, most professors say the same thing in slightly different words.

What went wrong? How did institutions which were once dedicated to intellectual freedom and the development of the individual become instruments of coercion, conformity, and mediocrity, committed to goals which are antithetical to education, liberalism, and humanism?

In principle, the answer is rather simple. One cannot separate any person or institution from its society. The trends and pressures in the universities mirror similar ones in American society. We have become a nation of bland conformists, willing to trade our freedom and intrinsic satisfaction for security and social acceptance. The universities and professors have made the same bargain. They have traded their intel-

[4]M. Stein and A. Vidich, "Identity and History: An Overview," in M. Stein, A. Vidick, and D. White (eds.), *Identity and Anxiety*. New York: Free Press, 1960, p. 25.

lectual independence and sense of contribution for the money and prestige that bland conformity guarantees.

Professors, deans, and college presidents have the same appetites and weaknesses as other men. In earlier times they were protected not by their character but by the lack of opportunities. Like the girl who preserves her virginity because no one wants it, they could preserve their ideals because no one was interested in corrupting them. They were in a world apart—free, but ignored and underpaid.

World War II changed all that. The government, military, and corporations learned that professors were not useless, and the professors learned that there was much more money and prestige in prostitution than in education. They found they could double or triple their incomes, increase their prestige, and exert more power if they ignored their students, published in the right places, and said the right things.

The basic causes for the decline of the universities are, then, the same as the causes for most human problems—greed, a lust for money, power, and especially prestige. Professors, who have often criticized businessmen as moneygrubbers, are themselves "prestige-grubbers". Perhaps prestige-grubbing is more noble than money-grubbing. Perhaps it is more moral to sell out for prestige than for money, but I cannot see much difference.

In addition to this basic human weakness, most academics have two other undesirable characteristics: provincialism and incompetence.

Most modern professors are very narrow men. They know a great deal about some tiny area, but very little about the rest of the world. Furthermore, their loyalties are almost invariably to their disciplines and their specialties, not to their institutions or students. They neither know nor care about what is done in other classes, nor are they interested in the relationship between their classes and classes taught in other departments. Students therefore encounter the same ideas over and over again, usually expressed in a different set of terms.

Perhaps we are naturally narrow; perhaps professors just aren't big thinkers, but I think that much of our provincialism is caused by the demands of the system. More than anything else, a professor *must* know the literature of his field. A man's work can be trivial, unimaginative, and repetitious, but, if he "knows the literature" and proves it by footnoting everything he says, he will be accepted by his colleagues. Conversely, if he does not know the literature, or if he fails to make the proper footnotes, no amount of originality or brilliance can protect him from criticism, editors' rejections, and a limited career. Again and again and again one sees commentaries and reviews in which the primary criticism is: "he obviously is unfamiliar with Professor _____'s work," or "he obviously does not realize that Professor _____ took the same position in 1932."

Since no man can read the hundreds of books and articles which are written each year in every field, professors learn to limit their work to an area which is small enough to let them master the literature. This superspecialization guarantees academic respectability, but it also guarantees provincialism.

The other basic academic characteristic, our insistence on remaining amateurs, has even more serious consequences. Lawyers, doctors, *public school* teachers, and almost every other professional, as a normal part of their professional training, learn how to perform their basic tasks. In fact, college teaching is the only profession which does not require its members to prepare for their life's work. Very few professors have ever taken a course in learning or teaching. The net result is that "colleges . . . are institutions run by amateurs to train professionals."[5]

Then, with logic which would confuse a confirmed sophist, we make a virtue of our amateur standing. We not only do not study the science of learning and the art of teaching, *we are not supposed to study them.* Doing so is considered unprofessional, and any suggestion that we be required to learn something about our profession encounters massive resistance. We are amateurs and want to remain amateurs, despite the consequences our incompetence has for our students.

Our amateur standing as teachers is matched (if not surpassed) by the administrators. With very few exceptions college administrators have no professional training in administration. Often they are men who did not make it as scholars and turned to administration as a last resort. Since most professors and students have very little respect for these men, they are constantly on the defensive and try to demonstrate their importance by making, changing, and enforcing rules.

[5]Herbert Simon, "The Job of a College President," *The Educational Record*, Winter 1967.

Because they have no training in administration, they do not know that force does not work very well—so when they use force, the results are frequently tragic.

In other words, our greed, provincialism, and incompetence have caused us to fail as educators. But then, since we do not like to believe that we have failed, we adopt all sorts of defences to protect ourselves from the truth. We say that students do not know what they want, that they cannot separate good teaching from entertainment, that the value of our teaching can be measured only later, etc. But the students know the truth—they resent our hypocrisy and try to get through to us by yelling louder. We resist, put greater pressure on them, and escalate the tension. Sooner or later a demonstration or other serious incident is too dramatic to be ignored, and we are surprised to learn that the students really had legitimate complaints.

Now that we have an overview of the basic problems of the system, let us look at various aspects of it in more detail.

WE HAVE YOU BY THE CREDITS

The similarity to a more vulgar expression is not accidental. Both expressions mean that one party has almost absolute power over another, and that is certainly the case here. The colleges and universities are monopolies: they alone have the power to grant degrees[6] and the degree has become virtually indispensable.

The university's control over degrees and credits gives them incredible power over you, and they use that power ruthlessly. There are very large fists inside those velvet gloves labeled "the rule of reason" and "law and order," and they do not hesitate to use these fists.

Berkeley and Columbia proved that they were even willing to take off the gloves and beat up the students, but the gloves usually stay on. When the gloves come off, professors are appalled to see policemen clubbing students. How could this happen in an institution dedi-

---

[6]Universities respond to the charge of monopolism by arguing that students can choose between different schools. Their arguments are essentially irrelevant because they do not provide potential students with the information they need to make a choice. Once the student knows what he is "buying," he is usually locked-in and cannot change without suffering severe penalties.

cated to the rule of reason? But, in one sense, the violence has been a good thing. It has caused severe backlash problems, but it did expose the basic inhumanity of the system and the coercive foundation on which it is based. Presidents Kerr and Kirk therefore performed the same service for education that Jim Clark and Bull Connors[7] performed for the Civil Rights Movement. They helped some people to see that the academics' plea for the "rule of reason" was as hypocritical as the Southerners' call for "law and order."

The students were not surprised by the violence of the repression; they had been getting clubbed for years, but nobody had noticed it before because the bleeding was internal. For example, I was once threatened with *expulsion* from Berkeley for not paying a 25 cent library fine.

Obviously, a man who would deprive a person of a Ph.D. degree for 25 cents should work in a concentration camp rather than in a university, but his actions were far from exceptional. I have heard many similar stories from other students—applications for graduate school which were rejected because of minor clerical errors, courses which were not transferred because they had the wrong name or course number, dissertations which were rejected because the original sponsor had died and requirements had changed, students who failed exams because they disagreed with their professors, etc.

Since these atrocities occur again and again, we must conclude that academics are somehow morally inferior to other men or that there is a fundamental flaw in the system. I believe that academics are no more (and no less) evil than other men, but we have been corrupted by the absolute power which is placed in our hands. We have, in effect, a gun in our hands—and it is silly to expect us not to use it.[8]

This monopoly power is un-American in the most fundamental sense of that word. The most basic principle of the American system is *free choice.* Current conditions limit free choice, but it is still the foundation of our system. Voters can choose between different candidates and political parties; consumers can choose between different

---

[7]Two southern "law officers" who attracted national attention by their brutality.

[8]From what little I have seen of European universities, it appears that things are worse over there (except in England). Professors are even more powerful and irresponsible. I doubt that this is much consolation, but at least it may prevent you from romanticizing the European schools or running off "to a place where I can be a free thinker."

products. This right of free choice gives people real power, and this power is the best defense against corrupt politicians and unsatisfactory businesses.

Because they violate the principle of free choice, monopolies are usually regulated. The government and economists of all ideological camps recognize the danger of monopolies and have regulated them to protect the public interest. The universities, however, have been able to resist regulations and most other forms of "outside interference".[9] Since they are unregulated monopolies, they can ignore your needs and make you do whatever they wish.

This immense, unregulated power is, I think, a major cause for inhuman administration and inadequate teaching. The market system does have its faults, but it is an efficient and equitable allocation mechanism; consumers' decisions determine what goods are produced; satisfactory producers get rich; poor ones fail. Because the universities are monopolies, the students have no power, and the universities can make them comply with ridiculous regulations and force poor teaching down their throats.

Professors do not have to interest their students because they can coerce them. They can be as dull, irrelevant, and disorganized as they wish because they control grades, credits, degrees, and—ultimately— jobs and admissions to graduate school. Textbook writers do not have to write in language the students can understand and enjoy. In fact, they deliberately do not do so because they must satisfy the people who make the buying decisions—other professors. Textbooks are therefore written for professors, and students find them dull, uninteresting, and irrelevant.

Many professors go a step further and feel that any book which is enjoyable can't be very good. They are so completely committed to coercion that they cannot understand that some people don't need it. So they criticize the few academics who write books that students and the general public enjoy reading.

---

[9] It is rather amusing that two groups with monopoly power—the police and the professors—have similar views on "outside interference." They both feel that they should be free from reviews, regulations, and other actions by outsiders. "Academic freedom" is essentially the same thing as "freedom from civilian review boards." But they both think that the *other* group should be supervised by some public agency.

For example, John Galbraith, adviser to President Kennedy, Ambassador to India, and author of *The Affluent Society* and *The New Industrial State*, has helped millions of people to understand economics, but many professors regard his work as illegitimate. The late Eugene Burdick, author of *The Ugly American, The Ninth Wave, Sarkhan, A Nation of Sheep*, and many other books, taught political science much more effectively than most of his colleagues, but he was rejected by many of them and had severe political problems at Berkeley.

There are, of course, many professors who object to the monopolistic, coercive educational system. We have proposed changes which would give the students some power over their courses, professors, and institutions, but these proposals are usually rejected (and their supporters are usually criticized). One "radical" proposal (it is only 2400 years old) was to create a free market for courses and professors. Students could be free, within limits, to choose courses or professors, and the courses offered and professors' salaries would depend, at least partly, on the student choices. Socrates, Plato, Aristotle, St. Augustine, and many other great educators used this system, but most American professors are horrified at the idea.

The reaction of some groups is actually funny, in a macabre sort of way. Many economists preach the virtues of the market system, but are unwilling to work in one; psychologists advocate participative leadership, but teach autocratically; and political scientists endorse democracy in principle, but do not practice it.

THE AMORAL ACADEMICS

Since professors are ready to work for anyone, and they repeatedly avoid their responsibilities as educators, many people feel that these men are immoral. But they aren't really *im*moral; they are *a*moral. They are generally oblivious to the moral consequences of their actions. They are, in a sense, moral idiots—men who do not realize what they are doing. They are so obsessed with their own work and their own careers that they do not even think of the impact they have on other people.

They are like the men who made the atomic bomb ("an interesting, challenging, scientific problem"): they made the bomb, turned it over to the military, and then felt they had discharged their moral responsibility by signing a petition asking the president not to use it! Let me make an even more shocking comparison: many professors resemble the Nazi doctors who performed experiments on concentration camp prisoners and justified the suffering in the name of science.

In fact, if we look at some of the experiments which psychologists are *now* performing on students, the parallels to the work of the Nazi doctors are much greater than the differences. There is not much difference between cutting up a man's body and twisting his mind. Some psychologists have made students believe they were providing dangerous and extremely powerful electric shocks to other students. Others have given students a wide variety of potentially dangerous drugs. One Berkeley professor even measures students' reactions as they watch films of a child's penis being cut (I saw that one, and it is a terrible experience which could have a devastating impact on some people). Any one of these experiments could cause permanent psychological damage. The drug experiments could even injure unborn children if a student did not know she was pregnant (remember what happened with thalidomide). But the dangers to students have been minimized or ignored. What is a little suffering or a few deformed children compared to science—that great, all-consuming, supermoral goal?

Since these men obviously do not realize what they are doing, we cannot call them immoral. Immorality is the willful violation of an accepted moral code, and these professors do not have such a code. This entire book contains examples of their amorality, but let us look at a few other examples to illustrate the principle.

Anybody's Money for Any Purpose

The universities have taken billions of dollars from the military. They have conducted research on atomic, chemical, germ, psychological, and biological warfare, trained CIA agents, and allowed the CIA to use the National Student Association as a front of spying activities. They have allowed professors to use university computers and students (the computers are more valuable, of course) for private research and consulting. They have used their position and prestige to promote dubious inventions (such as cigarette filters) and sell them to the government and public.[10] They have accepted money from anyone for any purpose, and, by doing so, they have violated every principle they are supposed to support—free inquiry, an impartial search for truth, open communication of scientific results, etc.

To the best of my knowledge, the Mafia is not currently support-ing academic research. If it should decide to set up a dummy founda-tion to support research, I have no doubt whatsoever that universities and professors will take their money and conduct whatever kind of research the Mafia requires. In fact, some of their problems would fit right in with some professors' research interests.

If we switch a few variables around, current research models would easily solve such problems as: What is the optimal price for a prostitute's services? How should heroin be diluted to maximize profits? What is the proper differential between the bribes offered to high- and low-level police officers?

Degrees for Sale

Anybody can get a Doctors' degree—if he has enough money. All he must do is to give enough money to a school, and they will give him an Honorary Doctorate for his "distinguished contribution to educa-tion." From time to time a few people feel uneasy about selling de-grees; it is dishonest and cheapens the title "doctor." But what is a little dishonesty compared to all that lovely money?

If the Mafia should decide to support research or contribute to universities, I am sure that they will be well rewarded. In fact, I would not be too surprised to see some prominent gangster receive an honor-ary Doctor of Laws for his "distinguished service to the community."

Helping the Underprivileged

In the past few years the universities have suddenly discovered that we have underprivileged people in America. Universities are sup-posedly repositories of knowledge, but that little fact escaped them for more than a century. Not surprisingly, they discovered these people

---

[10]For a more complete report on these activities, see J. Ridgeway, *The Closed Corporation*, Random House. It will anger and sicken you.

just when it was fashionable and profitable to do so. The poor have always been with us, but the universities were not interested until the government and foundations put up money for research and action programs.

On this issue the universities are far behind the corporations, even though they usually criticize the corporations as being reactionary. Many corporations are *spending their own money* to train people the educational establishment has ignored and to provide jobs and housing for the disadvantaged. The universities are sitting on a mountain of money, tens of billions of dollars, but they still refuse to invest in projects which could help the poor. Sure they help the blacks, Mexicans, and Puerto Ricans—just as long as it is profitable and fashionable to do so.

Plagiarism

If the student gets caught stealing someone's work, he is punished (and deserves to be). If a professor does it, he will probably be promoted. Plagiarism is the great silent scandal of academic life, the equivalent of medical fee-splitting and Congressional graft. Everyone knows it is widespread, but all the insiders are afraid to discuss it.

Even when a man is famous for plagiarizing, faculty committees refuse to consider the issue. Formal investigations are extremely rare, and suggestions that charges be investigated can actually cause trouble for the man who makes them. For example, a member of the CMU policy committee suggested that the recurrent charges that another professor stole students' work be investigated. The policy committee refused, attacked the person making the suggestion, and asked if he had concrete evidence that the charges were true. Since many men have been maligned by rumors of this sort, the man may well be innocent, but it is a rather novel theory of justice that one must be certain that a man is guilty before one begins *to investigate!*

Because it is so hushed up, I have no idea how widespread plagiarism really is. I do know that some very big names are involved. Many of the men who run large research institutes on university campuses insist that their name be attached to every publication that comes out of their organization—regardless of whether they worked on it. Many best-selling textbooks are written or revised by ghost writers. Many,

many professors publish their students' work under their own name.[11]

Plagiarism is, of course, a part of our times. Very few business-men, union leaders, or politicians write their own speeches or their own books. But it is less acceptable (in my opinion) for a professor than it is for a politician or a businessman. And it is certainly dishonest and hypocritical of us to punish students for plagiarism when it is so widespread among the professors.

Naked Exploitation of Students

Closely related to the plagiarism issue is the overt exploitation of students which occurs at most research institutions. As one professor put it: "Graduate students are slaves who help us to build our publica-tion lists."

Virtually every graduate student knows that many of his classes are run not for his education but to help the professors' research. Some professors assign books for students to summarize for the professor's files. Others give students projects which contribute to their books and articles. A few professors even assign projects which are related to their *private consulting*.

Exploitation also occurs at the undergraduate level. In most uni-versity psychology departments students are required to act as unpaid guinea pigs for the psychologists' experiments. If they take an under-graduate course in psychology, they must serve as experimental sub-jects for as many as six hours, even though there is almost no educa-tional value in doing so.

What is particularly shocking about these practices is that they are accepted as being legitimate. We *know* that they are immoral; we *know* that they are a clear violation of our responsibilities as educators; but we allow them to persist. We allow them for the same reason that we allow plagiarism—because publications based upon exploitation, plagiarism, or any other immoral practice build prestige, and prestige is everything in the universities.

There is no chance whatsoever of ending plagiarism and student exploitation. They will continue as long as professors value prestige

---

[11]Plagiarism is even more blatant in Europe. Many of my Belgian colleagues are required to sign contracts stating that they will not publish under their own names. Apparently academic exploitativeness is international in scope.

more than their responsibilities. However, we all feel a little uneasy about these practices. We all know that they are wrong, and we try to avoid confronting the moral issues. Our uneasiness makes it possible for you to avoid being exploited. In simplest terms: don't let us get away with it. For example, if a professor assigns you a project which helps his research or consulting, but doesn't teach you very much, ask for another one. He will probably back down because he wants to avoid a confrontation. If he insists that you do his work for him, drop the course, complain to the administration, perhaps even send a "letter to the editor." These exploitative practices thrive on secrecy, and the professors and administration will do everything they can to avoid publicity and open confrontation.

THE OUTSIDERS

The charge of "outside influence" is very popular these days. Deans and policemen blame student demonstrations on "outside agitators." Liberal professors worry about the impact of the army, CIA, government, and corporations. Teachers deplore the money and attention lavished on athletics.

Clearly, the universities are no longer ivory towers, isolated from the world. For better of worse they have become involved in the world and subject to many of its pressures. Since we cannot turn back the clock and these pressures are going to affect you, you must understand them and the impact they can have upon you.

The Leftists

When the man on the street talks about "outsiders," he usually means the leftists—the communists, socialists, black militants, and "other assorted kooks" with long hair, dirty clothes, and beards. The public doesn't like them, and it usually blames student demonstrations on "outside agitation."

Most students resent this position. They know that one should not lump together all factions of the left wing (they fight with each other as much as with the right). They ridicule the logic which equates political opinion and bathing habits. They are acutely aware of the legitimacy of their grievances, feel that their demonstrations are a spontaneous reaction to these grievances, and point out that most people at demonstrations are registered students.[12]

As in most controversies, both sides are partly correct, and both have oversimplified the situation. Students do have grievances, and these grievances are the basic driving force behind complaints and demonstrations. Most people at demonstrations are students, but the leftists have often worked very hard to get them there. They could not bring out the crowds if there were not real issues, but many student revolts have not been "spontaneous reactions to repression" or any of the other nonsense you read in the left-wing press. Demonstrations are often organized well in advance, and incidents are deliberately created to start things rolling. The left has years of practice at creating and exploiting incidents, and they are helped immensely by the predictable stupidity and repression of the police and administrators.

Daley's police did run amok. They did violate every rule of civilized police conduct, but they were deliberately provoked in ways which would cause most of us to lose our self-control. What would you do if someone threw a bag full of urine at you? How would you react to being called a "m . . . f . . . pig?"

I am certainly no apologist for the police and administrators, and I am not trying to justify their inexcusable conduct. But you should realize that many of the incidents which make you so furious are deliberately created for that purpose.

And, if you let your emotions take over your behaviour, you are going to be as manipulated by the left as you have been manipulated by the establishment. Since the goal, the ultimate end, of education is to make you independent, you must understand *both* the establishment and the people who are trying to tear it down. They are both trying to use you, but you really do not want to be used by anyone. This book will help you to understand and to cope with the establishment. Several other books can help you with the left.[13]

---

[12]This fact can be substantiated by the record of arrests at any demonstration. The overwhelming majority are invariably students. However, policemen, who have made the arrests, still emphasize the role of the outsiders, the "nonstudents."

[13]A sympathetic portrayal of the left, but one which clearly illustrates its manipulative tactics, can be found in John Steinbeck's *In Dubious Battle* (New York, Modern Library). J. Edgar Hoover's *Masters of Deceit* (New York: Holt, Rinehart and Winston, 1958) is highly propagandistic, but it can give you a quick overview and refer you to original sources. Many of these original sources were written by communists, including Lenin. A few hours spent with them can keep you from being exploited.

The Money Men

The leftists may be the most visible outsiders, but they are certainly not the most influential ones. They make the most noise and attract the most attention, but the money men have much more real power. The government, military, foundations, and corporations put up *most* of the schools' operating budgets. They provide nearly all the research funds, and, through loans to students and grants to institutions, most of the tuition and endowments as well. The universities pretend that they preserve their operational independence, but, since *no* institution or individual can be operationally independent when it is financially dependent, we should not be deceived by their public statements.

The men who control the money will inevitably control or influence decisions about how it is spent, and it is naive to pretend otherwise.[14] Sometimes, this influence is direct, but more frequently it is quite subtle and indirect. The direct influence is much better known, but the indirect is really more dangerous. When a university does classified research, trains CIA agents, or uses its prestige to promote cigarette filters,[15] the men involved *know* that they are violating academic principles. But some men will always prostitute themselves, and there are probably fewer prostitutes in academia than there are in most places.

The real tragedy is that men of integrity, men who would never willingly sell out, unwittingly allow themselves to be manipulated so that their work is used for purposes they dislike. They do not mean to help the establishment; they may even be opposed to it, but academic pressures and their own naïveté cause them to become, consciously or unconsciously, "servants of power".[16] They are not interested in politics or economics. They just want to do their work, write their articles, and be left alone.[17] But to do research, one needs money.

[14]The critics of federal aid to education have been saying that for years, but, since they are conservatives (and therefore unrespectable in academic circles), and we love all that lovely money, we have not bothered to listen.

[15]As Columbia has done.

[16]This issue is discussed much more fully in *The Servants of Power* (New York: Wiley) by Loren Baritz.

[17]These characteristics of scientists and the privileged position of scientists in Russia have caused some scientists to defect to Russia. Among all other groups, far more

Researchers must therefore learn the "grantsmanship game"—who has the money and how to get it. They must learn what topics and approaches are "supportable," and then work on supportable projects.

At first they may resist these pressure and try to follow their own interests, but after they find that they cannot get research money, and after the dean explains the facts of life, they get the message and play the game (or get out of academia). The money men therefore control research at its most sensitive point, at the planning stages. Ideas which might lead to real breakthroughs are dropped because they are too new or different to appeal to the money men, and many professors automatically drop ideas which are unlikely to receive support.[18] The money men and the journal editors occasionally work together to squash new ideas (see "The Censors," below).

This problem is aggravated by the fact that so much research money comes from the military. The Pentagon spends billions on research each year,[19] but not all of this money is spent on research directly related to weapons and military developments. The Pentagon also supports research in medicine, biology, anthropology, sociology, psychology, and many other fields. For example, the 1968 budget for behavioral and social science research was 45 million dollars,[20] much of which went to universities and professors.

This huge amount of money obviously gives the military enormous power over the universities and professors. The men who take this money (or try to) may utter all the academic platitudes: "We only do basic research" or "We insist on retaining the right to pick our own projects and control our own research," etc., but the military is obviously not going to support research which is not useful to them, and many professors will select, consciously or unconsciously, problems and methods which appeal to the generals.

---

people defect from Russia to the U.S. than *vice versa,* but more scientists move East than West. See S. De Gramont, *The Secret War* (Dell, 1962, pp. 354–359).

[18]One reason that "wild ideas" are dropped is that it takes a great deal of time and effort to submit a request for research funds. For example, the forms for a Public Health Services grant weigh more than a pound. No one wants to do all this work if he has little chance of getting a grant.

[19]The 1968 research budget was 8 billion dollars (*The New York Times,* July 19, 1968).

[20]*The New York Times,* July 19, 1968.

The Athletic Promoters

Europeans are often amazed when they learn how much emphasis we place on college athletics. One of my Belgian associates, after a trip to the U.S., asked: "What sort of universities do you have over there where they care more about winning football games than they do about research and teaching?" He obviously overstated the point, but I could not answer his question.

There is something fundamentally wrong with a school which allows itself to become a football factory. Sure, it's fun—a great way to spend Saturday afternoons. But what price do we pay for those afternoons?

We let ourselves be distracted from the basic purposes of the university, and we let basic principles be violated. We all know that many athletes are employees rather than students.[21] We know that some schools have changed students' grades to protect their athletic eligibility, that athletes are recruited dishonestly and paid under the table, that many athletes (especially black ones) never get their degrees.[22] By ignoring these problems we give our students another example of our cynicism, hypocrisy, and opportunism—and then we wonder why they don't respect us!

We ignore these problems and emphasize sports because sports are both profitable and prestigious. A winning team earns money, attracts attention, keeps the alumni and legislators happy (and therefore ready to contribute), and brings business into town for sporting events. The role of businessmen is especially disturbing. The very men who complain about "outside agitators" on campus use the universities to sell their products.

College football and basketball games are televized as purely commercial ventures. They sell beer, cigarettes, and dozens of other products. The TV revenues are so important to schools that they go out of their way to keep broadcasters and sponsors happy. The Berkeley

[21]The NCAA has even passed a rule which allows a school to fire an athlete (withdraw his scholarship aid) if he does not satisfy the athletic department. Even before this rule was passed, many athletes had lost their scholarships when they didn't make the varsity.

[22]For example, all five starters on the Texas Western basketball team that won the NCAA title in 1966 have not received their degrees. Let's not hear any more of that rationalization: "sports help poor boys to get an education".

businessmen, who are constantly complaining about outside agitators, get a lot of business from football crowds and have exerted a great deal of pressure against attempts to deemphasize football or to make Berkeley into a school with few or no undergraduates.

Notre Dame even provided the background for a Ford TV commercial! Ara Parseghian, the head football coach, walks around the campus, points out a few landmarks, and then drives a Ford into the football stadium. It may be profitable or "good public relations," but I think there is something infinitely obscene about a university renting itself out as an advertising prop.

Many other outsiders influence the universities, but the leftists, money men, and athletic promoters are the most important ones. Interestingly, each group criticizes the others for exploiting the universities, but ignores its own actions. The sports promoters criticize outside agitators; the left condemns military research; the foundations deplore the emphasis on athletics; and all of them use the university for their own purposes and destroy its independence. Thanks to them and to our own greed and naïveté—"the 'independent' university is a myth, or rather a memory."[23]

> "Freedom of speech is meaningless if
> everyone says the same thing."

THE CENSORS

Professors are allowed to speak much more freely than most other Americans, but they have far less freedom than is commonly believed. The professor who speaks out too boldly is punished severely, but very subtly. A corporation might fire an executive for making an unpatriotic or controversial speech. The universities exert almost as much censorship, but they usually do it subtly so that they can claim that they respect academic freedom.

Sometimes they do fire someone openly, but usually they just refuse to promote or to raise the salary of professors who get out of

[23]Jacques Barzun, *The American University*, Harper & Row, 1969.

line. They can also make life generally unpleasant by giving these men inconvenient class hours, extra committee service, and various dirty jobs. Unpleasantness and rejection would force out most sensitive men, and inflation and the rapid rise in professors' salaries give the universities enough power to exert fairly tight control.

The case of Professor Genovese of Rutgers University (a state-supported institution) is an almost perfect example of this principle. He became a major political issue in the 1966 New Jersey gubernatorial campaign when he stated his sympathy and support for the Viet Cong. One candidate wanted him fired; the other "stood firmly for academic freedom." Rutgers cloaked itself in academic piety and supported his right to speak freely. After the noise had died down, Genovese quit because his salary had been kept below standards.

Violations of academic freedom do not always involve the left. An even more flagrant violation was the blackballing of Professor Walter Rostow, an advisor to Presidents Kennedy and Johnson, who outraged the academic community by his hawkish stand on Vietnam. Despite his outstanding reputation as a scholar, he was not allowed to return to his old job at MIT, nor could he work at any other major university. His case was even more shocking than Genovese's because his scholarly production was so great that there was no academically legitimate reason to blackball him. It was a blatant case of overt censorship.

This case clearly shows how hypocritical the major universities are. *More than half* of MIT's entire budget comes from the Pentagon,[24] but they rejected Rostow because he *openly* endorsed military force. Their attitude toward him is rather like the call girls' attitude towards streetwalkers: they're all in the same business, but the streetwalker is too "obvious" about it.

The cases of Genovese and Rostow show very clearly that professors are expected to be wishy-washy, middle-of-the-road semiliberals. They should be somewhat antimilitary because academia is anti-military, but they cannot be so far left that they create unpleasant controversies.

I disagree strongly with Rostow's actions as a Presidential Advisor, but I respect him more than the men who blackballed him. His

[24] *Newsweek*, November 17, 1969, p. 58.

political beliefs are his own business, and he was honest enough to state his position clearly and unequivocally, while his critics have been hypocrites, hiding behind rationalizations and secret blackballs.

One may, however, argue that academic freedom does not refer to political or other controversial issues; it is simply the professors' right to take any position on issues related to their own specialities. Unfortunately, professors have much *less* freedom here than they do on controversial issues. It is much easier to say something outrageously controversial then it is to do something truly creative, and the academic system is more tolerant of political controversy than of professional originality.

Professors learn very early in their careers that they cannot say anything original, that doing so is academic suicide. Because different schools and journals have different emphases, professors do not have to follow any *particular* party line, but they must follow *some* respectable party line to survive.[25]

The Journal Editors

There are several levels of censorship, but the editors are the ultimate censors, "the definers of the truth." Truth is what they say it is, and anyone who disagrees with them is dead. They are the final court; there is no place to appeal their decisions.[26] If they refuse to publish a professor's work, he cannot survive, and they refuse any paper which does not follow one of the acceptable party lines ("schools of thought", is the academic euphemism for "party line").

Usually the editors justify their decisions in a very plausible manner. Every article has some flaws, and an editor can always make a reasonable case for rejecting any article. Occasionally, they slip up and let authors see naked censorship. By an almost unbelievable coincidence some of my own work was *openly* censored right after I had

[25]These statements must be qualified. Censorship is exerted most heavily in the humanities, somewhat heavily in the social sciences, and rather slightly in the sciences. As data become more important, censorship and academic authority become less important. Furthermore, some men who become big names by doing unoriginal things for many years are occasionally allowed to say something original.

[26]There are, of course, books and other places to publish. Books are rather hard to do, especially for research reports, because they have a limited market. Articles in other places are usually of no value to a professors' career and may even have a negative value because professors are not supposed to write "popular trash."

drafted this chapter. I had been censored repeatedly in the past, but this was the first time I could prove it.

A graduate student and I had written an article (naturally, she did most of the work). The article reviewed over fifty studies of smoking and heart disease and suggested that the Surgeon General might be incorrect in concluding that smoking caused heart disease. The relationship between smoking and heart disease might be caused by emotional stress. (Stress affects the heart directly, and it also causes people to smoke more heavily.) The paper was very tentative because the evidence is far from clear, but we did make a reasonable case that this hypothesis deserved to be studied more closely.

We were turned down by a couple of journals with the usual justifications, but then one journal accepted the paper very enthusiastically. I wish that I could give a verbatim copy of the letters revealing this censorship, but the publisher's legal department has advised that letters can only be reprinted with the permission of the person who wrote them.

Since the editor in question had violated his scientific responsibility and the ethics of his profession by repressing the publication of an article, I did not even bother to ask him for permission to reprint his letters.

The first letter accepted the article in an unusually enthusiastic manner. Most journals have a long backlog of articles to publish, and each accepted article must wait for its turn to be published. Editors rarely pull an article which has been scheduled for publication in a particular issue to make room for a different one, but the acceptance letter stated that he was intending to pull one and perhaps two articles so that our article could be published in the very next issue. Even more surprisingly, the editor said that he was "grateful" to us for giving him a chance to publish the article. Editors almost never make such statements.

A month later we received an incredible letter. The editor stated that he had sent the article to the Surgeon General of the Public Health Service for an opinion, and the article "now stands rejected." He also noted that we "must have predicted the consequences" of allowing the Surgeon General to rule on the acceptability of the article.

The *only* thing that is unusual about this entire affair is that the censorship is so obvious. The editor blew it. He accepted the article on its merits before he cleared it with the Public Health Service. Then, when the PHS killed the article, he did not cover his tracks with the usual academic nonsense: "We have re-examined your article and noted that you did not refer to the article by Professor Schlockenheimer. Since his work is so basic to this topic, we have decided not to publish your paper."

Instead of covering himself, he let us see, clearly and unequivocally, that papers on smoking, even those critical of the Surgeon General's position, must be cleared. And, in his own words, we can "predict" the results of giving the SG veto power over publications which criticize his position. It is, of course, a violation of the entire tradition of scientific inquiry and discussion to allow anyone to have this veto power, especially when the power resides in a person with a vested interest,[27] but the Public Health Service controls billions of dollars in research funds, owns lots of professors, and can do as it pleases. It is an open secret in academic life that they have killed other investigations which criticized their position, but no one will confront them because they are too powerful.

All journal editors have censorship powers, but the editors of the "prestige journals" are especially powerful. There are only a few prestige journals in each field, and a professor must publish in them to stay at the major schools. These editors therefore determine who will work at the major schools.

Editors can exert this vast influence because contract renewal and promotion decisions are generally based on the total *number* of publications and the *number* published in prestige journals. Most personnel committees do not read the professor's work; they simply count the titles on his publication list and give extra credit for the ones published in prestige journals. A good article is one which is placed in a good journal. A bad article is one which is published in a bad journal or is not accepted for publication.

Professors therefore study the journals, find out what they are

[27]People who are not familiar with scientific reporting may believe that the editor was justified in asking the PHS to advise him on the article, but asking for that advice would be the equivalent of allowing a defense attorney to judge the quality of the prosecution's evidence. That is, in science as in law the evidence should be judged by impartial third parties.

"buying," and design their work to fit the market. This is an obvious sell-out which takes away the integrity and originality of the work, but professors still let the journals dominate them. When I talk to a professor who is clearly designing his work to match the market, I sometimes wonder: Is there any real difference between the TV scriptwriter who turns out marketable junk and the professor who does the same thing?

This emphasis on the number of publications has some other unpleasant consequences. Most of us have only a few ideas, but we need lots of publications. We obviously can not develop our ideas too thoroughly, because we need those articles. We therefore prepare "partial publications": we publish things a bit at a time. In fact, proposed research projects are often evaluated in terms of the number of publications that can be squeezed out of them. A good project is one which yields several articles, even if the articles don't say anything. Some professors have even developed standardized formats for research and writing. They are like lawyers' forms. One just fills in the blanks and mails them to the editors.

We also learn how to rewrite our own articles and to publish them in more than one place. We might have an article in three or four different places which says almost exactly the same thing, but it gives four titles on the publication list. The academic term for this sort of work is "grinding out garbage."

Colleagues

One's colleagues also censor his work. Like most other men, professors want the approval and respect of their associates. Since their associates will generally criticize them for not working on the proper topics, most professors do socially acceptable research.

The Club

The jobs at the major schools are almost always arranged by the "club," the powerful inner circle. These men are spread all over the country, but they know each other, think the same way, and determine who gets the good jobs. Without the support of at least one of them, it is almost impossible to get a job at a major school.

The club also has an enormous influence over what gets published. The entire editorial boards of most journals are club members, and they will publish their friends' papers and reject papers from outsiders. There are even issues of journals in which *every* article has been written by an editor.

The academic club acts like all other clubs: it does not accept people unless they think the same way as the older members. It therefore filters out the independent, unconventional men who could make original contributions.

Graduate School

From the moment a student applies to graduate school till the day he completes his doctoral dissertation, he is watched closely to make sure that he is safe, that he won't rock the boat by doing anything original. For example, the Carnegie-Mellon psychology department rejected applications from two qualified students because they "wouldn't fit in here." One was interested in military psychology and expressed strong right-wing sentiments on his application. The other said that he thought he could make his "major contribution to the work of Jesus Christ by working as a psychologist." Our rejection of these two students was a blatant violation of several Civil Rights Acts, but none of us even considered that issue.

As a student at Berkeley I was worried about being able to read all the material for the qualifying examination. One of the examining professors reassured me by saying: "Don't worry about reading all the material. Just make sure you understand the biases of the examining committee and match your answer to their biases". Subsequent events proved that that principle applied to nearly all my exams.

Academic hiring policies are even more revealing. The very first thing we want to know about a potential professor are his thesis advisor and institution. This information usually tells us how he thinks because he could not survive if he didn't think the way his professors do.

The Basic Cause

The basic cause for censorship is, of course, the academic obsession with prestige. Safe, unoriginal publications in prestige journals guarantee prestige. Work which does not conform threatens professors and institutions. Original research might reveal that some cherished myths are incorrect, that some professors' reputations are undeserved. Popular writing is unacceptable because it does not contribute to institutional prestige.

Usually this obsession with prestige is hidden behind rationalizations about "standards," "contributions to knowledge," "thoroughness of research," "command of literature," etc., but a few people are more honest and explicit about why they want to act as censors. The Dean of Business School at Boston University once said that he did not want his faculty to write for the general public because: "I'm trying to build up the prestige of this place, and that sort of writing has negative prestige."

The Consequences

Because academic censorship is exerted subtly, many professors ignore it or pretend that it does not exist. But ignoring it does not reduce its effects, and these effects are obvious and predictable. Overt censorship stifles the students and junior faculty. They spend most of their time meticulously verifying what we already know.[28] The senior faculty are less vulnerable, but men who were selected as graduate students because they fit in, who had to flatter their professors to get their degrees and jobs, who have spent years selecting projects that appeal to the money men and journal editors are not likely to do original work. As one professor put it: "After 20 years of grinding out garbage, I *can't* say anything original."

They are much more likely to play the game, to grind out the publications, and to suppress their occasional discomfort about selling

---

[28]For example, there are dozens of published studies of the relationships between job satisfaction and turnover. These publications contain all of the academic mumbo-jumbo—correlation coefficients, obscure symbols, mathematical models, literature reviews, etc.—but the conclusion that emerges from them is obvious to everyone: people who don't like their jobs tend to quit!

out. One professor expressed these doubts openly, but said that he was going to play the game for all it was worth: "I haven't had an original idea in two years, but I still grind out four articles a year."

Most professors dislike selling out so completely. They want to be at least a *little bit* original, but they know that original work probably will not get published. Since their ideas must not be truly original, they express their originality in the worst possible way, by coining new terms for the same old ideas: "cognitive dissonance," "synergy", "status incongruence," "surgency-desurgency", and similar terms sound original and confuse students, but they refer to old ideas.

Although they would not admit it, professors play a game which is quite similar to the game played by popular recording artists. To make it big in the pop world you have to be *slightly* original. You must sense the trends and be very close to them, but just different enough so that you stand out. That is exactly what the professors do. They fall into some well-organized school of thought, but make minor changes in terminology, approach, or theory to establish their own identity.

Censorship is also a cause for the professors' famous narrowness, a characteristic that can have devastating effects upon you. You will be exposed to one narrow specialist after another, learn and forget several sets of jargon, but rarely get a chance to see how things fit together. Unless you take direct action to overcome our narrowness, you may never get that "broad perspective" that the college catalogues promise you.

The academics' censorship, narrowness, unoriginality, and emphasis on quantity are related to the trends we discussed earlier. Like most other Americans, most professors have given up their right and ability to make independent evaluations and decisions; they have substituted the approval of other people for their own judgment and originality; they have treated research as a commodity which can only be evaluated by the market.

Since they cannot judge the value of their own work, they cannot let you judge yours. The system censors them, and they censor you. Therefore, if you want to develop your own creativity and independence, you must find the professors who have not sold out and avoid or resist the ones who have. You must find the independent men because only they will value and help you to develop your own independence.

> "There is no conflict between teaching and
> research."

TEACHING, THE DYING ART[29]

This very popular faculty folk saying is the academic equivalent of: "The darkies are happy down on the plantation." Both are obviously untrue, but both make people feel better. They solve moral dilemmas by pretending that they do not exist. They allow men to ignore the consequences of their own selfishness by pretending that they are really acting for the benefit of the people they are exploiting.

Because both teaching and research are hard to measure, and there has been little research on college-level teaching, there is not much scientifically acceptable evidence, either pro or con, on this issue. However, professors who are proud of their objectivity and their ability to evaluate evidence, repeatedly assert that there is no conflict and accept supporting "evidence" which is too weak to be accepted on any other issue. They do so, of course, because they want to deceive themselves, students, and the public.

The "Evidence"

They point out that some great researchers are fine teachers and that some poor researchers are poor teachers. Occasionally, they go further and conduct more formal investigations, most of which find no clear relationship between professors' teaching and research. For example, Virginia Voeks, who evaluated the teaching and research of 193 professors, stated: "No trace of relationship was found between amount of publications and quality of teaching in any field."[30]

[29]This section will describe what is wrong with the teaching system. The chapter on learning will discuss ways to learn despite the system.
[30]"Publications and teaching effectiveness," *Journal of Higher Education*, vol. 33, pp. 212–218, April 1962.

To a layman these data might indicate that there is no conflict between teaching and research, but any social scientist should know better than to draw that conclusion. The fact that there is no relationship is really evidence that there *is* a conflict because research has shown positive relationships between virtually all intellectual activities. People who are good in mathematics are also good in English, foreign languages, spelling, history, and other subjects. Positive correlations have been found between virtually every possible pair of intellectual activities—except teaching and research.

These correlations occur because there is an underlying common factor: brains. More intelligent people can perform almost any intellectual activity better than less intelligent people.

While I have seen lots of mindless research and teaching, I doubt very much that any of my colleagues would claim that a professor's teaching and research are unrelated to his intelligence. Yet that is exactly what they do when they assert that the absence of a relationship indicates that there is no conflict between teaching and research. It really indicates that policies which emphasize research have suppressed the natural relationship we should expect between these two intellectual activities.

Their willingness to cite such nonsensical evidence to support their position indicates how morally and intellectually bankrupt professors have become. They are willing to violate their own standards and to ignore or to distort the evidence to preserve the fiction that their selfish behavior does not hurt the students.

The Basic Issue

Furthermore, they are distracting attention from the basic issue, which is not whether researchers are or are not good teachers, but whether *each* professor is a better or a poorer teacher because of his research. Students have the right to the best efforts of each professor, regardless of how talented he is; the basic question is, therefore, whether emphasizing research improves or harms teaching.

On that question, the answer is quite obvious. A few professors are better teachers because of their research, but most are poorer. Their research takes time that could be spent preparing for classes or working with students, and it causes them to focus on such narrow topics with such specialized jargons that students cannot understand them. We will consider the issue of time allocations in several other places, but let me give a horrible example of the way a man's research can ruin his teaching.

At Berkeley I was a graduate teaching assistant to Professor X., who had devoted his life to watching pigeons peck at various objects. Outside of a narrow group of cultists, nobody cares about pigeon pecking, but he found it fascinating. One day he lectured to his introductory psychology class about some of his experiments. Because the students knew his experiments would be on the exams, they tried to follow him, but it was impossible. He was up in the clouds, in a world of his own, drawing graphs, writing numbers all over the place, citing authorities with whom he agreed or disagreed. He obviously enjoyed himself immensely, but, when it was over, not one of the 10 *graduate assistants* understood what he had been talking about. And, if we couldn't understand it, how could the freshmen? After checking with my classes and the other assistants, I told him that no one could understand him and suggested that he be less technical in his lectures. He was outraged at my rudeness and stupidity.

"If you can't understand the lecture, you haven't been reading enough. Read my articles."

"But beginning students can't read original articles, and this is a class for beginners."

"That is too bad. You can't expect me to lower myself to their level. This isn't high-school you know."

"But they have no foundation for the points you are making. They don't understand the basic principles because you are losing them in the details."

"The details are important to the theory, and I don't intend to let you or them make this into a superficial survey course."

For the rest of the week he stood in front of 800 people, talking to himself, while the students sat there, copying the numbers and graphs. They did not know what it meant, but they hoped they could give it back to him on the exams. In a school that believed in teaching, he would have been dismissed for incompetence. At Berkeley he was soon promoted to full professor, presumably for his research on pigeon pecking.

He is an extreme example, but this sort of thing happens all the time. Most academic research is so narrowly specialized that it has no value at all to undergraduates,[31] and most researchers are so involved in their work that they cannot understand how irrelevant and uninteresting it is to students. They simply use their power to make the students listen to their lectures and read their articles, even though doing so is often a waste of time.

Academic Rewards

The academic hierarchy reinforces this tendency by rewarding research heavily, ignoring student evaluations of teaching, refusing to make any systematic or objective evaluation of teaching effectiveness, and *using a man's research to evaluate his teaching*. Alexander Astin and Calvin Lee,[32] who surveyed all the American colleges and universities, found:

> The professor's scholarly research and publication—not information based on classroom visits, systematic student ratings, student performance on examinations and similar sources—are currently the primary consideration in evaluating his *teaching* ability. . . . The heavy reliance on scholarly production as an indication of teaching ability greatly confuses the distinction between teaching and research and exaggerates the importance of research and publication.

Using publication as an index of teaching quality is particularly shocking because the study cited earlier (as well as a few other studies) indicates that there is no relationship between a man's quality as a teacher and researcher.

Astin and Lee concluded from their data that: "most institutions, unwillingly perhaps, engage in evaluation practices which, because they emphasize other academic activities, stand in the way of improving undergraduate teaching."

[31]The situation is quite different for graduate students, who sometimes get a great deal from professors' research.

[32]"Current Practices in the Evaluation and Training of College Teachers." *Educational Record*, Summer 1966.

It should be noted, however, that the importance of research and publication depends on the type of school. The universities rely most heavily on them, while the junior colleges hardly use them at all. This difference has important implications for your choice of college.

Since professors are directly rewarded for publishing, are considered as good teachers if they publish, and are not evaluated directly as teachers, is it any surprise that many of them ignore their teaching and concentrate on their research? And, given these facts, can any honest, objective individual claim that there is no conflict between teaching and research?

In Defense of Research

A word should be said, however, in defence of academic resarch. It does fill an important social function: the creation of knowledge. Even though much of it is trivial and repetitious, professors do conduct research on many topics which no one else will touch. Nearly all research conducted outside the universities is in applied areas, and our society also needs basic research. Our society would probably get more for its investment in basic research if more time were spent on genuine research and less time on grinding our repetitious publications, but we really do not have much choice. Since the professors are the only ones who are doing basic research, we shall have to tolerate their wastefulness (or develop a better system, a most unlikely possibility).[33]

The social importance of academic research does not, however, justify the price which students have to pay for the emphasis on research. Society gets the benefit, but students pay the price. From their standpoint, it would be much better if research were deemphasized and professors were rewarded for doing good teaching. Unfortunately, it is highly questionable that deemphasizing research would result in much greater emphasis on teaching.

Nearly all colleges, even those that do not emphasize research, have an unwritten rule that professors' teaching is not to be evaluated in any systematic or meaningful way. Long-term follow-up studies (the most meaningful kind of information) are extremely rare. Alumni opinions are hardly ever solicited. Student ratings are being used in an increasing number of schools, but they are usually done unofficially and are not taken very seriously by the administration or the profes-

---

[33]However, much of the research done in the universities, especially the work done for the military, is not basic, and could easily be done elsewhere.

sors. Since genuine research on teaching effectiveness is almost nonexistent, and systematic evaluations are taboo, it is almost impossible to measure the quality of a professor's teaching.

The most probable effect of deemphasizing research would therefore be to increase the emphasis on seniority and campus politics. Salary and promotion decisions have to be made on some basis, and, if that basis can not be either teaching or research, it would probably be seniority and politics. These factors, of course, exist at all schools, but they are more important when other bases for judgment and personal advancement are minimized.

At least researchers care about their work. They may care *too* much and bore students by talking excessively about their work, but some of their enthusiasm may rub off, and the smarter and more dedicated men get most of the rewards. In most of the nonresearch schools, the *only* things that count are seniority and politics, and this creates an unhealthy environment for everyone. Dead wood dominates the faculty, and political intrigues are the center of attention.

Research has also helped to attract better men to the universities. In earlier times (and even today at many small schools) some professors wanted to be businessmen, military officers, or independent professionals, but they failed and turned to teaching as a last resort. Professors were therefore less talented than successful men in other fields. Today the picture is quite different, at least at the research schools. Nearly all professors have deliberately chosen and prepared for academic life, and many of them regularly turn down high-paying jobs in industry and government. A professor who is dedicated to research may not be as good for students as one who is dedicated to teaching, but he is probably a lot better than a man who teaches only because he can't make a living any other way.

The Method Is the Message

"In education, the method is the message."[34]

That is a flippant phrase, but an important one. With it the Rappings have summarized their most important point:

[34]L. A. Rapping and E. A. Rapping, "Politics and Morality in Academe," *Saturday Review,* Oct 19, 1968.

There is only one really useful thing a teacher can communicate—not a set of facts, or formulae, or the "true meaning" of a poem, but an intellectual method or style of apprehending the world.

If they are correct (and I think they are), then the most important contribution we can make to your development is not to give you a set of facts which you can repeat on exams or a set of skills which you can sell on the market place.[35] It is to help you to understand and to use the ideal academic approach—detached, objective, and impartial.

If that should be our major contribution, we must know and use this method ourselves. We obviously cannot communicate it to you if we have not mastered it ourselves, and the only way to master it is to conduct our own research.

It seems obvious that research is an essential part of a teacher's responsibilities. He need not publish anything, of course, but anyone who does not use the methods of his discipline regularly or find them relevant to his own deepest interests, is not likely to maintain the ability to teach them for very long.[36]

In an ideal sense the Rappings are unquestionably correct. The method is the message, and a professor is going to be a better teacher if he can use the intellectual method and teach it to his students. Unfortunately, research is almost never encouraged on these grounds. It is encouraged because it is profitable and prestigious for both the universities and the professors, and this emphasis negates most of its value.

Some professors do, of course, maintain their detachment and objectivity, but many others do not. They realize that publications, not research, are valued, and they do whatever is necessary to grind out publications. The emphasis is therefore not on objectivity and detachment, but on finding out what the journal editors are "buying" and giving them what they want.

Even if research is conducted in a detached, objective way to satisfy the professor's intellectual curiosity, its value to the students is generally lost because we rarely let them see *how* we have proceeded.

[35]Your employers will provide the skills. Even if you go to a skill-oriented institution (such as an engineering school), your employers will still spend a great deal of time and money developing the skills they want.
[36]Rapping and Rapping, *op. cit.*

Instead of letting them see our minds at work, we show them the product of our thoughts. They see the results, not the process; the publications, not the sweat that went into them; the lectures, not the thoughts we had when we prepared them.

On the rare occasions that we discuss the way we reach our conclusions, we edit the process to make ourselves look better than we are. Every researcher knows how many blind alleys he has wandered into and how long it has taken to find his way out, but we rarely tell our students about them. We talk and write about our successes, partly because we are vain, partly because the journal editors do not allow us to be honest. They will only publish the stories of our successes. The failures get buried in our files.[37]

There are a few professors who "tell it like it is." They let their students in on the excitement, confusion, frustration, and logic of their research, and thereby help them to develop both the intellectual method and the desire to use it (the desire is, of course, at least as important as the skill itself). B. F. Skinner, the eminent psychologist, is one of the most prominent examples. He has written about his research in such a way that students can see how his conclusions emerged—and they see the whole process, including the false leads, incorrect conclusions, and sloppy thinking, as well as the underlying commitment and method that resulted in a major scientific contribution. He also cuts through the mystical mumbo-jumbo about "the" scientific method and acknowledges the importance of "following your nose" and "being lucky."

But men like that are very rare; most of us use very different methods and communicate very different messages. We may not mean to communicate them, but what we are and what we do communicates much more clearly than what we say. These unintended messages are a prime cause of student dissatisfaction and campus unrest.

FORCE IS LEGITIMATE   Perhaps the clearest message is that we believe not in objectivity, detachment, and reason but in *force*. We do

---

[37]The policy of publishing only the successes causes many scientific fields to become very distorted, a fact which has caused hundreds of scientists to propose a *Journal of Negative Results.* Alas, these suggestions have been made for decades, but such a journal has never been published.

not appeal to students' reason by presenting them with facts about courses, books, and professors and letting them make their own decisions. We say: "Take this course with this professor and read what he says—or else." If the student should ask: "Why?" (a perfectly legitimate question in institutions devoted to the rule of reason), we say: "Because we said so; if you don't like it, get out."

Since you have been taught that force is legitimate and have found that legitimate questions and orderly protests are ignored, is it any wonder that you use force against us?

EXPLOITATION IS LEGITIMATE   The exploitative practices referred to earlier (using students as guinea pigs, stealing their work, making them do our research, etc.) clearly communicate to students that exploitation is legitimate. Reactions to this message are predictable, and they have serious consequences for our society. Some students feel that ideals are obsolete and set out to exploit other people. They become the sorts of American who make us cringe—slum-lords, hucksters, etc. Other students cling more militantly to their ideals; they claim that the entire exploitative system must be torn down, and they take the destructive actions which have become so common. Professors generally dislike both types, but they feel no responsibility for creating either.

EDUCATION IS A BORE   By insisting that students do what they are told instead of helping them to enjoy the pleasures of the mind, we teach them that education is a dull waste of time. They do not enjoy it, and they look forward to graduation as the end to educational pressures.

THE WORLD IS CHAOTIC   In an ultimate sense, education is concerned not with facts but with relationships. It attempts to make sense out of chaos, order out of confusion. An educated man can see how things fit together, and this knowledge becomes an unshakable foundation of his life and sense of identity.

Our system rarely communicates that sense of relatedness. Students do not study the world they live in; they study physics, chemistry, biology, economics, sociology, psychology, and so on, and these subjects are generally divorced from reality and from each other.

They study physics not because its principles can help them to understand the world, but because it is a required course. It is not a tool, not
an aid to understanding, but a complex crossword puzzle which they
must complete to receive their degrees.

Most professors create that crossword puzzle image. Instead of
relating their subjects to the students' lives, interests, and other
courses, they treat each course as a distinct unit. In psychology courses
students learn one set of terms and theories; in sociology they learn
another; in economics they learn a third. Very rarely do professors
ever refer to other fields, and the references they do make are usually
derogatory. "Economists don't understand human motivation," says
the psychologist; "psychologists are naïve," says the sociologist; "sociology is little more than common sense," says the economist. And
each professor insists that students accept his perspective in his class.
Students learn to play several roles, and give each professor what he
wants, but they don't care very much about any of these roles.

Since most course are related neither to their lives nor to their
other courses, students rarely get the broad perspective and sense of
relatedness of an educated man. They memorize several sets of terms
and theories, but they never put them together or use them to make
sense out of the world they live in.

The students have tried very hard to tell us that. They have asked,
again and again, for a "relevant" education, but we have done our best
not to hear them. "Relevant" has been translated as "vocational" or
"recreational," and we have rejected their demands as illegitimate:

"This isn't a trade school".

"We aren't entertainers".

"Some day you'll understand what is really important".

Some students undoubtedly have asked us for vocational training,
but many have simply asked us to do our jobs as educators: to help
them make sense of reality. They want and need help in understanding the world, and by refusing to give them this help, we have failed
to fulfill one of our most important responsibilities.

EXTRINSICS ARE EVERYTHING   We talk a lot about the importance
of intrinsics—truth, objectivity, love of learning, self-satisfaction, etc.
—but the entire system emphasizes extrinsics. We may say that learning is important, but grades are what really counts. We talk about

teaching, but evaluate men by counting publications. We pontificate about the intrinsic value of education, but publish statistics about college graduates' salaries.

Students are not blind. They see that we subordinate learning, teaching, and intellectual satisfaction to grades and publications, that catalogues sacrifice truth for prestige, that universities violate scientific and moral standards to get government contracts. So they get the message and become as obsessed with grades, degrees, and prestige as we are. Since they are moving into a society which is even more obsessed with extrinsics than we are, we may be helping them to become "adjusted," but universities once tried to do more than that. Many modern professors do, of course, care about intrinsics, but few of us would acknowledge the role we have played in undermining them.

STUDENTS: PASSIVE, DEPENDENT, AND CAUTIOUS   All of the pressures mentioned earlier communicate that students should do as they are told and keep their mouths shut. They learn that any sign of intellectual independence, any challenge to the professor's authority can result in severe punishments.

They therefore learn to be passive, dependent, and cautious. Instead of thinking independently, they try to "psyche us out" and tell us what we want to hear. Instead of reading a book to find out what the author says, they try to find out what the professor thinks he said. Instead of proposing new ideas, they parrot ours.

The few professors who try to develop independence find that this passivity training has been so strong that many students can not respond to opportunities to act independently. Some professors assign several conflicting books or articles and refuse to lecture or to explain what is in them because they want the students to think for themselves and to learn how to read critically. Some students welcome the opportunity, but many are uncomfortable. A few will even accuse the professor of being irresponsible because he is supposed to tell them *the truth.*

"You've given us all these articles, but which one is right?"

"I don't know. Most of these issues are still controversial".

"But which one do *you* think is right?"

Unfortunately, such questions are very common. After spending years as passive robots, many students are unable or unwilling to act independently, even when independence is encouraged. The situation has gotten so serious that some corporations are trying to make their executives more independent. They have found that they have too many "yes men," and have hired psychologists or sent their men to expensive independence-training programs. Since the universities are supposed to develop intellectual independence, and the corporations are generally regarded as encouraging comformity, I sometimes wonder:" What sort of mad world is this where the corporations have to overcome the dependence that the universities have created?"

STUDENTS ARE UNIMPORTANT   Virtually the entire academic system communicates that students are unimportant. Teaching is subordinated to research; professors do not study the principles of learning or analyze their teaching effectiveness; teaching quality is measured by research; students' evaluations of teaching are prohibited or ridiculed; popular teachers are fired; student demands for relevant courses are ignored; professors refuse to communicate in language the students can understand. These and hundreds of other everyday actions communicate to students that they and their needs are unimportant to the system.

Since one of the basic needs of every human being is to feel important, these actions cause severe psychological reactions. Some students become apathetic; the system is so indifferent or hostile to their needs that they protect themselves by not caring. Others "identify with the aggressor"— they emulate the professors, ignore their own needs, and become indifferent or hostile to the legitimate complaints of other students.[38] Others become openly aggressive—like the Negro who proves his manhood by "fighting The Man" and burning down his neighborhood, they assert their injured dignity by criticizing, picketing and demonstrating.

In the past few years open aggression has been the most visible

---

[38]Identification with the aggressor is a fairly common psychological phenomena which occurs in most severely frustrating situations. It was especially pronounced among Jews in Nazi concentration camps. Some Jews became violently anti-Semitic: they beat up other prisoners and copied the dress and manners of their guards.

reaction, while 10 to 20 years ago students were generally apathetic. They did not care very much about anything. They were "beat" and wanted only to be left alone.[39] People are rightfully frightened by student aggression, but, from a psychological point of view, aggression is often a more desirable response than apathy. Apathy can never solve a problem, while aggression, despite its undesirable side effects, does solve some problems. Certainly, student aggression has caused some reforms in our education and political systems. The systems were as bad and the reforms as necessary 10 years ago, but reforms were not made because students were apathetic.

STUDENTS CANNOT BE TRUSTED   In addition to communicating to students that they are unimportant, we communicate that they cannot be trusted. We have to make the decisions because students wouldn't make the right ones. We have to tell them what to study because they would not read the right things. We have to give them quizzes because they are too lazy to work without being forced. We have to tell them what is in the books they read because they are too stupid to understand them.

Many students get the message and never learn to trust themselves. They need grades to tell them that their work is good because they cannot evaluate it themselves. They need someone to tell them what is in the books they read because they don't believe they can dig it out themselves. They need someone to make their decisions because they have never developed the confidence that they can make their own. They need someone to reward them when they are "good" and punish them when they are "bad" because they have no personal standards or ability to look at themselves.

These are the people who go on to become "the organization men" and "the corporate wives." The "adjustment skills" they learn in the universities help them to fit right into the corporate system. Their educations prepare them for a life of cheerful mediocrity.

---

[39]Surprisingly, the public generally confuses beatniks and student activists. A beatnik is a person who endorses the beat philosophy—"go away; leave me alone; don't bother me, and I won't bother you." The last thing a beatnik would want is control of a university. Some beatniks and activists wear beards and dress sloppily, but their similarities are so superficial and their differences so fundamental that equating them reveals a rather primitive level of reasoning ability.

PROFESSORS ARE HYPOCRITES   Students look at what we do, hear *all* the messages we communicate, and contrast them with our public pronouncements. We use force, but endorse the "rule of reason." We ignore our teaching responsibilities, but insist that teaching and research do not conflict with each other. We exploit our students, but claim to care about the underprivileged. The contrast between our words and our actions is so great that students reach the only possible conclusion: professors are hypocrites.

They also generalize that everyone else in the establishment is a hypocrite. No one is to be trusted, especially people over 30. Since some 18 years in the system have convinced many of them that they cannot trust themselves, and our hypocrisy convinces them that they cannot trust us or other adults, they lack one of the most basic foundations of psychological security. They are alienated from everything, from the establishment, from their teachers, from their parents, and from themselves. They are adrift; they have nothing solid to lean on, nor do they know who they are or what they believe.

Alienation is probably the most common theme in modern literature because it is the most common human dilemma of our times. Young people feel alienated and isolated, and much of their behavior is caused by their crushing anxiety, aloneness, and bewilderment. They rebel against the establishment partly because they are frustrated, partly because rebellion seems to help them to define themselves. They follow a style slavishly because conformity helps them to relate, at least temporarily, to other people. They worry excessively about what other people think of them because they do not think much of themselves.

Nearly all professors are appalled by these behaviors, especially among our own students. Our students are often so different from the sort of people we had hoped to develop that we throw up our hands, say the situation is hopeless, and become even more obsessed with our own work. Very few of us realize how much our own selfishness, incompetence, and hypocrisy have contributed to the situation, and even fewer professors are willing to do anything about it.

CONCLUSION   Because we do not understand the teaching process very well, and have virtually no comparative research, I cannot say whether modern professors are better or poorer at communicating knowledge and ways of acquiring it than our predecessors of 20 to 30 years ago. The issue is open, and the question can never be answered. But, when I look at the students' attitudes and professors' behavior, it is clear to me that professors used to communicate a much better set of messages: a respect for students, a concern for their development, the importance of intrinsics, a love for learning, and, perhaps most important, a basic sense of their own dignity and decency.

Principles We Forget

One reason that we communicate so many unintended and undesired messages is that we do not know what we are doing. Very few college teachers have ever systematically analyzed their classes to discover what messages they were really communicating, and most professors have ignored the science and technology of learning.

Learning is, of course, very different from teaching, and it is a sign of our incompetence that we ignore the distinction between the two.

> It is a measure of our naivity that we assume implicitly, in almost all our practices, that teaching is the way to produce learning, and that something called a "class" is the best environment for teaching.[40]

Learning, in addition to being very different from teaching, is also much more clearly understood. There has been relatively little research on teaching, especially at the higher educational levels, but there has been a vast amount of research on learning. Learning is also affected by the techniques used to store and transmit information, and there have been some revolutionary improvements in these techniques. If professors understood learning research and information technology, they could be much more effective, but nearly all professors have ignored them and have continued to use traditional, ineffective teaching methods.

LECTURES ARE A WASTE OF TIME   As we have already stated, there is no rational reason for lectures to be used at all, but they are the

---

[40]Herbert Simon, "The job of a college president," *The Educational Record*, Summer 1966.

primary instructional method in most colleges and universities. The word "lecture" is derived from the Latin verb *legere*, "to read". Before the printing press was invented, books were too expensive for individuals to purchase and the teacher had to read them aloud to the students.

With the invention of the printing press, lectures became obsolete. Students could buy their own books, and reading is much faster and more efficient than listening. Students can read much more rapidly than professors can talk. In the same time it takes to hear a lecture they can read exactly the same material several times. They can comprehend written material more easily. If they get confused, they can revert back to points made earlier. They can underline or make marginal notes. And, because they are not frantically scribbling in their notebooks, they can concentrate on what the author *means*.

The academic world has, however, ignored all this evidence and has failed to take advantage of the printing press. Now that 500 years have passed and other improvements have been made in communications technology, they are doing their best to misuse the more recent inventions. Movies and visual and audio tapes are now being used extensively, but most of them feature *lectures*. These techniques, which offer such exciting possibilities, have been used to perpetuate the most wasteful possible instructional method! Furthermore, research indicates that taped and televised lectures are even worse than live ones.[41]

Some schools have even invested vast amounts of money in inventories of taped lectures that students can hear at the library. If they had any brains at all, they would transcribe the lectures so that students could *read* them and photocopy the portions they wanted, but the lecture tradition dies very hard.

When a tradition persists despite its obvious wastefulness, we must ask: Why? Social inertia and the professors' extreme reluctance to test their prejudices are factors, but there are other important causes. It is very easy for professors to lecture. We all have dozens of lectures on "mental videotape," which we can give without working or thinking. We also like to talk, and lectures provide a captive audi-

---

[41]McKeachie, "Psychology at Age 75: The Psychology Teacher Comes into His Own." *The American Psychologist*, vol. 23, pp. 551–557, 1968.

ence. Their years in the public schools have prepared the students for a passive role, and listening is very passive. Americans are oriented to tangibles, and a lecture is more tangible than independent reading is. In a lecture both students and professors can feel that they are working and "covering the material," even if very little is accomplished. A full notebook is tangible, while understanding is abstract. These feelings are strengthened by our high tuition fees: students and professors feel that there should be lots of class hours so that the students "get their money's worth."

EACH STUDENT LEARNS AT A DIFFERENT RATE   Everyone knows that there are huge individual differences in learning rates, but professors generally ignore these differences. The unit of instruction is the class, not the individual. Each person gets the same assignments at the same time as every other person. For some the pace is too fast; for others it is too slow. Most students therefore learn much less than they would if they proceeded at their own pace. Professors and administrators know that ignoring individual differences retards learning, but they generally believe that it is too much trouble to develop more individualized instructional methods.

There has been, however, a slight improvement in this situation in the past few years. These improvements have affected only the extremes, but they are a step in the right direction. Many schools or departments now offer Honors Programs for their best students, and many individual professors provide supervized reading and research, often on an informal basis. These programs have generally been developed without outside pressure because some professors like to work closely with the best students. They may identify with them and remember how bored they had been in slow-moving classes. They may also find that working with a few bright, highly motivated students is a pleasant relief from trying to teach large groups of students who could not care less. Unfortunately, some of the same professors who are most willing to work with the best students are most unresponsive to the others, making the other students even more indiffierent. Professors and schools have been much less responsive to the needs of the people from the other extreme. For years they rejected most culturally deprived people; then, in a burst of madness, the best schools in the country started accepting large numbers of students who were utterly unprepared for their competitive pressures. Boys from the ghetto, who had been given wretched teaching for all of their lives, were forced to compete with students from the best preparatory schools, with little or no special assistance. The result was predictable. The students felt the pressure, objected to being discriminated against, and demanded special programs. These demands were motivated by many other needs and values, especially the blacks' need to work out their identity and to relate themselves to a world dominated by whites, but the need to escape from unequal and unfair competition was usually an important factor also.

Unfortunately, students' sensitivities and defensiveness, our own rigidity, and a misplaced sense of delicacy have prevented most schools from dealing rationally with the problems of culturally disadvantaged students. It may be tactless to say that people from the slums cannot compete, at least in their first few years, with students from the suburbs and preparatory schools, but it is obviously true. Professors are in the truth business and should tell the truth, even when it offends people, even when the people it offends are the innocent victims of a vicious social system.

Keeping the facts buried has resulted in irrationality on both sides. Special programs have usually been developed in the worst possible atmosphere by the worst possible process. They have been based not on a rational analysis of the students' educational needs, but upon bargaining—usually bargaining under pressure. This pressure has occassionally been so severe that rational analysis or action by either party was impossible. For example, at Cornell negotiations about various educational issues were conducted while armed students were occupying some buildings.[42]

Because the great majority of students have no political clout and no particular desire for any kind of special programs, professors have been almost completely unresponsive to their needs to learn at their own pace. A few technical improvements have been made which allow individual pacing (teaching machines are the most conspicuous example), but most professors dismiss them as "gimmicks". They "know" that lectures and class discussions are the best methods; they

---

[42]These remarks should not be interpreted in a criticism of the *intent* of compensatory education. I agree completely with the intent, but virtuous intentions are no substitute for intelligent actions.

therefore set the pace for the entire class and tell the students, directly or indirectly. "if you dont' like it—leave."

LEARNING DEPENDS ONLY ON WHAT THE STUDENTS DO[43]   Learning is a change in behavior caused by experience. Since the learning must take place in the student, the important thing is what *he* does, not what the teacher does. The teacher can affect the student's learning only indirectly, by causing him to do the right things. Despite this principle, most professors devote all of their preparation to what *they* will do: what they will say in their lectures, the slides they will show, the references they will cite, etc. It would be far more effective to analyze what the students are doing and to plan activities which would help them to learn. If we analyzed students' behavior in classes, we would realize that they are usually doing little more than listening, an activity which rarely results in effective learning.

Once we start thinking about what students do, it becomes clear that we should define learning very differently from the way we do now. Now it generally means "covering the material." Students have a curriculum, a list of subjects and courses which must be "learned". Learning is measured by giving students examinations which usually measure nothing more than their ability to parrot the words of their professors and the textbooks.

Every professor knows that most students have not really learned in the sense of changing themselves in any significant way. They have covered the material, but it has not "touched" or changed them. Many professors are dissatisfied, and this dissatisfaction causes the endless curriculum committees and revisions that plague the academic world. Because these revisions are rarely stated in terms of what the students should do differently as a result of the new curriculum, they are usually meaningless.

The point is that to say the student should "know" electricity and magetism, or should "know" eighteenth-century French history is to say absolutely nothing. What should a person who "knows" these subjects be able to do? What questions should he be able to answer; what problems should he be able to solve; what inquiries should he be able to make; what intuitions—physical or historical—should he exhibit in his think-

[43]Simon, *op. cit.*

ing and speech? Until specific, operational answers have been provided to these questions, no learning environment has been designed.

For this reason, faculty deliberations on curriculum revision are mostly superficial and irrelevant. They are concerned with the relative "importance" of subject areas, when *no* subject areas are intrinsically important. It *is* important that students acquire skills—broad, transferable skills—of orderly, professional problem solving, imaginative thinking, and independent learning.

A wide range of alternative subject matters can be used as the problem material and as for-instances for learning these skills; but concern for subject matter per se will almost guarantee that they will not be learned.[44]

A LIBERAL EDUCATION REQUIRES TIME AND FREEDOM   If we define learning in terms of the changes which occur in students, it is clear that the most profound changes, the ones we associate with becoming a liberally educated man, require time and freedom, not classes and coercion. Certainly, no reasonable professor would argue that the ability to parrot professors on examinations equals an education, but that is the primary effect of most educational programs.

If we want our students to develop the tastes, habits, and skills which we feel are the essence of liberal education, we should allow them the time and freedom they need to wander in the wilderness, to think for themselves, to raise questions, and to try to answer them.

Time alone is not enough. We must also supply the support and stimulation students need to make their "wandering" profitable. As it is now, most students find the whole process so painful and unrelated to their needs and the pressures they face that they do not use their free time to develop themselves intellectually. In fact, they spend most of their free time escaping from pressures and reality.

They play cards, dance, go to football games, drink cokes, date, etc. All of these activities are a normal, natural part of their lives, of course, but we would prefer that they spend more time on intellectual activities. We all know that they rarely visit libraries or attend the lectures by distinguished visitors which the universities advertise so proudly, and they almost never talk about the content of their classes

[44] *Ibid.*

during their free time. They do talk about their grades, exams, and papers, but those are very different topics.

Since learning is a completely natural process which occurs at all times, and students spend 5 or 6 hours outside of class for every hour inside it, it is clear that the current emphasis on classroom activities is ineffective. Most professors try to extend their influence beyond the classroom by giving homework assignments, but students regard homework as just another chore. They do it, in a more or less indifferent way, because they have a gun at their heads, but it rarely stimulates them to learn on their own, nor does it change them in any significant way.

On this point the psychotherapists are far superior to professors. They are educators too, and their job is essentially the same as ours —to help people to understand themselves and the world, and to use this understanding to live more effectively. They strive for the same sort of changes as we do—more openness to experience, more honesty and objectivity, more interest in understanding, more ability to learn —but their approach is much more effective than ours. Instead of making the "student" adjust to their pace, they let him set his own pace. Instead of telling him what is important, they let him make his own choices. Instead of trying to force him to learn new things, they create an environment which encourages his natural curiosity. Instead of lecturing, they listen.

All of the principles of successful psychological counseling have been published extensively. Substantial research—much more research than has been conducted on college-level teaching—has demonstrated that these principles stimulate the sort of changes the educators claim to want. Yet very few educators understand or use these principles.

STUDENTS WANT TO LEARN   *All people,* even mental retardates, have a natural desire to learn. Even lower animals and babies have this basic desire. A starving rat will explore a new cage before eating; monkeys will solve difficult problems just for the fun of it; children read cereal boxes at the breakfast table. My three-year-old daughter spends most of her day learning—picking things up, dropping them, tasting, ripping, feeling, and breaking them, asking questions, and imitating adults. Sometimes I look at her, see how much she enjoys learning, and wonder: How did we ever design a system that takes enthusiastic learners and makes them into uninterested college students?

LEARNING REQUIRES FEEDBACK ABOUT RESULTS[45]   Students (and everyone else) learn most effectively when they do something and observe the effects of their actions. Without feedback, learning rarely occurs. People continue to make the same mistakes over and over again because they do not know what their mistakes are. Feedback is especially important in learning skills. One must get specific information about his successes and failures to master any skill.

Professors generally deplore the low level of student skills, especially their inability to study effectively, to separate essentials from trivia, and to present their ideas in an understandable form. Very few professors, however, provide the feedback students need to develop these skills. The only feedback they receive is in the form of grades —and grades do not help them to learn. They know they did something right or wrong, but usually do not know what it was or what they should do in the future.

PROFESSORS NEED FEEDBACK TOO   Professors can improve their performance only if they get informative feedback, but they usually cannot or will not get it. Large classes prevent two-way communication; status and age differences act as barriers; students have learned to be passive and may even be afraid to say what they think of professors. If they do say anything, it is usually on some sort of rating form, and ratings are no more helpful to professors than grades are to students. Even if specific comments are solicited or given freely on questionnaires, they are usually given long after the event occurs, and feedback is most effective when it is immediate. For example, we drink too much because the immediate pleasure of the drink has more impact on us than the headache we will have in the morning. We cheat on diets because taste is an immediate pleasure, while fat takes a long time to build up. Since most professors rarely get immediate, informative feedback, it is not surprising that they never learn how to teach.

Teachers in other settings sometimes get very useful feedback.

[45] *Ibid.*

The army's teacher-training unit at Fort Monmouth, New Jersey, is hardly a center of intellectualism, but it does a much better job of developing presentation skills than any university I have ever seen. Teachers are videotaped and observed while they are giving presentations; they can then see their own performance while the observers point out their strengths and weaknesses and make suggestions for improvements.

Management training programs are generally low-status teaching assignments, but their general level of instruction is much higher than that of the universities. Nearly always there is an observer in the room whose primary job is to maintain instructional quality by providing feedback to the instructor. He makes his own observations, talks to the class, and distributes questionnaries about *each* lecture or exercise. He and the instructor then discuss this feedback and plan later sessions. At times this feedback can be very painful, but it is the best way to improve teaching.

REWARDING SUCCESSIVE APPROXIMATIONS AS A TEACHING TECH-
NIQUE   Psychologists have demonstrated that extremely complex behaviors can be taught to rats and other animals simply by rewarding them every time they move in the right direction. A psychologist can make a rat with electrodes implanted in its brain walk towards the spot the experimenter wishes merely by rewarding him every time he takes a step which brings him closer to the goal—even if that step is not *exactly* in the right direction. The rat therefore proceeds in the correct general direction, and soon ends up at the right place.

Similar techniques have been used to get mice to perform incredibly complex behaviors that can not be taught by any other system.

They can, for example, be trained to pick up a marble in the fore paws, turn around three times, and then place it in a hole in the wall. The same general principle has also been applied to human behavior, and has demonstrated its value for teaching people. Unfortunately, very few professors have ever heard of it, and almost no professors use it.

In fact, they often use the opposite principle. They punish approximations. If a student who has been doing very poor work improves slightly, they are more likely to punish him by saying "not good enough" than to reward him by praising his progress. If a student has a "bad attitude" which changes slightly, they are less likely to reward him for moving in the right direction than they are to punish him for not moving far and fast enough.

MEANINGFUL LEARNING IS MUCH MORE EFFECTIVE THAN ROTE LEARNING   The emphasis on rote learning, especially the learning of terms and definitions, is extremely inefficient. It destroys student interest, is much slower than meaningful learning, is forgotten more quickly, and is tranferred to new situations less readily. Despite its wastefulness, a huge percentage of the time in most college courses is spent in memorizing relatively meaningless facts. Students are so busy learning new vocabularies and memorizing facts that they rarely deal with the important question: What does it *mean?*

CONTINUANCE OF EFFECTIVE LEARNING   Effective learning will continue after graduation only if students are motivated and have learned how to learn. The conflict between the academic system's purposes and practices is revealed very clearly in its term for graduation. Nearly all academic practices focus on the 4 years that the student spends in college, yet we call the final ritual the *commencement* —the time when students leave to *begin* their educations.

We were supposed to use the 4 years not to cram students' heads full of facts, but to develop their desire and ability to continue their education for the rest of their lives. Clearly we have failed. Most students view graduation not as the commencement of their education, but as its *conclusion.* Most will never read another serious book or discuss an abstract idea. Many still do not know how to read a book or to write a report. Very few know how to learn, or how to create environments and experiences which provide them with the feedback they need to change themselves. We have failed, then, in our most basic task. We have failed to create the hunger for learning and the ability to learn that characterize an educated man. The violence of the late 1960s has made everyone aware of the extent of our failure, but the system was bankrupt long before the violence began.

CONCLUDING REMARKS

When a colleague saw a draft of this manuscript, he said: "You will only increase the students' frustration. First you tell them they can't change the system. Then you describe it in the most unfavorable possible terms."

He has a point. Knowing the harsh realities of your situation, knowing that you are stuck with a totally inadequate system, may well increase your frustration. But, since recognizing reality is the first step in coping with it, you must understand the system and its basic message: "Shut up! Do as you're told!" Do that for 4 years, and you will get a degree, a ticket to enter the bureaucracies, a license to become a typical, mediocre, middle-class American.

You must understand that message, but you do not have to respond to it. The overall system is a desert, but there are oases of decency, freedom, and individualism in it. Many, perhaps most, professors will try to dominate and to manipulate you, but some professors do care passionately about your education. If you know your way around, you can find these men and use their talents, strength, and dedication to become a better person. You can find your way through the insane maze we call the higher educational system and come out of it with something worthwhile.

This chapter concludes the general portion of the book. Now we shift to specific problems, such as overcoming loneliness, developing satisfying sexual relationships, and getting into graduate school. Read only the chapters which refer to problems that *you* have now and refer to the other chapters as problems develop.

THE FRESHMAN YEAR

"Typically, freshmen arrive . . . filled with
enthusiasm. . . . by the end of the year not a
few will have dropped out and a large
proportion of the remainder are ready
for . . . the 'sophomore slump.' ".[1]

The "sophomore slump" (which often occurs in the spring semester of the freshman year) occurs because Freshmen expect so much and get so little. To help you through this difficult transition period, I shall analyze some things which freshmen dislike and show how certain common reactions are self-defeating.

This entire chapter will be quite negative because freshmen's expectations are usually unrealistically positive, and excessive expectations are the major cause for disillusionment and disappointment. The chapter will also ignore most of the specific problems which trouble freshmen and other students (such as loneliness, studying, sex and drugs). These problems will be covered later; now we are concerned solely with the transition problems.

[1]Joseph Katz and Nevitt Sanford, "Curriculum and Personality," in Nevitt Sanford (ed.), *College and Character.* New York: Wiley, 1964, p. 126.

IMPERSONALITY

Many freshmen are appalled by the impersonal atmosphere. They had believed the propaganda about "joining a community of scholars," but suddenly find themselves ignored by their professors.

This transition is so abrupt that you may find it upsetting. In high-school you were Bob or Nancy, and your teachers may have known something about you as a person, while here you are Mr. Jones, Miss Brown, or perhaps just a number. Your high-school teachers were quite upset if you didn't learn or do your daily assignments, but we don't care that much. We give you the material and assignments, and you can do them or not. It's your decision and your problem.

Some of this impersonality is caused by our selfishness and desire for convenience. We don't want to spend the time it would take to get to know you as a person because, unlike your high-school teachers, teaching is not our only professional responsibility. Your high-school teachers were concerned only with the transmission of knowledge, but we are also committed to its discovery. We have been trained in research, and one of our most important responsibilities is to conduct it. Furthermore, many of us enjoy research more than teaching and devote most of our attention to it.

While our selfishness and the conflict between teaching and research are unquestionably important factors in our impersonal attitude, you should realize that our explicit commitment to preparing you for independence is at least as important. To understand this commitment requires a brief analysis of the purposes of different educational institutions.

PURPOSE

High-schools are part of the compulsory public-school system, while colleges and universities are attended on a voluntary basis. The purpose of the public-schools is to provide people with the basic skills (such as reading and writing) and values (such as honesty and patriotism) which one needs for *low-level* social roles.

Colleges and universities try to prepare students for much higher and more complex social roles which can only be fulfilled by people who have all the skills and values acquired in the public schools *plus* a substantial degree of personal and intellectual independence.

Because our task is to prepare you for rules in which you must think and act independently, it would be *irresponsible* for us to act as paternalistically as your high-school teachers. If we held your hand, did your thinking, and exerted the external discipline[2] of high-school, you would never get ready for the roles you must assume.

There are, of course, better ways to prepare people for independence than suddenly exposing them to a harsh, performance-oriented, impersonal environment, but most college professors don't know them. They try to develop independence the way some people teach swimming—by throwing you into deep water and saying "it's up to you to sink or swim."

Since both our research responsibilities and our conception of our teaching responsibilities require us to be rather impersonal, you will just have to learn to live with impersonality.

LEFT-WING INDOCTRINATION

Many freshmen resent professors' attempts to indoctrinate them with left-wing ideas, and nearly all students are disturbed when professors point out that the U.S. constitution was ratified by less than 5% of the population or that there is no acceptable historical evidence that Jesus Christ ever existed.[3]

Some students reject the professors' point of view and many students become very anti-American, but both reactions are unjustified and unintended. We disagree with the things you were taught as a child not because we want you to burn down the country, but because we have a deep commitment to the truth and because our job is to increase your independence and objectivity.

Public-school teachers, who have much less commitment to the truth[4] and a very different purpose, are the real indoctrinators. They use their subjects, especially history, as tools to inculcate patriotism

[2] In my opinion we exert too much discipline, but it is still much less than in high-school.

[3] The stories about him were not written down until long after His death, and there were so many conflicts between stories that various church conferences rewrote the Bible. Incidentally, many early Christians (50–100 A.D.) were named Judas (because he had not yet been "convicted").

[4] And much less understanding of it.

and passivity. Students learn that the Pilgrims came to America to establish religious freedom, that Washington could not tell a lie, that Lincoln regarded abolishing slavery as a sacred duty, that we graciously accepted the Phillipines so that we could prepare the country for independence, and so on. These myths serve an important social function: they help people to identify with the country, and this identification helps to hold the country together.

Educated men naturally sneer at these myths, but without them *no* society could exist. People must be held together by a common set of beliefs, especially a belief that their society is superior. Without these beliefs, the society would fall apart.[5]

However, college graduates must do more than simply preserve stability. I dislike being repetitious, but the point deserves all the emphasis it can get: you are being trained for leadership or professional roles, and these roles require independence and objectivity. We therefore try to tell you the truth, even if it hurts.

We do, of course, have our own biases, and these biases will influence our teaching, but we do *much* less indoctrination than did teachers in the public-schools. We just seem to be indoctrinating you because the truth is so different from the myths you have already learned.

PACE AND PRESSURE

The social roles for which you are preparing also require the ability to cope with heavy pressures, and we give you lots of practice. Some pressures are caused by the sheer amount which you must learn, but most of them are just part of the "initiation rite for separating the upper-middle from the lower-middle class."[6] If you can't cope with the pressure, we *want* the system to weed you out.

That attitude may seem cruel or irresponsible, but I think it is both humane and justified. College pressures are *much* less severe than those which college graduates must face, and, if a person is unable to

[5]The "revolutionary societies" are particularly dishonest in the indoctrination procedures. It is rather amusing that so many young people feel a moral obligation to educate the ignorant masses when the societies they seek to emulate work so hard at distorting history.

[6]David Riesman and Christopher Jencks, "The Viability of the American College", in Sanford, *op. cit.*, p. 39.

cope with the pressures of the upper-middle class, both he and society would be better off if he didn't enter it. Far too many people are killing themselves trying to compete in leagues in which they are hopelessly outclassed.

There is, however, another side of the story. College pressures are less severe than the ones you will face as a college graduate, but, because so many high-schools are a joke, you may be totally unprepared for *any* pressure. In fact, if you have never learned how to study or to discipline yourself, you may feel overwhelmed and inadequate.

Some schools have tried to reduce the transition problem by minimizing or suspending grades for the freshman year. Most schools, however, refuse to do so because they feel that the people who will receive the benefits of a college degree should make some sacrifices. They also feel that the problem is not that the colleges are so difficult, but that the high-schools are so easy. If the high-schools had done their jobs, you would probably be ready for the demands of college life and the far greater demands which will come when you finish it.

The problem is further complicated by the fact that these pressures hit you at exactly the wrong time. At your age you have so many other problems that you may be unable to cope with these increased demands. If you do feel out of your depth it might be a good idea to drop out of college for a year or two to work out some of these other problems. If you drop out properly,[7] you can easily resume your education when you are ready.

ANTI-INTELLECTUALISM

Some freshmen are extremely disappointed when they find themselves in an anti-intellectual environment. Having been bored by high-school, they had looked forward eagerly to intellectual stimulation. Then, when they arrive on campus, they find that their professors may be intellectuals, but the system is not. It emphasizes grades and requirements, not genuinely intellectual activities.

The system also breaks down the social relationships which could convert classroom material into intellectual discussions. Professors

[7]If you are considering dropping out, turn immediately to the brief discussion on this topic at the end of the chapter called "Miscellaneous Issues."

rarely see students outside of class, and the fact that one is in class inescapably removes the freedom and intrinsic interest which are indispensable parts of all genuinely intellectual activities. Furthermore, even if students should be excited by classroom ideas, they rarely get a chance to discuss these ideas outside of class.

> The majority of students develop friendships with others whom they know as persons but not as students (in a scholastic sense). If peer groups include individuals who are sharing the excitement of academic-intellectual discovery it is almost a matter of chance. . . . Individual students who know each other well, and who are important to each other outside of classroom, have become less and less likely to share excitement *within* the same classroom. . . . Most college faculty members offer it [intellectual excitement] mainly in social systems where whatever excitement they *do* offer is little shared by students outside the classroom.[8]

Ideas are therefore something to be learned to satisfy the professors, not something to be savored and shared with one's friends.

The student culture is even worse; it is *actively* anti-intellectual. Serious students are criticized and rejected; social skills are valued more highly than intellectual abilities; and social activities are infinitely more important than intellectual issues.

Although there are many other factors involved, I think that the "free universities" are partially caused by the failure of the universities to satisfy some students' intellectual needs. Of course, some "free university" courses fall into the advanced-basket-weaving category, and many others are obvious manifestations of a need to rebel against the establishment, but I think that many students attend "free universities" to satisfy their intellectual hunger.

If you are upset about the lack of intellectual stimulation, I can offer you little more than sympathy. Most students will always be anti-intellectual, and the establishment will always use its power to make you conform to anti-intellectual and nonintellectual requirements.

You can reduce their power and increase your intellectual freedom by finding a few intellectual students, and by deemphasizing grades—but I'm afraid that you will just have to resign yourself to a few more years in an anti-intellectual environment. The only consola-

[8]T. M. Newcomb, "Student Peer-groups Influence," in Sanford, *op. cit.*, pp. 143 f.

tion is that someday you will get a degree which may help you get a job which satisfies your intellectual hunger.

PSYCHOLOGICAL REACTIONS

Because college is so new, different, and demanding, students have a wide variety of reactions to it—and many students respond more to their feelings than to the objective situational demands. Here I shall analyze a few common reactions and suggest better ways to cope with your problems.

The Freshman Jitters

After a few weeks on campus many students become anxious or depressed. Some had always gotten good grades easily, but now they find that they must work hard to get mediocre marks. Others had been forced to work hard in high-school and now feel that the work load and competition are too much for them. These feelings are the natural result of changing leagues. The demands are greater and the competition is harder.

Many students respond directly to their feelings of inadequacy by working compulsively or by giving up. These reactions look different and cause different responses from the authorities, but neither solves your problem. Unless you are extraordinarily well-disciplined, you can not work excessively for 4 years,[9] and, if you do so, you lose most of the values of college life. Giving up is obviously even less effective.

Both working compulsively and giving up are primarily reactions to one's own feelings, not to the objective situation. The compulsive worker and the psychological drop-out are both trying to cope with the same feelings of inadequacy, but attempts to deal with feelings directly are much less effective than rational responses to your *objective* problems. In this case the objective problem is coping with college-level demands and competition. They are difficult, but they are certainly not overwhelming, and an intelligent learning strategy can make your life much easier.

[9]Many students overwork so much in the first semester or year that they become exhausted and flunk out as sophomores. They are like the man who does the first hundred yards of a mile race in 10 seconds flat: he looks good for a while, but he doesn't have a chance.

You need a different strategy, a different approach because college demands are not simply greater in quantity; they require a different *quality* of thought, analysis, and writing. If you try to respond to these demands by doing more of essentially the same things you did in high-school, you will not get anywhere. I therefore suggest that you use the strategy outlined in the chapter on learning. It is certainly no panacea, but it will reduce your work load, improve your grades, and boost your spirits.

Dependency Conflicts

After the extraordinary regimentation of high-school, your new-found independence may be both exhilarating and frightening. It is a heady experience to be free to cut classes, to come home as late as you like, to ignore your homework assignments, etc., but it can also be profoundly frightening. Your high-school teachers' and your parents' demands and regulations were irritating, but you knew what you had to do. Now you have the freedom that you have always demanded, but you may not know what to do with it.

Welcome to the world! No one else does either. We all want freedom when we don't have it, and, when we get it, we are afraid of it. Man needs both freedom *and* security, and one is usually purchased with the other. Since people are motivated primarily by their *un* satisfied needs, they are often willing to trade whichever they have for the one they feel they need.

The history of mankind is largely a series of reactions to this conflict, an endless cycle of trading security for freedom, then freedom for security. For example, the French revolted against the Bourbons, but soon became tired of anarchy and turned to Napoleon. After 150 years of vacillation between strong and weak governments they turned to a latter-day Napoleon, Charles de Gaulle, but soon tired of him and forced him out. The American colonies threw out the British, but soon found that the colonies could not exist independently and establish a strong central government. The conflict between the states and the federal government is still very powerful, and there have been several reversals in emphasis.[10]

[10]Because of this fluctuation between strong and weak governments, terms such as "liberal" and "conservative" are essentially meaningless. Modern American liberals,

Please excuse my historical digression, but I want you to realize that virtually all men experience the same conflict that you do, and that we all move back and forth from demanding greater freedom to demanding greater security.

This conflict is most obvious among the student demonstrators, but all students use less dramatic forms of the same tactics. They rebel against authority and demand greater freedom, while conforming slavishly to the tyranny of the group. But neither rebellion nor conformity relieves the underlying anxieties.

Having left the security and tryanny of your family and high-school, you must work out a new relationship to the world, one which provides you with both freedom and security. Rebellion, conformity, and similar actions don't work. I have no easy solution, but the general approach outlined in Chapter 2 is, I think, a reasonable one.[11]

Disillusionment

Your feelings of insecurity may be greatly increased by our ruthlessly ripping away the myths which have supported your faith in yourself and America. This faith has been one of the basic sources of security, and learning the truth about the Pilgrims, the Indians, and the Phillipines, and so on can make you feel terribly alone and insecure.

The social necessities for telling you the truth have already been discussed, but you should also realize that the truth may hurt, but you can never be secure without it. You will be as hollow as a balloon— one prick of the truth and you'll explode. The Chinese Communists proved that by using selective versions of American history as a basic brainwashing technique. They told American prisoners part of the truth about our history, and the men just folded up.

However, the Chinese Communists also realized that this technique would not work on people with a solid understanding of the truth. They therefore *didn't even try* to brainwash most officers and college-educated men. The experiences in the Korean prisoners-of-

---

for example, want a strong central government, but so did Alexander Hamilton, who despised the common people.

[11]For a more thorough and systematic analysis of dependency conflicts see the works of Erich Fromm, especially *Escape from Freedom* and *The Art of Loving*. His concepts are discussed further in the chapter on loneliness.

war camps are one of the most dramatic illustrations of a principle we college professors never tire of pointing out: *knowledge, real knowledge, not myths, or propaganda, is the firmest and surest foundation for psychological security.*

Your disillusionment is therefore part of the price of becoming a secure, adult individual. And, if you are unwilling to pay that price, if you cling tenaciously to the myths, you will have to spend an inordinate amount of time and energy deceiving yourself, and you will *never* be secure.

Furthermore, if you learn to live with your disillusionment, if you approach our history and the history of other countries with an open mind, you will realize that America is not so moral as the myths about it, but it has been *much* more moral than other powers. We did exploit the Philippines, but our exploitation can not compare to the Belgians' actions in the Congo. We did grab large chunks of Mexico, but the Russians have grabbed more countries than I can recall. We have been cruel and unfeeling toward blacks—but racism is the norm, not the exception, in virtually all societies.

If you are open-minded, you can avoid the stupidity and self-deception of the right and left wings. They both distort history, deceive themselves, and claim to have a monopoly on the truth. And they both spend most of their time and energy preserving their self-deceptions.

CONCLUSION

Even if you follow all of these suggestions, it is going to be a hard year. You will feel anxious, tired, frustrated, lonely, confused, and disillusioned. You will vacillate between enthusiasm and depression, between working compulsively and goofing off. You have doubts about your own abilities and the value of college. You will long for the simpler life you have left and think about dropping out and going back to it.

These feelings are natural and inescapable, so don't be afraid of them, or try to hide them, because doing so would just make it harder to cope with them. The best way to handle your feelings and to preserve your balance is to express them openly, both to yourself and to other people.

If you express them openly, other people will do the same, and you will realize that you all feel the same way. Then you won't feel nearly so bad, and you will be much more able to cope with your feelings and situation.

LONELINESS

"The deepest need of man . . . is . . . to leave the prison of his aloneness."[1]

If you look honestly at yourself and your friends, you will find that you are constantly trying to escape from your aloneness, but do not succeed very well. The escape is sometimes from the aloneness itself and sometimes from the awareness of it, but the release is temporary and the feeling soon returns.

Sex, romance, parties, bull-sessions, and similar activities ease the pain for a moment, but you rarely achieve real closeness. You usually feel that you do not know what other people are really like and that they do not know the real you. You feel cut off and alone, even when you are in a crowd, perhaps even when you are making love. Somehow it just does not seem as good, or as close, or as warm as you want it to be.

Drinking, drugs, bridge, movies and other escapes blot out the awareness of your aloneness, but do not affect the underlying reality. Sooner or later the truth catches up with you; you realize how alone

[1]Erich Fromm, *The Art of Loving.* London: Unwin, 1957, p. 14.

you are; and this realization may drive you to even more frantic escapes. You drink more, or see more movies, or work harder to improve your bridge.

You are not the only person who feels and acts this way; most other young Americans are trying to escape from the same feelings. You live in the loneliest era of the loneliest nation on earth. Almost every aspect of American culture is affected by the frantic, obsessional need to escape from aloneness. No other national group talks so much about personal relations or has so many problems with them. We are inundated with appeals to love each other, to be popular, to make friends and influence people. We spend billions on toothpaste, deodorants, and cosmetics; read books on ways to adjust to each other; let immature children go steady for "Saturday night security"; take billions of tranquilizers; and carry radios everywhere to listen to idiotic disc jockeys telling us that we are not alone. But none of it works, and the loneliness continues.

Since loneliness is an inescapable part of our times, you must find better ways to deal with it. Sex and drugs and popularity have failed, but there is a solution to the problem of loneliness; there is a way out of the prison of your aloneness. My purposes here are to show why the problem is so serious and to provide a solution.

THE LONELY CROWD[2]

Conformity is the modern solution to the problem of anxiety, but it does not work. We live in a group-oriented age, a time in which people are more concerned with adjustment than with individuality. The American rhetoric is still individualistic, but almost no one takes it seriously. Instead of making their own decisions, most people try to learn and to adjust to what other people want or expect. They ask: "What is in? What is out? What are *they* wearing? What record is number one? How does this candidate stand in the polls? Is this book a best-seller?"

They need other people to tell them what is right and good and true because they are afraid to make their own decisions—afraid to be

[2]This phrase is from the book, *The Lonely Crowd,* by David Riesman. The ideas in this section come from that book and from Erich Fromm's *The Art of Loving* and *Escape from Freedom.* I recommend reading all three books.

different because difference implies aloneness. Their lives are based on a simple premise, which may or may not be expressed:

> If I am like everyone else, if I have no feelings or thoughts which make me different, if I conform in custom, dress and ideas to the pattern of the group, I am saved; saved from the frightening experience of aloneness."[3]

Of course, not everyone is a conformist, and even the conformists pretend to be individualists. A few people even try to prove that they are nonconformists, but the proofs are usually pitiful—a beard, dirty clothes, long hair, or casual sexual behaviour. In fact, these people often prove how individualistic they are by joining groups in which everyone conforms to the same pattern of nonconformity!

These comments do not apply to the very few people who are actually *doing* something different—working on civil rights projects, starting Utopian communities, living in Grecian caves, and so on. But for every one of them, there are a hundred people who have pasted an individualistic, nonconformist veneer onto a solid bourgeois, conformist reality. They let their hair grow long, sleep around, perhaps even smoke a little pot, but they depend on regular checks from long-suffering, often-criticized parents.

These minor differences make some people think they are individualistic, and they frighten the complacent majority, but they are silly symbols that mean nothing at all. The fact that some people claim to be individualists on such flimsy grounds and that others can not tolerate such minor distinctions indicate how conformist our society has become.

Conformity is not necessarily a vice; in fact, if it solved the problem of aloneness, it would actually be a virtue (regardless of what the philosophers think of it). Unfortunately, it has failed completely. Americans are conformists, but they are lonely conformists, members of a lonely crowd. Why? Why doesn't merging oneself with the crowd solve the problem?

First, relationships based upon conformity are always insecure. The conformist's security comes from the crowd's acceptance, and this acceptance can be withdrawn at any time. He can never be sure that he is accepted, nor can he know whether he will be accepted

[3]Fromm, *The Art of Loving*, p. 16.

tomorrow. Fashions change, and the man who is in today may be out tomorrow.

Second, these changes alienate individuals from themselves. The individualistic person has a set of internal standards—a "psychological gyroscope" which provides a sense of continuity. His opinion of himself depends upon his own actions; if he lives according to his own standards, he respects himself. Because his standards remain the same, he knows who he is, and he is the same person today as he was yesterday. The conformist does not have this sense of continuity; his opinion of himself depends on what *other* people think, and he can not control their opinions. Furthermore, they will reject him if he does not satisfy their *current* expectations. As these expectations change, he must change or be rejected. He is therefore divorced from his own past—different today from what he was yesterday, and he must change again tomorrow. This constant changing confuses him; he does not know who he really is, nor can he respect himself. He is alienated—not just from other people but from himself.

Third, a conformist knows that other people do not respect him. People like him not for what he is but for conforming to their standards. He is accepted not for himself but for the masks he wears, and relationships between masks leave people feeling empty and alone.

THE ROMANTIC ILLUSION

The masks are especially common in romantic relationships. Nearly everyone wears a mask on dates; each person tries to convince the other that he is something "better" than he really is—stronger, smarter, richer, sexier, and so on. Each plays a role, and neither gets to know the other as a real person.

If they should fall in love, the romantic illusion becomes greater. They may try to be honest with each other, but the habits of a lifetime prevent them from doing so. They want to take off their masks, but are afraid that they will lose the other person if seen as they really are. Even if a person should take off the mask and present himself honestly, he may be seen not as he is but as the other person wants him to be.

The awful danger to the young is that of projecting their romantic wishes onto real people, so that they see them as they would like them to be, not as they really are. . . . A romantic relationship is not a real relationship between people; it is essentially an attachment to a notion, a stock conception, a feeling. The other person is just a convenient peg on which to hang the romantic picture."[4]

In addition to causing lovers to distort what they see, romantic conceptions are communicated to each other with a clear implication that the other should change himself to fit the illusion. "If you loved me, you would not be so aggressive, or so fat, or so talkative." Each person realizes what is expected of him and tries, consciously or unconsciously, to change himself. Their relationship therefore becomes a charade, a melodrama in which each plays a role, but neither plays himself.

The romantic illusion has been a problem in all societies and all eras. Lovers have always deceived themselves and each other. But the deception is greater today because our society is so obsessed with the romantic side of love. We have made romantic love into the great escape, the all-purpose cure; Hollywood, television, best-sellers, and advertising tell us that the goal of life is romantic love, that all our problems will be solved if we could just find the right person, if we were just prettier or smelled better.

Some physicians and sexologists add to the romantic illusion by making sex into a technical accomplishment. The marriage manuals have performed a real service by helping people to understand their bodies and the mechanics of sex, but sex is a *human*, not a mechanical act. The manuals' emphasis is upon achieving sexual adjustment (simultaneous orgasms) rather than relating to another person. Orgasms are certainly important, but the obsession with technique and the physical side of sex can rob it of all meaning. It becomes just another area of competition, a place where one can prove how good he is. A good lover is like a good dancer, only better. Points scored in bed count more than the ones scored on the dance floor. As one wife put it, "When we make love, I can see Henry turning the pages in his mind, making sure that he follows all the instructions."

[4]Kenneth C. Barnes, *He and She*. Baltimore, Md.: Penguin, 1958, p. 91.

When sex is regarded as a technical accomplishment, each person remains alone. They may give physical pleasure, but they do not give themselves. Their bodies interact, but their selves remain aloof, untouched by the act itself. As some of you have already learned, and as many more of you will soon find out, even when it is physically satisfying, sex can be a profoundly lonely experience.

EXPLOITATION

Sex is particularly lonely when it is exploitative, which is a rather common occurrence. Girls have always been used to satisfy men's physical desires, but now both sexes exploit each other. It may be a more balanced situation, but it is certainly not a healthier one.

Boys still use girls to satisfy their sexual needs, but they also use them to build up their ego and status. Many boys are insecure and have to prove that they are attractive, manly, and virile by exploiting girls sexually. Some boys are so unsure of themselves and so desperate for status that they use sex as a status symbol. They tell their friends, often in great detail, how far they have gotten with each girl.[5] These actions may build a boy's status, but they take all the meaning and humanity out of sex and physical affection.

Even if the sexual side of the relationship is kept private, girls can still be used as status symbols. A pretty girlfriend is a status symbol in exactly the same sense as a nice car, and many boys try to build their status by possessing the "best" girls.

Girls do exactly the same thing. A football player, a BMOC, or a rich boy are status symbols, and many girls use their dates to build their status. In fact, on most campuses there is a crude "market": most people know their approximate market value and try to get the best possible deal. The prettiest girls get the most prestigious boys, and vice versa. A fairly pretty girl gets a fairly prestigious boy, and so on. This entire approach to what is supposedly a human relationship takes away its human meaning. Boys and girls relate to each other not as people but as pretty faces, sexy bodies, nice cars, and football players.

[5] These stories are often lies, of course, but true and false stories are told for exactly the same reason: insecurity; and they have essentially the same effect on a girl's reputation.

THE PURITAN HERITAGE

Conformity, romantic illusions, and the use of people as status symbols are fairly recent developments, but the roots of American loneliness go back much farther, to the insane moral code of our Puritan and Victorian ancestors. This code has essentially the same effect as the other developments: it prevents us from relating to each other as we are.

The original Puritans were sick. Some American history books have idealized them and said that they came here to establish religious freedom, but that story is utter nonsense. They came here because the English would not tolerate their attempts to tell everyone how to live and to worship. They were dictatorial because they were obsessed with guilt, convinced that their natural impulses were evil, and unable to accept themselves as complex human beings who loved, hated, and desired each other. They were constantly trying to beat down their own guilt feelings by dominating other people and pretending to be holy. They created one of the most repressive societies in human history, and we live in the shadow of that society.

Today the pendulum has swung to the other extreme. We live in an age of permissiveness, promiscuity, and violence. Some people therefore believe that the Puritan heritage is dead, but nothing could be further from the truth. Most Americans, especially young people, are still tormented by guilt and shame; many women are frigid; many men think that sex is dirty; most people can not express aggression honestly; and the very acts which seem so "free"—nudism, promiscuity, and so on—are essentially irrational overreactions to the irrational pressures of our Puritan heritage. This heritage has affected our attitudes toward almost every issue, but its effects on our attitudes toward sex and aggression have especially serious consequences.

Our Bodies

Almost all Americans feel uncomfortable with European habits of elimination. We see men urinating by the side of the road, walk past *pissoirs* on Parisian boulevards, see men and women use the same toilets in Belgian restaurants, and say, "What is wrong with these people? Don't they have any decency?" But there is nothing wrong with them; there is something wrong with us. They deal with the natural elimination function in a natural, unself-conscious way, while we are ashamed of it. We reveal our shame in our reactions to Europeans and in our silly euphemisms for toilets, urination, and defecation[6]—"bathroom," "powder room," "powder my nose," "wash my hands."

We are self-conscious about elimination because it has been confused with sex, the taboo topic. Sex is so taboo that any exposure of the body is suppressed, even for children. On almost any European beach one can see small children running around naked. They are not ashamed, of course, and neither are their parents, because nakedness is natural for children. American children would like to do the same thing, but their parents would be mortified.

European adults are also able to change clothes in a natural, relaxed way. They simply wrap a large towel around themselves, slip off their clothes, and put on their bathing suits. They don't show anything; in fact, one sees less of their bodies than he sees when they are wearing their bathing suits, but Americans are usually shocked by their "indecent" behavior.

The difference between the Europeans' matter-of-fact attitudes toward elimination, changing clothes, and children's nakedness and our constant concern with nudism, topless waitresses, and so on shows that the current wave of nudism is not a genuine acceptance of our bodies, but an irrational overreaction to Puritanism. The people who take off their clothes say, in effect: "Look at me, you hung-up Puritans; I am free and uninhibited." But if they were really free, they would not be so self-conscious about their nudity, nor would they try so hard to attract attention.

The Purpose and Meaning of Sex

If the topic has been discussed at all (and it is generally not discussed), young people have usually been told that the sole purpose of sex is reproduction. Their parents and teachers are too embarrassed to talk about sex as an expression of love or a physical desire. The books and

---

[6]We use even sillier euphemisms for the parts of a chicken: "white meat" and "dark meat" were used by the Victorians because they were ashamed to say "breast" or "leg."

sex education courses deal with the physiology of sex and its God-given purpose of perpetuating the human race, but no one ever tells students about the power and urgency of sexual desires or the closeness that can come from sexual relations.

Since children soon realize that their desires are unrelated to reproduction, they feel dirty, guilty, and ashamed. Sex is for making babies, but they have this terrible, sinful feeling which has nothing to do with children. This guilt often continues for all of their lives, creates serious marital problems, and finally gets passed on to their children.

Even if these attitudes are rejected they will continue to exert their effects. Promiscuity, the most dramatic form of rejection, is often an overreaction to this guilt and shame. Some "free-lovers" are doing the same thing as the nudists: they are proving that they are not "hung-up." Others are deliberately trying to "liberate" themselves. They enjoy talking about sex, and these remarks often indicate that sex is not an expression of love or a physical pleasure, but a duty, "an up-lifting experience," "an act of creation," "an expansion of consciousness." People who talk this way are as hung-up as the Puritans; they must make sex into something else because they can not accept it as it is.

The Idealization of Women

Many, perhaps most, American men place women on a pedestal, treat them as pretty little dolls, and dislike the fact that they have to urinate, defecate, and menstruate. Somehow it does not seem right that these dainty little creatures should be human, nor can men accept women's natural sexual desires.

We still have a double standard, and many men want their wives to be virgins before marriage and faithful after it, but feel that they themselves should be free to play around whenever they wish. Other men are upset or afraid of sexually demanding women; it does not seem right for a woman to want or to initiate sex. A few men divide women into "good" and "bad" categories, feel guilty about having sexual desires for "nice" girls (including their wives), and can satisfy themselves only with prostitutes or other "bad girls."

This same idealization affects many other aspects of the male-female relationship. Men feel protective toward these weak little creatures, even though they live much longer than we do and can stand much greater pain (childbirth is more painful than any male experience, but women often look forward to their second, third, and subsequent children). We keep their dainty little eyes and noses away from nasty sights and smells, even though they are much less affected by them than we are (most men feel sick when they change dirty diapers, something women do every day). We assume that they are too weak and childish to discuss politics and economics, even though they control most of the money. In other words, we do not treat them as adult human beings with brains, courage, and sexual desires.

Women are also conflicted about being put on a pedestal. It has its pleasant features, but they often realize that their men are reacting to a romantic ideal which exists only in their own minds, instead of loving them as living, thinking, wanting adults. They therefore feel empty and alone; guilty about their sexual desires and afraid to express them; eager to assert their independence and intelligence, but afraid of being "unfeminine."

The Masculine Stereotype

Men are not much surer of themselves. Female idealization has its counterpart in the masculine stereotype—smart, brave, powerful, sexually demanding. Men's excessive concern with sex is partly a compensation for doubts about themselves, partly the result of an inability to integrate sex into a total personality. Puritans can not deal with sexual desires as an integral part of a normal person. They try to remove it from women, and they exaggerate it (and its "evilness") in men. They spiritualize females and bestialize males. Women are above human sexual desires; men are below human tenderness.

Sex is thought of as an evil lust, of which most men feel both ashamed and proud. They are ashamed to have these nasty desires, especially toward such divine creatures, but afraid that they do not have enough of them. It is a dirty little part inside them that they must keep from running wild, but they make sure that other people know how powerful it is (especially when it is really not very powerful at all). They tell dirty stories and brag about conquests. They are afraid to be tender because tenderness is not part of the stereotype. They cannot cry because they are too strong. They can not date a girl without trying to make her because people might think they are "queer." They play out the role and imitate the stereotype, but then feel lonely because women do not relate to them as they really are.

In the past few years there has been a massive reaction to the male and female stereotype. An increasing number of young people have rejected them and gone to the opposite extreme: they attempt to deny the differences between the sexes by looking and acting like each other. The girls' hair gets shorter as the boys' gets longer; girls wear jeans and men wear beads.

Taken by themselves, these developments are harmless, but the underlying (and often unconscious) goal of obliterating the differences between the sexes is impossible. Girls are not dainty little dolls, but they are not boys either. The masculine stereotype is inaccurate, but it is much more accurate than the idea that men are the same as women. Denying the differences between the sexes has essentially the same effect as the stereotypes: it prevents people from relating to each other *as they are.*

Aggression

The effects of the Puritan heritage on sexual desires and behavior are obvious, but it has almost as significant effects on aggressive feelings. We have been conditioned from birth to regard aggressive feelings or actions as *bad:* "Don't hit your sister!" "You don't hate her; you love her." "If you can't say something nice, don't say anything at all."

This training has made us feel guilty about our natural aggressive feelings, and we usually can not express these feelings in any reasonable way. We may bury them inside ourselves, or explode angrily, or sulk, but these actions do not solve our problems. If we sulk or bury our feelings, the other person will continue to do things which irritate us, and our irritation can turn to hatred (it can also cause migraine headaches, high blood pressure, and heart attacks). If we explode, the other person will become more aggressive; the tension will escalate; and we will probably feel ashamed of ourselves.

Aggressive feelings are especially hard to acknowledge or to express toward the people we love. Our culture does not recognize the ambivalent nature of love, the fact that love and hate *always* go together. They go together because frustration causes aggression, and the more we care about a person, the more he will frustrate us, and the more we will hate him.

Since our society forbids us to express or even to have aggressive feelings, most Americans feel guilty about their hostility and express it indirectly. If a man is angry with his wife for talking to a stranger, he may criticize her cooking or yell at the children. A girl may dislike her boyfriend's habit of monopolizing the conversation, but express her annoyance by saying, "I'm not in the mood," or by being cold when he tries to kiss her. This kind of action expresses the feelings and releases the tension, but it does not solve the problem.

Summary

By suppressing honest expressions of sexual and aggressive feelings our Puritan heritage has strengthened the walls of the prison of our aloneness. We cannot accept ourselves or other people as we are, as loving, hating, wanting human beings. We cannot relate to each other as people, nor can we express ourselves honestly with either our words or our bodies. We cannot have the substance of real relationships and must act out a charade of roles, images, and stereotypes.

THE SOLUTION

There are, however, two solutions to the problem of aloneness; *creative work* and *love*. Creative work bridges the gap between you and the world, and lets you express yourself in the process of creation. You express what you really are, what you really feel, and you merge yourself with the thing that you have created. This expression and unity come only from *creative* work, work which you do for the joy of creation, which you plan and execute yourself. This sort of work is very rare in our society, especially among students. You must spend most of your time responding to external pressures, and you may not get many chances to do the things that are really important for you —to build a boat, or to write poetry, or to make a special dress.

But you *must* do these things. No matter how great the pressures are, you must use some of your time to create. You must preserve some of your self for yourself. If you do not, if you let the system make all your decisions, it will squeeze the life right out of you, and you will become a robot, passively following orders, rather than a real person who controls and expresses himself.

And, if you are not a real person, you cannot have real relationships. You may fall in love a dozen times, have many sexual affairs, be a BMOC or a campus queen, but you will still remain alone. You will not have enough inner security and sense of self-hood to share yourself with another person. And without that sharing, there can be no love.

Love is a giving, not a taking, and only people who are sure of their selves can give that self to another person.

> All [a person's] ... attempts for love are bound to fail unless he tries most actively to develop his total personality so as to achieve a productive orientation.[7]

Obviously, this definition of "love" is very different from the popular and romantic ones that refer primarily to *falling* in love—to the sudden, intoxicating experience of closeness, an experience which rarely lasts very long. The love referred to here is a much more permanent state, and it can occur between any two people, regardless of their sex; it is a human, rather than primarily a sexual state.

This kind of love contains five elements: *giving, care, responsibility, respect,* and *knowledge,* and each element is essential. *Giving* refers not to losing something, but to sharing one's self, an act which enriches both people. The giver expresses his self, and in doing so makes himself stronger and more human. "Giving is more joyous than receiving, not because it is a deprivation, but because in the act of giving lies the expression of my aliveness."[8] This expression also enriches the other person and makes him more aware of his own aliveness and humanity. "In the act of giving something is born, and both persons involved are grateful for the life that is born for both of them."[9]

Though the *care* element is most visible between parents and children, it is an essential part of all love relationships. *"Love is the active concern for the life and growth of that which we love."*[10] Love and exploitation are therefore antithetical; people who use each other for

---

[7]Fromm, *The Art of Loving,* Preface.
[8]*Ibid.,* p. 23.
[9]*Ibid.,* p. 24.
[10]*Ibid.,* p. 25.

sex or status may be deeply infatuated, but they do not love each other.

Responsibility refers not "to duty and obligation, but to an entirely voluntary act; it is my response to the needs, expressed or unexpressed, of another human being. To be responsible means to be able and ready to respond . . . to the . . . needs of the other person."[10]

Many people equate *respect* with esteem, status, or power, but it is none of these things.

> It denotes, in accordance with the root of the word (*respicere*, to look at), the ability to see a person as he is, to be aware of his unique individuality. Respect means concern that the other person should grow as he is. Respect, thus, implies the absence of exploitation. I want the loved person to grow and unfold for his own sake, and in his own ways, and not for the purpose of serving me. If I love the other person, I feel one with him or her, . . . *as he is,* not as I need him to be as an object for my use.[11]

Respect is impossible without *knowledge;* one must know what the other person is like before he can respect him. "There are many layers of knowledge; the knowledge which is an aspect of love . . . does not remain at the periphery, but penetrates to the core."[11] This kind of knowledge is impossible if the other person does not present himself honestly, or if you are so concerned with yourself that you cannot understand the picture he presents. Conformity, romanticism, and Puritanism prevent this kind of knowledge, thereby preventing both respect and love.

Many people will reject the preceding analysis and definition because they are unrelated to the delicious sensations that most people call "love." There is no need to accept it as *the* definition of "love," but whatever you call it (and "love" seems to be a reasonable term), this sort of relationship is the best and most lasting solution to the problem of aloneness. It lets you experience genuine closeness without losing your own identity. You and the other person can communicate and share your uniqueness and humanity without losing either.

Even if you agree with the preceding analysis, you may feel that this kind of relationship is so unobtainable that it is irrelevant. Fromm's position may look like Christian ethics: beautiful, noble, perhaps even perfect, but impossible; a wonderful set of rules for

[11] *Ibid.,* p. 26.

perfect people, but too demanding for mere mortals like yourself. It requires too many things that you do not have—genuine independence, the courage to be yourself, respect for yourself and other people, honest communication, and so on. This kind of love may seem so difficult that you give up on it and continue in your old habits.

Although love is very hard to attain, it is certainly not impossible, nor is it an all-or-none phenomenon. The ideal state is too high for anyone to reach all of the time, and you may not even come close, but the closer you come, the more alive, human and satisfied you will be. Conversely, the more you follow the conformists, romanticists, and Puritans, the more lonely and unhappy you will be. In other words, you really do not have a choice, unless you regard being lonely as a reasonable alternative.

If you accept this assertion and really want to develop your ability to love, you must do three things: *take chances, be honest with yourself,* and *be honest with other people.* Giving yourself always involves risks; you may be rejected, a very painful experience. Most people are so afraid of rejection that they hold back and wait for the other person to give himself first; they need proof that the other cares before they can commit themselves. The other person does the the same. Since neither will move first, they remain apart. But, because their loneliness is so painful, they continuously try to force the other one closer to them, and they keep testing him to see how far he has gone. They demand more and more proofs of affection, and the more they demand, the less willing the other person is to give them. This causes them to become more separate, more unhappy, and more demanding. The only way out of this vicious cycle is to commit yourself, to give yourself first. Perhaps you will be rejected, but a clean rejection is better than a lifetime of loneliness.

You may not, however, know *how* to give yourself. It is fairly easy to say: "I love you." It is much more difficult and risky to give yourself as a person. You must let the other person see you as you are, and this disclosure requires that you be honest with yourself. If you cannot accept yourself as you are, if you do not respect yourself, you cannot present yourself honestly, nor can you respect another person. Now it is easy to say: "Know thyself," but, as you know very well, it is terribly hard to do it. You want to look beneath the masks you wear, but are afraid of what you might find. Some people try to deny or to conquer this feeling; they try to rip off their masks, but the fears are too strong for that. The masks will remain until you feel safe enough and sure enough to let them go, and the only way to acquire this feeling of security is to develop honest, supportive relationships with other people.

In other words, you must know yourself to give yourself, and you must have relationships which make you feel safe enough to give yourself in order to know yourself. There is therefore not a simple sequence, but a continuous cycle of increasing self-knowledge, increasing honesty with other people, and increasing ability to give yourself.

You probably need help to develop this kind of cycle. You and your friends have been taught to avoid the truth, and you do not know how to express your feelings. You must therefore *learn* how to express yourself, and this learning requires a special climate which you do not know how to create.

Fortunately, on many campuses you can get help. Many psychology departments and other campus organizations (such as the YMCA) now offer programs which create this kind of climate by reducing social inhibitions and encouraging honest expressions of feelings. It takes time and skill to create this environment, but there is a growing body of specialists who know how to do it. Since the details of the method have already been discussed, there is no need to repeat them here, but I should like to repeat that T-groups and similar programs can help you to become more honest, more genuine, and more able to love yourself and other people. They are not an all-purpose cure, of course, but, since they do help a lot of people, I urge you to consider attending one.[12]

---

[12]If no such programs are currently offered on your campus, you may be able to go to an off-campus organization or to form your own group and to find a trainer. The counseling center or the psychology department can probably refer you to organizations or competent individuals. You might also try to start a group without a trainer. If you can find enough people who really want to work on these problems, a leaderless group can sometimes be productive.

SEX

Sex was discussed at several points in the last chapter, but always in relation to its effects on loneliness. Since sex is a human act, loneliness will come up occasionally in this chapter, but only as a peripheral topic. Here the emphasis is on specific sexual problems which young people often have, but for which they usually cannot get information and advice.

This chapter may offend some readers by discussing premarital relations, homosexuality, birth control, and unwanted pregnancies, but these things are problems for many students who usually cannot get the help they need because of the Puritan heritage. They get sermons on the importance of virginity and the evils of homosexuality, but they do not get the factual information they need to make their own decisions, nor does anyone relieve their embarrassment by discussing these problems in an unemotional, matter-of-fact way. They therefore feel guilty about perfectly natural feelings and behavior, and their guilt and ignorance cause them to act foolishly.

My purposes here are to help you to become less guilt-ridden and more able to make your own decisions; accordingly, I shall provide some information, tell you where to get more of it, and discuss these issues as personal problems rather than moral imperatives.

CHASTITY, PRO AND CON

Premarital sex is much more common than it used to be, especially among college students. It is also much more open. A few unmarried couples live together openly, and many others are less worried about keeping their sexual behavior private. I have mixed feelings about these developments. The openness is generally a healthy sign: people have always violated sexual codes, and modern young people are less hypocritical about it. On the other hand, some of these people are more honest than intelligent. They have expressed themselves honestly, but they may be sorry that they did not remain chaste.

My purpose here is not to try to convince you to remain a virgin; it is simply to help you make a more reasonable decision by clarifying the implications of your actions. Far too many people do not really think about this issue. Some let their desires dominate them; others are ruled by irrational guilts and fears. Neither reaction is mature, adult, or honest. Since this decision can profoundly affect you, it deserves some thought.

This decision has always been a problem in our society, but several social changes make it especially difficult today. First, social pressures have become quite inconsistent. The Puritans and Victorians exerted much more pressure than we do, but the pressure was all in one direction. There was, therefore, a crude balance between sexual desires and social prohibitions. Now the social pressures are less extreme, but very contradictory. Boys and girls are exhorted by their parents and other adults to remain chaste. But their friends may brag about their adventures; a few people argue that "everyone is doing it"; and the pseudo-Freudians tell them that virginity causes neuroses. These conflicting social pressures make it much harder to decide what is right.[1]

[1] The fact that the pressures conflict does, however, have its positive side. It makes it much easier to accept your actions if you should have intercourse, either intentionally or accidentally.

The problem is complicated by the fact that improved health and diet have caused you to mature sooner than your parents or grandparents. Long before your parents had to cope with sexual feelings you were physically (but not psychologically) ready for intercourse and parenthood.[2] These natural desires cannot be satisfied within marriage because you must finish your education. The biological pressures are increased by the modern American habit of early dating and going steady. Sexual experiments are progressive: after you have tried something, you go a little further the next time. Because children today start dating and going steady very early, they have often tried everything except intercourse by the time they are 15 or 16 years old. When they have gone that far, and done so regularly, it is really difficult to keep from going all the way.

The American obsession with sex also increases these pressures. Everything from movies to deodorant ads tells you that you must be sexually attractive, and many people feel that sexual relations are a proof of their attractiveness.

Finally, you have more opportunities to have intercourse than people have ever had. You are rarely chaperoned, and cars and drive-in movies present opportunities to go as far as you like. This combination of opportunities, desires, and pressures is too much for most people. They have intercourse, often accidentally, which they may later regret.

Only 14% of the boys and 15% of the girls said it was planned, compared with 84% of the boys and 82% of the girls who said it was unpremeditated.[3]

Since you may not think about these issues when you get excited, I suggest you consider them now. The following argument is addressed primarily to girls because they are more concerned about this problem, but some points also apply to boys. Despite the double standard, some boys do feel that they should remain virgins, and biological and social pressures have confused and troubled them. If

[2] A girl today may expect to menstruate about 10 months earlier than her mother and 20 months earlier than her grandmother. Boys now complete their growth at age 17, compared to age 23 in the year 1900. (Michael Schofield, *The Sexual Behavior of Young People*. Baltimore, Md.: Pelican, p. 27.)
[3] *Ibid.*, p. 65.

you are a boy who is troubled by this issue, I hope that you realize that the male stereotype and your friends' pressure is based not on confidence or genuine sexuality, but on insecurity. They are unsure of themselves as men and doubt that they are doing the right thing. They therefore try to beat down their doubts by forcing you to conform. Since you have to live with yourself and to follow your own moral code, I suggest you read the following discussion.

The Case for Chastity

MORAL   Moral factors are by far the most common reasons that people give for remaining chaste. Most parts of our society regard premarital intercourse as wrong, and many people accept these attitudes. Breaking the moral code can lower your self-respect and the respect that other people have for you.

SELF-RESPECT   If you honestly think sex is wrong, you will lose respect for yourself. Your friends or lover may tell you it is all right, but, if you really do not believe them, having intercourse becomes the worst type of conformity. You will have abdicated your responsibility to make your own decisions and allowed someone else to impose his moral code upon you. Knowing that you have let someone else do that to you will increase your self-contempt, and it may also damage your relationship. The other person may lose respect for you, and you may resent him.

RESPECT OF OTHER PEOPLE   Despite all your precautions, your actions may become public knowledge, especially if you are a girl. A shocking number of boys do not have the decency to keep quiet, particularly if they break up with a girl. The act you thought was so private may become another topic at the boys' bull-session. Even if no one talks, there are dozens of ways for the information to leak out, and you may be punished very severely. Our society is extremely hypocritical: we do not worry much about immorality as long as it is kept quiet, but the person who is found out is punished for everyone else's transgressions.

Many schools will expel you. Some friends may reject you. Your parents may be critical, and they will feel hurt and embarrassed, especially if your behavior is widely known. If you are a girl, boys will regard you as "easy," and many will "try their luck."

YOUR CHANCES FOR MARRIAGE   The boys who try their luck will probably regard you as a sexual object, not as an attractive person or a potential wife. This problem is especially acute if you do not marry the boy with whom you had relations. The desire for virgin wives is based in part upon men's lack of confidence about their ability as lovers. Many men will be afraid that you will compare them unfavorably to your previous lover; they may also feel that girls who violated the moral code before marriage will do so afterwards, particularly if their husbands are not satisfactory lovers. These fears can prevent them from marrying you or cause serious problems if you do get married.

Premarital relations can also lead to broken engagements. Your fiance may have begged you to sleep with him, but once you do, he may lose interest or respect for you, and he may be afraid that you will cheat on him after marriage. Such a man may not be much of a loss, but you will not feel that way when he first drops you.

EXPLOITATION   Many girls allow themselves to be exploited sexually. Some violate their own moral standards because their boyfriends demand that they "prove their love." Even if he does not actually demand intercourse, he may hint that he will go out with others girls or visit prostitutes if she does not give in. If a girl should yield to these pressures, she cheats herself out of something very precious. She gives her virginity not as an act of love but as a response to blackmail.

A variation on this theme is the "big date." Many boys feel that taking a girl to a big dance or spending a lot of money entitles them to sexual favors. Girls may not like this system of trading kisses and petting for dates, but they have lived with it since high-school. If a date is really special, a girl may go further than she wants because of gratitude for the nice time or fear that it will not be repeated. She probably will not plan to go all the way, but she may go too far to stop.

This entire system is symptomatic of the problems we have already discussed. Under these circumstances petting or sexual relations are not acts of love; they are essentially prostitution. The girl lets the man touch and even enter her body not to express her love, not to satisfy her own needs, but to reward him for the dates.

POPULARITY   This system would not be so common if we had not glorified popularity. From the time you were six years old you have been told to seek popularity. You have been graded on "adjustment," manipulated by the advertisers, and pushed by your parents. Popularity is the proof that you are a worthwhile person, that people really care about you.

Nonsense! Popularity is valued because it is visible, not because it means anything. Americans are so unsure of themselves and of other people's feelings about them that they need lots of friends and dates to prove that people really like them. But that proof is an illusion, a fraud, because it says nothing about how people really feel about you. Popularity is visible, but it is no substitute for a few people who really like or love you.

Popularity based on sexual permissiveness is especially empty. Dates and boyfriends are only a shadow and a symbol of what you really want: love and respect. If you buy the symbol with your body, you may lose the real thing. Men do not respect prostitutes, not even the ones who simply pet to pay for their dates. They want love, even if they only know how to ask for sex. And they know, usually in a confused, unconscious way, that they cannot love girls whom they exploit.

CHANGING THE RELATIONSHIP   Even if you do love and respect each other, having intercourse may disrupt your relationship. Sex may become dominant; you stop talking to each other and spend most of your time doing it, thinking about it, or looking for places to do it. Since you want more from a relationship than just sex, you may find that you lose more than you gain by having intercourse.[4]

NEUROSES   In our sexually conscious, psychological oriented society, many people believe that chastity causes neuroses. Articles in popular magazines point out the dangers of frustrating your natural

---

[4]However, some people spend less time on sex after they have had intercourse, a point we shall consider in "the case against chastity."

instincts; your friends may even argue that certain teachers are nasty because they are frustrated old maids.

These arguments are drivel. There is no evidence that chastity per se causes neuroses. Not satisfying your sexual desires may make you uncomfortable; it may even make you unpleasant from time to time; but it will not have any permanent effects. The nasty-old-maid argument is even sillier. Some unmarried women are nasty; others are not. And, if one is nasty, cause and effect are probably reversed. She is not nasty because she is sexually frustrated; she is unmarried (and perhaps frustrated) because no one wanted to put up with her nasty disposition.

A few people approach the neurotic issue from another angle. They argue that virginity may not cause neuroses, but that it is a symptom of them—a sign that you are inhibited, frigid, and generally neurotic. In our adjustment-conscious age these are frightening charges, and many girls have had relations to prove that they were not neurotic. Their reasoning is faulty, and their behavior is pitiful.

Neuroses are not diseases; they are simply convenient terms to refer to certain patterns of behavior and feelings. No one *has* a neurosis in the same sense as one has a cold, and everyone is more or less neurotic. More importantly, you can never *prove* that you are not neurotic. In fact, trying to prove it indicates that you are unsure of yourself, a major characteristic of the people whom we call neurotic.

A variation on the neurotic theme is the argument that "everybody is doing it; why shouldn't we?" First of all, everybody is *not* doing it.[5] A substantial number of girls and a few boys do remain virgins until they get married. Second, the argument is silly and irrelevant. You are not everybody. You are you—an independent, self-respecting individual with your own beliefs and standards. It is no more reasonable to let the crowd make your decisions than it is to let another individual do so. You are a responsible individual, and the responsibility for this decision belongs entirely to you.

PREGNANCY   Many girls and a few boys are restrained by the very reasonable fear of pregnancy. An unwanted pregnancy is a disaster for

---

[5] A Gallup poll reported in *Newsweek* (December 29, 1969, p. 36) indicated that only 50.8% of college students had had pre- or extra-marital relations.

everyone concerned, and it happens far too frequently. You probably know several people who have had to leave school to get married, and you may even know a few girls who have had abortions or borne illegitimate children. Even if you use some method of birth control (and many people get so excited that they forget to use them or use them properly), there is always some risk of pregnancy. You should consider this risk carefully before making your decision. (This topic will be discussed more extensively later.)

VENEREAL DISEASE   Research indicates that very few people are deterred by fear of becoming infected with a venereal disease. Ignorance is a major cause of this lack of concern. You probably do not know very much about the VD, and you therefore do not worry about it. The chances of getting it are rather slight, but they are much greater than you realize. VD is unpleasant, and, if you do not realize you have it, it can kill you or drive you insane.

COMPATIBILITY TEST   Many people argue: "We can't have a happy marriage unless we are compatible sexually. We should therefore have relations to find out whether we satisfy each other." On the surface this argument sounds logical. Sexual compatibilty *is* important in marriage. However, it does not follow that you should have compatibility tests.

The circumstances under which such a test would occur are so unfavorable that the results will probably be misleading. The physical conditions are usually far from ideal; you may be uncomfortable and afraid of being caught. One or both parties will feel at least a little guilty and ashamed. The fact that it is a test may make you feel even more apprehensive than usual about proving yourself. Indeed, "sometimes a girl breaks down and cries . . . because she feels she is not coming up to scratch."[6]

These differences, as well as experience with hundreds of couples, has led a prominent marriage counselor to conclude:

> Whether a man and a woman are physically suited to each other has seldom been determined from pre-marital sex experiences. Sex relations before marriage differ in many ways from those engaged in by husband

[6]Kenneth C. Barnes, *He and She*. Baltimore, Md.: Penguin, 1958, p. 145.

and wife. For one thing, the anxiety, strain, and awkward conditions surrounding pre-marital experience often make it entirely unsatisfactory for a man and a woman, who might find themselves ideally suited under the normal conditions of marriage.[7]

The Case Against Chastity

Although the arguments in favor of chastity are impressive, one can make a fairly good case against it, at least for some people. You should look at both sides before making your decision.

MORAL   It may offend some people, but there is a moral case against chastity. The case rests on the very sound principle that each person must act according to his own moral code, and the code which prohibits premarital intercourse applies only to people who accept it. This argument is supported by the fact that virginity is certainly not valued in all cultures, nor has it been valued in the European culture during all eras. Many cultures, in fact, regard it as a nuisance or a proof that a girl is unattractive.

In other words, the demand that you remain a virgin is not natural, nor does it come from God; it came from people, and they have no right to tell you what is right or wrong. You have to develop your own code and to make your own decisions.

Note that this position is not nearly so rigid as the one that regards all premarital intercourse as immoral. It does not say that intercourse is right, only that you must decide whether it is right for you. It places the responsibility for your conduct and morals where it belongs, on your own shoulders, and by doing so it shows much more respect for you as an adult. If this position makes sense to you, and if you really believe that sex is not wrong, having intercourse may actually increase your self-respect. You will know that you are making your own decision instead of letting other people dominate your life.

Although this position allows some people to have sexual relations, it actually increases the pressure against other people's doing the same. It says, in effect, if you do believe it is immoral, it is *really* wrong to do it. You cannot plead that you have only violated an artificial or

[7]Samuel Kling, *How to Win and Hold a Mate,* Perma books (paper bound).

imposed code. You have taken the responsibility for developing your own code and have been unable to live by the code you have developed. You may therefore feel an even greater loss of self-respect than if you violated the traditional code.

LOVE   Many people argue, with considerable justification, that sex is an expression of love that is as valid and meaningful outside of marriage as it is within it. The prudes say that this argument is simply a convenient rationalization for yielding to your animal desires. Some people (especially girls) do use love as a rationalization for an act which is committed for other reasons, but others express their deepest, most human feelings by making love.

RESPECT FROM OTHER PEOPLE   Although the responsibility for the decision is yours, you are still concerned with the opinion and respect of other people. The reaction of your lover is probably most important to you, especially if you are a girl. Many men lose respect for a girl who yields to them, but many others do not. Their reaction depends primarily upon their own attitudes toward sex and their acceptance of the double standard. It is hard to give a general rule here, but I think you will find that the less experienced he is, the more likely he is to retain or to increase his respect for you (especially if it is his first time). It will be something special for him, and he may feel more warm and respectful toward you.

On the other hand, if he is a "ladies' man," you can be fairly certain that giving in to him will lower his respect and interest. Ladies men are *invariably* neurotic. They do not respect themselves, nor do they respect or care about women. They are unsure of themselves as men, and they may even be trying to suppress latent homosexual desires. They have to prove themselves by seducing girls, especially virgins. They do not express love, nor do they feel it. They simply exploit girls to build their own egos. If your boyfriend has had relations with many girls, you will probably lose his respect and you may even lose him entirely.[8]

If your friends should find out, they may be much less horrified than you expected. Young people have become much more permis-

---

[8]In my opinion he is not much of a loss, a point that will be discussed in a moment.

sive about other people's sexual behavior, and in some groups sex is a status symbol. Of course, status is not a good reason for having relations; in fact, the person who has sexual relations to enhance his or her status is doing the same thing as the ones who restrain themselves because of fear of other people's opinions. They are all living according to other people's codes, not their own.

CHANCES FOR MARRIAGE   Although it may decrease your chances for marriage, this effect is much less pronounced than it used to be. Fewer men insist or expect that their wives be virgins, and girls overestimate the importance that males place on virginity. The importance of virginity is especially low among college-educated men, the people in whom you are most interested.

NEUROSES   Quite a few of the advocates of chastity claim that having relations can cause neuroses. There is some truth to their position, but not much. A few people do feel so guilty that they have psychological problems, occasionally serious ones. Guilt is the primary element in many neuroses, and anything which increases guilt can cause psychological problems.

On the other hand, surveys clearly indicate that most people do not feel guilty. In fact, the majority of people who have had premarital relations indicate that they have no regrets. Kinsey found that 69% of the unmarried females said that they did not regret having had premarital intercourse; 13% had some minor regrets. For the married females that percentage was even higher: 77% said that they had no remorse, and 12% expressed minor regrets. Kinsey concluded:

> The regret . . . appeared to depend on the nature of the pre-marital experience. For the most part, those who regretted it most were the females who had the least experience.

Percentages are, of course, misleading. You are a human being, not a statistic. Perhaps most people are not sorry, but that is very little consolation if you feel guilty and miserable. You must therefore consider your own personality. If you are the sort of person who tends to feel guilty, if you have strong beliefs that premarital intercourse is wrong, you should probably restrain yourself.

DISRUPTING THE RELATIONSHIP   Although having relations can cause sex to dominate the relationship, the usual effect is just the opposite. Many virgins neck and pet for hours, but it is physically impossible to have intercourse as long or as frequently. Furthermore, satisfied desires have much less effect on people than frustrated ones. People who do not have relations may think about sex almost constantly, while people who are sexually satisfied can think of other things.

PREGNANCY   Although fears of pregnancy are justified, modern birth control methods are fairly safe—*if* they are used properly. The fact that the first intercourse usually occurs by accident can cause birth control to be forgotten or misused, but the methods themselves can provide *almost* complete protection. Therefore, if you make a conscious decision instead of just letting nature take its course, you may run little danger of becoming pregnant. (This topic will be discussed more fully in a moment.)

LOSING A LOSER   Many girls are afraid that they will lose their boyfriend if they give in to him. Although this fear is justified, especially with ladies' men, any man who will drop you for giving in to him is a poor prospect anyway. Since you probably would not be happy if you married him, losing him is more of a blessing than a loss. In other words, if he is that kind of man, good riddance. It cost you your virginity to find out, but better your virginity than the rest of your life.

I am not advocating that you have relations to find out what kind of man he is. I am simply objecting to the common belief that losing a boyfriend is a tragedy and to the system of using your body (or the promise of it) to seduce a man into marriage. If all you have going for you is that he wants to sleep with you, you have nothing at all, and the sooner you find out the better.

FREEDOM   The net effect of the points made above is to increase your personal freedom. Our society is still struggling with its Puritan heritage, but more and more people have come to accept chastity as a personal decision rather than a moral imperative. This freedom is increased by modern birth control methods. You can make your decision on the basis of your desires and values instead of letting other people or the fear of pregnancy dominate you. In my opinion, these are healthy developments, regardless of the decision you make. Neither virginity nor nonvirginity is meaningful or important by itself. What is important is that you know what you really want and have the courage to live according to your own code.

Remaining Chaste

As Robert Burns phrased it: "The best laid plans of mice and men gang aft agley."

If you decide to remain chaste, you may find that it is very hard to carry out your decision. The temptation is strong, and the further you go, the stronger it gets. This increase is particularly great for women, and they often do not realize how powerful their desires are. Most boys know the strength of their feelings; they may even have had orgasms from necking. But many girls do not realize the driving, demanding nature of their own impulses. The fact of the matter is that women's desires are harder to arouse, but, when they are aroused, they are often *stronger* than the man's. Once a woman passes a certain point, it is extremely difficult for her to stop.

The only solution to this problem is to avoid situations in which you get too excited. If you want to remain chaste, you should avoid long parking sessions, heavy petting, and so forth. Otherwise, whether you like it or not, you will probably lose your virginity.

MASTURBATION, PORNOGRAPHY, AND HOMOSEXUALITY

These three forms of sexual release are quite common among young people, but many individuals feel guilty about yielding to their impulses. Since this guilt creates more problems than the acts themselves, the following discussion is an attempt to put these acts into perspective and to help you to cope with both your sexual needs and your guilt feelings.

Masturbation

Masturbation is completely natural and virtually *everyone* does it at one time or another. Unfortunately, many young people think that they are the only ones who masturbate. You have been taught since infancy that your genitals are nasty things which should not be touched, and you may feel guilty about yielding to your "evil" impulses. You may also have heard all sorts of old wives tales about the damage masturbation causes, but these stories are utter nonsense. *"Masturbation never causes any physical or mental harm, either temporary or lasting."* [9] The only thing about it which can cause problems is the guilt caused by the Puritan attitudes.

Pornography

The same point can be made about pornography. Reading books and looking at pictures does not cause psychological problems, nor does it increase the number of sex crimes. Guilt about using pornography can, of course, cause problems, but this guilt comes from social training and reactions, not from pornography itself.

Purveyors of the Puritan ethic have argued that pornography causes sex crimes, but these people have no training in or understanding of psychology. Most psychologists who have studied this issue have, in fact, concluded that pornography and the masturbation which often accompanies it have exactly the opposite effect: they provide a sexual release which acts as a substitute for rape, child molesting, and so on. Collateral evidence on this point is the relatively low rate of sex crimes in countries such as Denmark, which allow pornography to be published and distributed rather openly. This conclusion is also supported by President Nixon's Study Commission.

Unfortunately, most people do not *want* to understand this issue or to deal dispassionately with the evidence. Pornography arouses desires in them which are so frightening that they cannot face them. They therefore try to force down their own desires by acting as censors for everyone else. Virtually every censor, whether official or self-appointed, is really trying to control his own impulses and

[9]Oswald Schwarz, *The Psychology of Sex.* Baltimore, Md.: Penguin, 1949, p. 38.

to relieve his own guilt. It is a tragic indication of the strength and irrationality of our Puritan heritage that people with such serious psychological problems are often given power over the public.

Homosexuality

The same tendency causes the extreme reactions to homosexuality, especially among males. Men make jokes about homosexuals, beat them up, and deprive them of their legal rights because they are trying to keep down their own homosexual desires. The guilt toward these desires is a natural result of the guilt which often causes these same desires to be aroused. Girls are so idealized that many boys are unable to relate to them, especially during early adolescnce. They feel unclean, unworthy of these embodiments of virtue.

Although they cannot express their sexual and other feelings toward the natural objects, the feelings themselves cannot be denied or completely suppressed. The usual expression is masturbation, but many individuals experiment with homosexuality. Such experiments are far from rare; authorities estimate that about 50% of all adolescent boys engage in one form or another of homosexual behavior, and that many other boys have some kind of homosexual feelings which they do not express directly. Unfortunately, very few boys know how common their feelings or behavior are; they see how antihomosexual all their friends act, think that they are different, and feel very guilty and ashamed.

This guilt increases their inability to relate to girls. They already feel that girls are too nice to touch, and now they "know" how evil and unworthy they are. They may therefore remain homosexual for the rest of their lives.[10]

The great majority of experimenters ultimately fall in love with a girl, but their homosexual experiences often remain a terrible secret and barrier between them. They have no perspective about their actions, nor can they talk to anyone about them. Feeling that these

[10]It is worth noting that the extreme social and legal pressures we exert have not been successful in keeping down the number of practicing homosexuals, but the pressures continue and are rationalized as protection for society. The Puritan conscience is as powerful and unstoppable as the desires it seeks to repress.

actions are too shameful and disgusting to discuss, they do everything they can to keep them buried (including criticizing and attacking "dirty queers").

Overt homosexuality is much less common among women, but it is far from rare. Authorities estimate that about 25% of adolescent girls engage in some form of homosexual behavior. These figures may be somewhat misleading because there is no stigma attached to actions which would be called homosexual in boys (for example, holding hands, sleeping in the same bed, even sleeping with their arms around each other). For girls these acts are not regarded as homosexual, and they often do not lead to mutual masturbation and other forms of overtly homosexual behavior. Adolescent girls have much weaker sexual desires than boys, and affectionate acts and "crushes" are usually enough to satisfy them.

The Puritan moral code plays a profound role in the development of female homosexuality. Many girls have been taught that their own sexual desires are nasty and that "men are beasts who want only one thing." Since they are unable to relate to boys, they naturally turn to the gentleness and tenderness of another girl. Sometimes these relationships become overtly homosexual; sometimes the sexual aspect is subtle; but in either case they may become unable to fulfill the female sex role, even if they should eventually marry. Their "crushes" or affairs with other girls, by adding to their guilt and confusion, may prevent them from relaxing with their husband or responding to him sexually.

If the authorities are at all acurate, about one-half of the boys and one-quarter of the girls reading this book have had some form of homosexual relationship. These statistics alone may make some people feel a little less guilty and ashamed, but I am afraid they will not help very much. Our culture is too guilt-ridden, punitive, and antihomosexual for a few statistics to do much good. If you have experimented and feel guilty about it, I urge you to see a counselor. This recommendation is based not on moralistic, but on pragmatic grounds. You probably cannot overcome your guilt feelings by yourself; these guilt feelings (and the homosexual desires you may still have) will undoubtedly interfere with your married life.

If you are currently a practicing homosexual, I am even more emphatic in my recommendation that you see a counselor. I am not speaking as a preacher trying to save your soul, but as a psychologist who knows that most homosexuals are extremely unhappy. They do not like themselves; they do not like each other; they do not have stable or satisfying sexual relationships; they face extreme social pressures; they are therefore lonely and miserable.

Regardless of the strength of your homosexual desires or the date of your activities, a counselor can help you. If you do want help, but are ashamed to ask for it, you should realize that a competent counselor will not betray your confidence, nor sit in judgment on you, nor try to turn you into something you do not want to be. He will simply try to help you to understand, to accept, and to live with yourself, regardless of what you are or want to be. If you want to remain a homosexual, he will help you to accept and to live with yourself and other people. If you want to assume a normal sex role, he will help you to become a better, more confident, more self-respecting husband or wife.

VENEREAL DISEASE

Venereal disease is another topic we adults have not discussed frankly with you. It is a "nasty" subject, and we are too embarrassed to discuss it. Unfortunately, we do not suffer the consequences of our timidity; you do. Some of you will unquestionably become infected, and you probably will not realize it or know what to do. The disease may therefore spread to other people, and it can become more serious for you.

In fact, if treatments for syphilis does not begin in time, the disease becomes incurable and will ultimately cause insanity and death. This problem is complicated by the fact that the symptoms go away, making some people think that they are healthy when the disease is really getting worse.

Since any venereal disease can be cured quickly, effectively, and painlessly if treatments begin soon enough, you should see a doctor if you have any reason to suspect that you have become infected. If you notice *anything* unusual in your genital area—a discharge, sores, painful urination, swelling, inflammation, or anything else—get to a doctor or clinic *immediately.* If you do not have VD, he may find some other problem that needs treatment. If you do have VD, one shot of penicillin now can save you and many other people (including your children) from months or years of misery.

There is no need to be embarrassed. Doctors have been trained to act impersonally and professionally. The doctor[11] you see will concentrate on your symptoms, not on your morals. If you are not infected, he will say little or nothing. If you are, he will cure you and may ask for the names of the people with whom you have had intercourse. By all means, give him the names. He is not going to have them arrested or expelled; he just wants to protect them and the community by curing the disease. These other people will be contacted discreetly, and there will be a minimum of embarrassment. You are therefore doing them a favor and fulfilling your responsibility to the community by giving him their names.

BIRTH CONTROL

Despite all the books and articles about birth control, thousands of students have unwanted children each year—with tragic consequences for everyone concerned. An innocent child begins his life under a cloud and may be rejected by his parents or blamed for every marital problem they ever have. He may end up in an orphanage or, if his parents cannot face the responsibility, he may even be murdered. Regardless of what happens to the child, the mother will feel guilty and desperate, especially if the father will not marry her. The father may have to quit school to support a family he does not want.

Even if the couple marries, the tragedy is far from over. They will be criticized by the gossips who count the days. They will hurt and embarrass their families by the early child and face the problems of parenthood long before they have learned to live with each other. They will know that their marriage was not entirely voluntary, a fact which often becomes an excuse to behave irresponsibly or a weapon in the eternal battle of the sexes. Again and again I have heard men say: "If she hadn't gotten pregnant, I would be a doctor today." or "Since she trapped me into marriage, I don't have to be faithful to her." Because of these problems "premarital pregnancy is more likely

---

[11]Girls might feel more comfortable consulting a woman doctor, and there are many listed in most telephone books.

to be followed by divorce than postmarital pregnancy."[12]

Even if they do not have a baby, a couple who has intercourse without protection is placed under a terrible strain. They count the days until her period and become frantic if it is late.

When we analyze the availability of birth control devices, the consequences of not using them, and the number of unwanted pregnancies, we realize that some powerful irrational forces must be at work. Perhaps the most powerful of these are the romantic illusion and the desire to preserve it. People want to believe that love conquers all, even when they know that it cannot conquer biology. Their feelings are similar to those of soldiers under fire: "It can't happen to me." Soldiers feel this way because their own deaths are too frightening to think about, and to many young people, pregnancy is almost as frightening. But ignoring something doesn't make it go away; in fact, ignoring the possibility of pregnancy greatly increases its chances of occurring.

Guilt and shame also play important roles, especially for girls. They want to believe that sex "just happens," and taking precautions would weaken their rationalizations. But, if you "just happen" to have intercourse, you may "just happen" to have a baby.

The general guilt and shame of the rest of our society keep many adolescents ignorant of sex and birth control. Parents are so hung-up that they abdicate their responsibilities to teach their children about sex. Teachers are as inhibited as everyone else, and they are afraid to say anything that might offend the parents. Many schools do not offer sex education courses, and the ones that are offered are hopelessly abstract and intellectual; topics such as birth control and the demanding nature of sexual desires are almost never mentioned.

Students therefore do not understand their own feelings and must learn about birth control on their own. They ask each other questions and read junky books, but they learn very little and are confused by misinformation. Some of this misinformation would be funny if its consequences were not so tragic. For example, one boy said: "There's the Greek method. Apparently one can temporarily sterilize oneself by heating one's sex organ in boiling water."[13]

Even if an unmarried person should get good information about

---

[12]H. T. Christensen, *Eugenics Quarterly*, 1963, vol. 10 no. 3, p. 127.
[13]Schofield, *op. cit.*, p. 88.

birth control and decide to use it, he or she will encounter the Puritan conscience in its most irrational, vicious state. We adults *know* that fear of pregnancy does not prevent most people from having intercourse; we *know*, much better than you do, the terrible consequences of unwanted pregnancies; we know that innocent children suffer; but we say, in effect: "If you are going to sin, you must take the risks." That is the "logic" behind the refusal of many doctors and clinics to insert interuterine devices (IUD) or to prescribe birth control pills for unmarried women.

Despite all these irrational forces, you must think rationally about birth control. This advice is *not* directed only to people who are having intercourse; it is for every person who is getting sexually excited through necking and petting—because you may get overexcited and have intercourse, even if you don't want it. If you do not think about birth control before you have intercourse, I guarantee you will worry about if afterwards! The information is readily available, and there is no rational reason for you not to read it—*now*.

There are so many books on this topic that a recommended reading list would be superfluous. You might also waste your time looking for a recommended book or give up because you cannot find it. I therefore suggest you go out right *now* and buy any book on sex or birth control which is *written by a physician*.

These books often tend to be abstract and intellectual, but at least they will help you to understand the basic biological principles. Their weakest point is that they cannot communicate the strength of sexual desires, nor do they tell you how these desires can reverse your good intentions. I cannot communicate that either, but I would like to discuss a few points which some books do not cover well.

1. Prophylactics, diaphragms, and withdrawal are *not* foolproof. If used properly, they are somewhat less dependable than pills and IUD, but people very frequently get so excited that they use these techniques improperly or not at all. Carrying a prohylactic in your pocket is no guarantee that you will be cool-headed enough to use it.

2. The rhythm method is *not* foolproof, especially for unmarried women. The method itself is unreliable, and unmarried girls often have such irregular menstrual cycles that the rhythm method becomes a sexual form of Russian roulette.

3. Birth control pills must be taken *every* day during most of

the menstrual cycle. Many people have the erroneous belief that taking the pill right before or after intercourse can prevent conception. This belief is absolutely unfounded; in that situation a birth control pill is no more effective than an aspirin.

4. Most of the birth control pills sold without prescription are worthless. Thousands of girls buy pills from quacks or pushers. These pills are almost invariably worthless, and some of them are even harmful. If you want to take pills, get a prescription.

5. You *can* find a doctor who will insert IUD or prescribe birth control pills. You may have to go a large city, or pretend to be married, or visit a few doctors, or suffer some embarrassment, but you can find a doctor or clinic that will help you. And the trouble, expense, and embarrassment are nothing compared to the problems of an unwanted pregnancy.

6. *No* birth control method is completely safe. The pill and IUD are almost 100% sure, but occasional pregnancies still occur. You must therefore realize that you are taking a chance, and, if the risk seems too great, you most avoid intercourse and situations which lead to such excitement that intercourse occurs.

7. Birth control pills can have some very unpleasant side-effects. Some girls become depressed; others get irritable, and a few have died. At least 250 deaths have been caused by the pills. The Senate hearings have publicized this point, but a counter-argument has been made by some distinguished gynecologists. Pills are so much more effective than anything else, including IUD, that a group of women using other methods will have more unwanted babies *and* more deaths from birth related problems than they would have if they used the pill. Neither this argument nor the contrary one is supported by adequate evidence. In other words, there are dangers in using pills, and dangers in not using them.

UNWANTED PREGNANCIES

If you or your girlfriend is pregnant, you are probably desperate. All kinds of ideas run through your head. You think about abortion, marriage, running away, suicide. Sometimes contradictory thoughts occur right after each other. One minute you are planning to get married; the next minute you think of suicide. Your mental state is perfectly understandable, and most people in your situation would feel the same way. The pressure is too much for you, and your emotions have overwhelmed your reason. Since you are irrational, you must recognize your irrationality and take steps to compensate for it. The situation is too much for you to handle alone, and you must get help.

The first help you need is medical. You must make certain that the girl is pregnant. Menstrual cycles are not always regular, especially in young girls, and guilt feelings or anxiety about being pregnant can delay periods for *weeks*. In fact, some authorities estimate that 50% of all abortions are performed on women who are not pregnant. You should therefore see a doctor immediately; his professional code requires that he keep your secret, even from your parents. If you do not want to see a local man, buy a ring and go some place else with a false name, but make sure of the pregnancy before you do *anything*.

If it is a real pregnancy, you should seek psychological help. You must sort out your own feelings so that you can make an intelligent decision, and, because of the pressure you are under, you cannot do that alone. You need someone to help you to understand yourself. Naturally, your girlfriend or boyfriend is the first person to talk to, but you are both going to be irrational. A girls' entire life and biology have conditioned her to want a husband, and guilt and other irrational feelings cause many boys to think that marriage is the only answer. Perhaps it is the right answer, but this decision is much too important to make in the midst of a panic. You are in trouble, but an unhappy marriage is a lot worse.

Since neither of you can realistically appraise your chances of a successful marriage, nor can you evaluate any other alternatives, you need an outsider. Your parents might help, but they are probably too conventional to help you to understand yourself. They "know" that marriage is the right thing and will probably increase the pressure you have to face. Since the pressures are already overwhelming, you should probably defer talking to them until after you have made your own decision.

On the other hand, if you are pregnant and the boy will not even consider marriage, talk to your parents immediately. You need psychological and objective support, and they are the best place to get it. You are afraid to tell them, of course, but most families pull together when one of them really needs help. In fact, thousands of girls who were convinced that their parents did not love or understand them have found that the people they feared so much can be tender and understanding. If you are pregnant and abandoned, you need your parents, and it is unfair to yourself and to them to keep it a secret. If you find that they cannot or will not help you, you can always leave, but give them a chance.

If you are considering marriage, I urge you to contact a professional immediately. Your problems are too difficult to be worked out without professional help. If you are uncertain of what you want to do, he will help you to understand your own feelings. If you are sure that you want to get married, he will help you prepare for the problems and stresses of married life—and these problems are much greater for a couple in your situation.

You can find professionals listed in the telephone book under "marriage counseling" or "family counseling." If you live near a large town, you may find a listing for the Family Service Bureau or The Jewish Family Service Bureau.[14] The Family Service Bureaus and other agencies are not quite so private as individual counselors because you must see a secretary or receptionist, but the professionals will respect your confidence. Furthermore, the receptionist will usually only take the most basic data, and will not ask personal questions. The agencies' fees will be more moderate than individuals', and their personnel are quite familiar with this problem.

If you prefer an individual, you must be very careful because most states allow anyone, even a quack, to call himself a "marriage counselor." Doctors' degrees are usually listed in the phone book, but an M.D. or Ph.D. is not essential, and other degrees may not be advertised. Some excellent counselors have the M.S.W. (Master of Social Work), frequently with a psychiatric or counseling specialty. There are a few other degrees that are acceptable, but do not go to any counselor who does not have at least a Masters from a *recognized* university (too many people have "Doctor's" degrees from diploma

---

[14]The Jewish Family Service Bureau will usually help people of any faith.

mills). If you contact a counselor, ask him about his professional training and credentials. If he is legitimate, he will not mind your questions; in fact he probably wishes everyone asked them. If he does not
have the proper degrees or is evasive about his background, do *not* go
to him. A quack can do an enormous amount of harm.

Any professional will help you to understand yourself, your feelings toward each other, and the chances for success in your marriage.
They can also clarify your alternatives, and refer you to hospitals
where you can have the baby or to agencies which will arrange for
adoption.

Unfortunately, many people will ignore this advice. They will be
too embarrassed to see someone or too panicky to think before they
act. I therefore feel obliged to comment on some fairly common, but
very foolish actions.

1. Attempts at self-abortion are extremely dangerous. Poking
   sharp objects into the uterus is insane. It probably will not
   cause an abortion, and it can cause hemorrhages, infection, and
   death. Use of drugs is equally foolhardy. Most drugs will not
   cause an abortion; they will just make the mother very sick,
   and they may deform the child. Furthermore, any drug which
   is strong enough to kill an embryo is strong enough to kill the
   mother.

2. Abortionists are extremely dangerous. Most have no medical
   training, and the operation is performed under the worst possible conditions. The absence of proper sanitary facilities, the
   need for secrecy, the unwillingness to refer patients with com-
   plications to reputable doctors, and the abortionists' general
   incompetence can cost you your life.

3. Medically sound abortions can be arranged. Abortions can be
   objected to on both moral and psychological grounds. A human life is destroyed and the act often causes the mother or
   father to become deeply depressed; a few people even commit
   suicide because of their guilt feelings. But we must be realistic.
   Some people will get abortions, and they are better off in the
   hands of a competent physician.

So, if you are going to get an abortion, do it right. The sooner you
do it, the safer and easier it is. Furthermore, the law in some states
regards abortion in a later month as a much more serious crime,

presumably because they regard the older fetus as a person instead of a ball of cells.

If you are rich enough, go to Scandinavia, Japan, or England, or some other country where abortions are legal. There are also some states where legal abortions can be arranged. You will be much safer because these people will know what they are doing and have all the necessary facilities. If you are not rich, see your family doctor.[15] He may be upset, but practicing medicine makes a man realistic. He has seen or heard of dozens of abortions, and he can help you. Perhaps he may even consent to do it, but he will probably refer you to someone else.

4. Many adoption agencies are unethical. If you are going to let your baby be adopted, get a reference from your doctor, clergyman, or The Family Service Bureau. Don't just answer an ad in a local paper for "girls in trouble." Perhaps the people placing that ad are legitimate, but there is a black market for babies, and you do not want your child to end up with a family that cannot satisfy the requirements of a legitimate adoption agency. Furthermore, a few organizations may even try to blackmail you.

5. Most important of all, think before you act. You got into this mess because you let your emotions overrule your reason. Don't make the same mistake again.

---

[15]You should see him even if you plan to go to a state where abortions are legal. He can help you to find a competent, ethical doctor, and if you go there without his help, you may end up with a quack.

MARRIAGE

"For many students marriage is more an
attempt to establish a suitable self-conception
than the expression of a well-formed
personality's natural bent."[1]

Marriage is one of America's greatest failures. We have one of the
highest divorce rates in human history, and the divorces are only the
tip of the iceberg. Millions of people are dissatisfied with their marriages, and countless children grow up in homes which are little more
than battlefields. Detailed statistics could be cited, but you have seen
so many divorces and domestic battles that statistics are unnecessary.
Everyone knows that the problem is serious.

Unfortunately, most students see it as a problem for *other* people.
They know intellectually that many marriages fail, but feel certain

[1]Nevitt Sanford, "Freshman Personality: A Stage in Human Development," in
Nevitt Sanford (ed.), *College and Character.* New York: Wiley, 1964.

that their own will succeed. Lovers' natural delusions are one factor, of course, but our obsession with romantic love and our refusal to think about the more enduring aspects of the marital relationship are even more important. People of most other nationalities regard courting as the preparation for marriage, but Americans usually regard dating as an end in itself. Children enjoy themselves, but they do not prepare themselves for marriage, nor do they think seriously about marital problems. They simply go out, enjoy themselves, fall in love, and get married. They make the most important decision of their lives on a purely emotional basis. Then, when the inevitable problems arise, they ask: "How could I have been so blind?"

My purpose here is to help you to think clearly about this decision. Most readers will not take my advice seriously because the American cultural pressures and their own feelings are so strong that they can not think rationally. Having been taught that "love conquers all," they feel that rational analysis of marriage is unnecessary or even improper, a violation of the romantic ideal. While I realize that most readers will ignore this advice, I do hope to help a few people to avoid hopeless marriage and a few others to lay a better foundation for the marriages that do occur.

Problems will be stressed, and the entire chapter has a rather negative tone for two reasons: First, romantic love creates such a euphoric state that negative factors are usually overlooked. Second, the decision to marry is much harder to reverse than the decision to break off or to wait. You can easily change your mind about delaying your marriage or breaking off a relationship, but once you marry, you are stuck—perhaps for life. The emphasis will therefore be on avoiding hopeless or premature marriages.

The chapter is divided into two parts. First we shall look at your readiness for marriage; then we shall consider the type of person you should marry and your chances for a successful marriage with various individuals.[2]

---

[2]This chapter is no substitute for premarital counseling or a course in marriage. The traditionalists, with their obsession for the irrelevant, object to such courses because they feel that anything as important as a successful marriage is not a proper topic for a university course. Despite their pressures, some schools have offered courses; if your school offers one, take it and, if you are on the brink of marriage, get premarital counseling.

*"When you marry is as important as whom
you marry."*

ARE YOU READY?

Not too long ago, marriage was grounds for expulsion from many colleges because marriage and education were regarded as being incompatible. Millions of World War II and Korean veterans destroyed that belief; they used the GI Bill to finance their educations and generally did quite well. Today about one-fifth of college students are married, but many of them are not nearly so mature as the veterans were. They are much younger, and they have spent all of their lives in school. They therefore lack the understanding and maturity one needs to make a success of marriage.

Despite the overwhelming evidence linking youth to marital failures, more and more students are marrying. Early dating and going steady are important causes for student marriages, but I think that the chief cause is the American cult of "instant happiness." Student marriages are, in fact, an extreme example of the "buy now, pay later" philosophy. Many Americans have been conditioned to satisfy their immediate needs and to ignore the long-term consequences of their actions. They marry before they are psychologically or economically ready, then pay for their impatience for the rest of their lives. They mortgage their careers and undermine their marriages.

It is, of course, an oversimplification to say that all students (particularly graduate students[3]) are not ready for marriage. Some students are ready for marriage, while some graduates are not. This discussion will therefore not be confined to the problems of student marriages, but will also consider the personal factors that are related to marital success.

Perhaps the most important personal factor is one's motives for marrying. Everyone says that he is marrying for love, but many young people are really trying to escape from unpleasant situations or their psychological problems. We shall discuss several types of psychological problems, but one general point can be made here. *The unhappier a person is, the more he is convinced that marriage is the only alternative,*

---

[3]Graduate student marriages will be discussed in the chapter on graduate school. These remarks refer primarily to undergraduates.

and the more desperately he wants to get married, the more likely it is that he is trying to run away from something (and the less ready he is for marriage). The very problems that he is trying to escape will prevent him from being a good husband and ruin his marriage, making him even more miserable.[4]

Because one must understand himself to know whether he is ready for marriage, the following discussion will focus on self-analysis. This analysis may prevent you from making a serious mistake, and it should also help you to be a better husband or wife. There is also a "Marital Readiness Questionnaire" in the appendix to help you with this self-analysis.

The emphasis here will also be on the negative because no one can say that you *are* ready; one can only say that people with certain kinds of characteristics and problems are *not* ready. Furthermore, marrying too soon has much more serious consequences than marrying too late.

The discussion considers two issues. First and most important: Are you psychologically ready for marriage? Second, would marrying soon help or hinder your progress toward your major goals?

Age

Age is the most obvious index of psychological readiness for marriage, and it is very closely correlated to marital success. Every major study has found that early marriages are more likely to fail, particularly when people are less than 18 or 19. The failure rate for the latter group is two or three times as great as it is for people who marry at 22 or 25.[5] These failures occur because younger people are usually not mature enough, and they may be trying to run away from themselves or from unpleasant situations. If you are still in your teens, and you want very much to get married, you should ask yourself: "Why?" You may find that you are trying to escape from something in yourself or in your life. Since marriage will not provide that escape and it generally will add to the pressures, you will probably end up much unhappier than you are now.

[4]Obviously the same principle applies to women.
[5]J. Dominian, *Marital Break-down.* Baltimore Md.: Pelican, 1968, pp. 130 f.

Time

The amount of time that you have known and been engaged to each other is closely correlated with your chances for a successful marriage. Nearly every study reveals that "a short period of acquaintance and engagement is associated with high incidence of marital unhappiness."[6] These studies indicate that "at least nine months of engagement provide an average probability for success."[6] The figures are especially negative for elopements, which usually occur between people who have not thought clearly about marriage, and who may have known each other for very brief periods of time. One study found that only 48% of the elopements led to happy marriages, compared to an average of 80%.[7]

Long acquaintances and engagements are important for three reasons. First, marriages based on short acquaintances are usually the result of physical infatuation or neurotic motives, poor bases for a marriage. Second, long acquaintances and engagements give you a chance to learn more about each other, and you may realize that you should not marry. Third, acquaintance and engagement periods give you a chance to lay a foundation for your marriage. You can start adjusting to each other without facing all the pressures and strains of married life.

It therefore seems obvious that you are probably not ready for marriage if you have known each other for a short time. Furthermore, if you want to marry a relative stranger, I suggest that you analyze yourself more deeply. Why are you willing to make such an important decision on so little information? What do your feelings say about the kind of person you are?

Inertia

Inertia plays an important role in many marriages, especially among very young people. People date each other for a while and then drift slowly toward marriage. They go steady, get pinned, buy an engagement ring, and finally marry, without ever making a real decision or

[6] *Ibid.*, p. 135.
[7] Popinoe conducted the study which was reported in *Marital Break-down.*

analyzing themselves. One stage follows naturally after another until they find themselves married, usually to the wrong person at the wrong time.

The going-steady mania and the insecurity on which it is based are the major causes for these inertial marriages. Young people grasp at the security of going steady long before they know anything about the opposite sex or their own desires, and going steady prevents them from learning very much or developing the independence they need to make a real choice. A few people drift into marriage with their high-school sweetheart; they have had time to get to know each other, but they have not learned much about the opposite sex or the way they get along with different types of people.

Even if they are lucky enough to have their early romances break up, many young people can not take advantage of their freedom and opportunity to learn. They date a couple of people, feel insecure and "out of it," go steady with the first person who appeals to them, and start drifting toward marriage.

If your life has followed this pattern, if you have gone out with only a few people, if you have gone steady most of the time, you may not be ready for marriage. You probably do not know enough about the opposite sex or your feelings toward them, and you may not be independent enough to be a good spouse.

Sex

Most young people overestimate the importance of sex in marriage. It is important, but it does not have the overwhelming impact that some people ascribe to it. Despite the mythology, sexual problems rarely *cause* marital failures, nor does sexual compatibility guarantee marital success. Sexual difficulties are often *blamed* for failures, but they are usually caused by other problems that the couple can not talk about (such as immaturity). Some couples rarely have sexual relations, but respect each other, share similar values, enjoy each other's company, and live rich full lives. Other couples have extremely satisfactory sexual relationships, but can not live with each other.

Since every scientific investigation reveals that mutual respect, similar interests, and many other factors have much greater effects on marital success than sex, I shall state unequivocally: *if sex is your primary reason for wanting to get married, you are not ready for marriage.*[8]

Your Choice

The person you choose often says a great deal about your readiness for marriage. There is a reason for your choice, and some reasons suggest that your personality is not well enough developed for you to be a good husband or wife. You may be running away from your own problems or acting out of your unconscious needs.

There are, of course, no hard and fast rules linking your choice to your personality; one person may choose another for a wide variety of reasons. Research has, however, uncovered some rather common relationships between choice and personality; certain kind of people tend to make certain kinds of choices. Space limitations prevent listing all of these relationships, but we can discuss a few of the more common ones.

If you want to marry a much older person, you may be looking for a substitute mother or father. If your choice greatly resembles your mother or father, the same principle holds true. You may be acting out the childish desire to possess your parent. Somewhat similar feelings cause a few people to choose more dominant mates; they want someone to lean on rather than an equal partner. The opposite alternative is equally dangerous: if you are ready to marry a submissive, dependent person, you may be expressing unconscious needs to dominate people; these needs will almost certainly interfere with your married life, even if the other person has a strong need to be dominated. Complementary neuroses are *not* a solid foundation for a happy marriage. If you want to marry outside of your race, religion, or social class, you may be trying to hurt or to defy your parents. This kind of symbolic defiance can be fantastically costly: long after you have defeated your parents and expressed your independence you may be paying for a silly gesture.

Perhaps the most general principle relating choice to readiness is that *people who choose mates who are extremely different from themselves are not ready for marriage.* They may be trying to defy their parents;

[8]And you are probably thinking of marrying the wrong person.

they may be deeply infatuated; they may be acting out any one of a wide variety of unconscious needs; but they are clearly not ready for marriage because they have not seriously considered the consequences of marrying a person who is too different from themselves. Therefore, if you want to marry someone whom your parents and friends regard as unsuitable, who has very different background, values, goals, interests, religion, etc., I urge you to reconsider. Something inside of you is driving you toward disaster, and you should see a competent professional to find out what that something is.

Independence

As the preceding comments clearly indicate, independence is crucially important. Without it, you can not make a real decision about marriage, nor can you be a good mate. Erich Fromm makes this point very explicitly: Love and the respect on which it is based are "possible only if *I* have achieved independence; if I can stand and walk without needing crutches, without having to dominate and exploit anyone else."[9] The author of *Marital Breakdown* is even more emphatic: "The failure to achieve a minimum of emotional independence is one of the main causes of marital breakdown."[10]

"Independence" is being used here in a very different sense from the popular one, which confuses counterdependence or dominance with true independence.[11] "Independence" is an ability to stand on your own two feet, to look beneath your own masks and defenses, to accept yourself as you are, and to relate to other people as they are, instead of leaning on them or using them for your own purpose. Without this kind of independence you can not make a real decision, nor can you be an adequate mate.

The question, then, is: How can you tell whether you are independent enough for marriage? Certainly, the opinion of your friends, which is based more upon your image than your substance, is not an adequate guide. There is no completely reliable test, but certain behaviors and attitudes are fairly accurate indices of emotional dependence. Most emotionally dependent people have an "acute need for the physi-

[9]Erich Fromm, *The Art of Loving.* London: Unwin, 1957, p 26.
[10]Dominian, *op. cit.,* p. 42.
[11]Chapter 2 discussed these distinctions.

cal presence of the partner who acts as a source of reassurance and reduces the *dread of aloneness.*"[12] If you are unable to act effectively when your partner is not around, if you feel anxious, uneasy, or just plain miserable, you are probably not independent enough for marriage.

Another sign is fear that the other person will leave you. This fear may be expressed by jealousy, concern that he will find someone else, excessive worry about his health, or visions of accidents when he is traveling or late for a date. However it is expressed, it suggests that you are emotionally immature and dependent. Your fears are, in fact, a carry-over from your childish dependence upon your parents. You are afraid of being abandoned because you need your parent substitute so desperately.

A strong need to dominate or to possess the other person is also a sign of emotional dependence, and it is based upon this same childish fear. You are unsure of yourself and the other person's feelings toward you and must dominate or possess him to make sure that your emotional needs are satisfied.

Submissiveness looks very different from dominance, but it is usually caused by this same dependency. Some dependent people submit so that they do not have to accept the responsibility for their own lives and decisions.

Constantly testing the other's love is another sign. If you keep rejecting or irritating him to see whether he will come back, or if you continuously demand reasurances that he loves you, you are too emotionally dependent for marriage.

Unfortunately, people who are dependent upon their partners, who are jealous, dominant, or possessive, usually feel that the strength of their dependence is really a sign of the intensity of their love, a proof of their devotion, while "it may only prove the degree of their preceding loneliness."[13]

Self-respect

Self-respect is closely related to independence. In fact, you must re-

---

[12]Dominian, *op. cit.,* p. 44.
[13]Fromm, *op. cit.,* p. 11.

spect yourself before you can be independent. If you do not accept yourself as you are, you will build a wall of defences around yourself and depend upon other people to help to preserve and to strengthen that wall.

All of your relationships, including marriage, will be part of a campaign to build up your self-esteem and self-confidence. Since preserving your image is the central focus of your life, you can give very little of yourself to someone else. Your need to build your self-esteem, and all the defenses you employ to satisfy this need—all the walls you build between yourself and the truth—will shut out the other person and leave you both alone.

It is impossible to say whether you have enough self-respect. You can not measure it the way you can measure your height or your weight, and there are no adequate psychological tests for it. You therefore have to look honestly at yourself and ask: Do I really like myself the way I am? If you do not like yourself, or if you are reluctant to look at yourself, or if you constantly try to change your personality or present a false image, you probably do not have enough self-respect to be a good husband or wife.

Situational pressures

Even if you are psychologically ready for marriage, the pressures of student life may destroy your chances for a happy marriage. Marriage is not easy under the best of circumstances, and the time, economic, and psychological pressures of student life have ruined many marriages that would have succeeded if they had been delayed until after graduation. There are a few positive aspects of student marriages, but the general picture is extremely negative.

ECONOMICS   Economic pressures are the most obvious ones, and they have destroyed many student marriages. Students rarely have much money, and Americans are not very good at economizing. We are so used to having cars, nice apartments, and various luxuries that living without them is usually seen as a real deprivation. I think that the antimaterialism of some students is a very healthy thing, but most Americans are psychologically dependent upon their possessions, especially if they have children. In fact, if you should have a child, your economic situation may become desperate. You may even lack money for essentials, including tuition payments. These economic pressures interact with most of the other pressures to cause many students to get on to the tread mill before they learn what life is all about.

TIME   Economic problems dramatically increase time pressures. Part-time jobs add to already heavy study schedules, especially at the graduate-school level. Wives often feel neglected, and their complaints add to the pressure.

FRUSTRATED PLANS   These pressures are so heavy that many students cut down on their studies, drop out of school, or decide not to go on for graduate work. Even if the economic and other pressures are not extreme, the responsibilities of marriage and the general conception that marriage is a time for settling down cause many students to become security-conscious at the very moment when they most need to explore themselves and the world. Instead of trying out new roles, thinking about new issues, and deciding what they want to be, many married students let their responsibilities narrow their vision; they concentrate on getting a degree and a good job, instead of an education and a chance to broaden their horizons. They settle into comfortable, secure ruts and remain in them for the rest of their lives.

PARENTAL INTERFERENCE   Many student marriages are subsidized by one or both sets of parents, who may feel that their financial support gives them a license to interfere. This interference takes many forms, from trying to control the couple's budget and spending habits to telling them where to live and what to study. Students usually resent this interference, but, if they are accepting financial support, they may feel guilty, obligated, or simply reluctant to object to it. Whether they object to it or not, it is almost certain to cause problems, and it can irrevocably damage the relationship.

ROLE REVERSALS   The wife is often the primary bread-winner, and this reversal of roles can make both individuals very uncomfortable. Even if you have tried to reject "out-dated" conceptions of the male and female roles, you may feel profoundly uncomfortable and find that your feelings do not agree with your rational analysis. For your entire lives you both have been conditioned to fulfill certain roles, and reversing these roles will probably make you feel confused, insecure, and anxious.

ISOLATION   Although the increasing number of married students reduces the isolation problem, married students can still feel "out of it" because they are excluded from most of campus life. Campus groups and activities are almost entirely for single students, and you will be out of place in them. Furthermore, because your interests and life style are so different, you and your friends will gradually grow apart. In addition to the discomfort exclusion causes, it may actually hurt your education because much of what you learn comes from your classmates.

OUTGROWING THE WIFE   If the wife should drop out or avoid beginning college in order to support her husband, the husband may outgrow her. She will be working at a low level, while he is developing skills that will move him into higher social levels. As he moves up the ladder, she may find that she does not fit in with his associates, and he may actually feel ashamed of her. Furthermore, when he is earning more money and occupying a higher social position, he may want someone more exciting, glamorous, and intellectual to share his new life.

Outgrowing the wife is *not* a rare occurrence; it happens all the time. In a society which appraises wives as well as husbands, which values degrees and social polish, the girl who worked so hard to put her husband through college often ends up with little more than his contempt. Even if he does not out-grow her, she may resent, consciously or unconsciously, having to interrupt or to terminate her education. Some very bitter wives and divorcees have learned that lesson too late. Therefore, if the wife would have to interrupt her education, I urge you not to marry.   •

Conclusion

Because most students are not psychologically ready for marriage and because marrying during your student days creates marital problems, harms your education, and narrows your horizons, I suggest that you delay your marriage until after graduation. You may find that you are not suited to each other; you will have a chance to become more mature; and you will face fewer situational pressures. It may be hard to delay your marriage; you may feel frustrated and lonely, but your marriage will have a much greater chance for success.

> "Opposites may attract, but they rarely
> enjoy living with each other."

THE RIGHT MATE

Most divorced people feel that their marriages failed because they chose the wrong mate. Sometimes they blame it all on the other person; sometimes they say that they had a "personality clash." But choosing the wrong mate is generally seen as the basic problem. Although many of these people are trying to cover up their own inadequacies, there is no doubt whatsoever that a poor choice makes marital success very unlikely. Regardless of how ready you are for marriage, you will be happier with certain types of people.

Unfortunately, the emphasis upon romantic love, the rejection of parental influence on this decision, and the pressures of our pluralistic society cause many young people to choose unsuitable mates. Parents used to make this decision, and, because they based it on much better criteria than their children do, they made much better decisions (as the differences in divorce rates clearly indicate). They knew that similar backgrounds, values, interests, and goals are the foundation of a successful marriage, and they looked for these similarities in their children's mates. They knew that marriage is not primarily romance, but living and doing things together, working together toward some goal, raising children, and building a life together.

Unfortunately, you probably do not realize that long after the intoxication has faded, you will have to talk to each other and to do something with your time. If you have nothing in common, you will bore and irritate each other, and your boredom and irritation will drive you apart.

The dangers caused by your naïveté are greatly increased by the "melting-pot" atmosphere of most colleges. This atmosphere makes a major contribution to your education, but it can also cause you to date people with whom you have nothing in common. Once you take that first step, your emotions take over, and they can easily cause you to marry someone who is utterly unsuitable.

My purpose here is to help you to think more clearly about the sort of person with whom you can be happiest so that you avoid hopeless marriages and select someone with whom you have a reasonable chance. I shall also describe some of the problems you can anticipate with different types of people to help you to prepare for these problems. The "Mate Analysis Questionnaire" in the appendix may also be useful. This discussion will not be very original or complicated. If anything, it will be too simple and repetitious. Again and again I shall stress the importance of similarity—not because the idea is difficult to understand, but because so many people ignore it and choose mates with whom they have nothing in common.

Raw Material

Some people deceive themselves to justify an irrational decision; they know that they are marrying an unsuitable person, but pretend that he will change to fit their needs. The potential mate is seen not as a distinct individual but as the raw material from which they will fabricate the person they need.

This sort of thinking reveals that they do not love or respect the other person; he[14] is valued not for what he is but for what she hopes to make of him. In addition to being disrespectful this kind of thinking is extremely naïve. People do *not* change very much after marriage, and the very characteristics that you dislike now will probably continue to annoy you for the rest of your life. If anything, people become even more irritating after marriage. They don't try so hard to put up a front, and, because you are in constant contact, the things you dislike become even more obnoxious. A glance at "Dear Abby" or "Ann Landers" should convince you that many people are infuriated by their inability to get their mates to drop such trivial habits as picking their nose, slurping their soup, or reading in bed. If years of complaints can not change

---

[14]Following normal grammatical usage, the pronoun "he" will be used in all situations to avoid the cumbersome "he and she," even though these remarks usually refer to both males and females.

such minor habits, why do you think that you can change such basic characteristics as drinking, laziness, moodiness, or coldness?[15]

Since the person you marry is the person you will have to live with, you had better take a good hard look at him and ask: Could I enjoy living with him *as he is?* If the answer is "no," it is time to say goodbye, and the sooner you say it, the better. The longer you wait, the greater the chance that you will let your emotions distort reality and lead you into a marital disaster.

Changing Yourself

Some people also regard themselves as raw material. Disliking themselves as they are, they try to change to fit some ideal or their mates' demands and expectations. Changing oneself is, however, only slightly less difficult than changing the other person. Your heredity and all of your experiences have made you what you are today, and no amount of will-power will change you very much.

If you try to change yourself or to reject your past, the most probable effect is to create a sense of discontinuity and alienation, and these feelings will make you less adequate as a mate. You must learn to get along with yourself before you can get along with anyone else, and the first step in that direction is to accept the fact that you are what you are.

Therefore, when appraising your chances for happiness with any mate, you must not think that either of you will change very much. You must decide whether you can live together happily *as you are.*

Presenting Yourself

Since neither of you will change very much, the more honest you are with each other before marriage, the better your chances of making a good decision and having a good marriage. You may be afraid to be honest—afraid that he will not marry you if he knows what you are really like—but a false image will just frustrate your real needs.

You need to be respected and loved for what you are, not for what

[15]Coldness is especially hard to change. In fact, a person who is inhibited about expressing affection before marriage is likely to become even more inhibited after marriage because intercourse has a greater amount of guilt attached to it than other expressions of affection.

you pretend to be. Being honest may drive him away, but an unhappy marriage is infinitely worse than a broken love affair. You can not pretend forever, and, if he does not like you as you are, your marriage is going to fail.

Family

One's family is usually the major influence on his values, interests, habits, and personality. Socioeconomic class, race, religion, and education also exert significant effects, but these effects are usually minor modifications of the basic pattern which the family has already established.

Although students work very hard at rejecting their parents' values and habits, underneath their veneers they are usually quite similar to them, especially on issues related to marriage. People who grew up in large families tend to have large families. If a boy had a father who believed in the double standard, he will probably accept it also. If a girl had a mother who believed in sacrificing everything for the children, she will probably make similar sacrifices.

Since your mate's basic values and conception of marriage are probably rather similar to his parents', you should make every effort to know them. And, if their values, habits, interests, and general approach to life make you uncomfortable, you have relatively little chance for a happy marriage.

Socioeconomic Class

"Class" is a dirty word to many college students. Believing that class differences and conflicts have been a major source of the world's problems, they attempt to rid themselves of "bourgeois" thinking by ignoring class differences. While I applaud this attitude as a general principle, I think it is very foolish to apply it to your choice of a marital partner. People from different classes usually have severe marital problems. Having grown up in different worlds, they do not share many values, interests, habits, or goals. They therefore can not communicate or enjoy living with each other.

You will probably be happier if you marry someone from your own class. Certainly, you should not marry someone from a class too far below or above your own. If your father was an unskilled laborer and you marry a member of the upper class, you will feel utterly out of place, and you and your husband will have very little in common. Conversely, if your parents are wealthy, and you marry someone from a poor background, it may be very hard for you to retain respect for him because all of his habits, values, and interests will seem "cheap" or "low."

Many students will reject this analysis because they have tried to reject their own pasts, but, whether you like it or not, the classes in which you both were raised have inculcated values, attitudes, interests, and habits that simply can not be erased. And, if you come from very different classes, your marriage is more likely to fail.

Religion

Religious differences can create some very serious problems. "A conclusion of all major studies appears to indicate that mixed marriages, especially when they involve a Roman Catholic and another denomination, do run a higher risk of marital breakdown."[16] These problems occur because members of different religions value different things and because the husband and wife often disagree about the children's religious training.

In our irreligious age, relatively few people pay much attention to religion, either before or after marriage. Young people date members of different faiths, and, if they should fall in love, get married, with or without their parents' blessing. Even if they should not practice their religions after marriage, when their children are born or become ready for school, these individuals may be surprised to find how strongly they feel that children should be raised as Catholics, Protestants, or Jews. If the other parent feels as strongly, they may fight about this issue for years. You would therefore be much better off to marry someone of your own faith.

Race

Surprisingly, interracial marriages often succeed. There are not many

---

[16]Dominian, *op. cit.*, p. 26.

of them, but the few that do occur seem to be rather happy. Despite the huge differences in backgrounds and the vicious social pressures, the divorce rate for interracial marriages is lower than the national average. Several factors seem to be involved.

First, race is so visible (both physically and psychologically) and the social pressures are so great that people think more carefully before marrying. Knowing that they will have problems that other couples do not have, they make a more careful choice and prepare more thoroughly. They compensate for their racial differences by selecting people with whom they share goals, values, and interests, and by planning for their problems.

Second, the people involved are probably more mature and independent. A few are defying their parents or convention, but many have thought about the problem and have the courage and self-confidence to make a difficult decision.

Third, they probably love each other more than most couples. Only people who feel very strongly toward each other are willing to face such extreme problems and pressures.

Fourth, the social pressures are so marked that they may turn more toward each other. Many couples blame each other for their problems, but interracial couples can work together against a common enemy—the vicious, racist public.

The preceding comments do not mean that you should run out and marry someone from a different race. On the contrary, the problems and pressures are so great that I advise against it. You may not be strong enough to handle the situation, and your motives may include a need to defy your parents or to prove your independence and liberalism. However, if you have really thought about all the issues, if you have talked to people who have interracial marriages, if you really love and respect each other (as people, not as symbols), I think you have some chance of a happy marriage. You are going to have some serious problems, but the evidence does not agree with the general public's belief that the situation is hopeless.

Values

True love, in the deepest sense of the word, can reduce or compensate for many problems, but it certainly can not make people with incompatible philosophies enjoy each other's company. We all have certain values—certain beliefs about what is right and moral and good. Although we may be intellectually aware of differences between our values and other people's, and although we may have learned in anthropology or other courses that there is no absolute right or wrong, we all believe that what we value *is* right. We may talk about moral relativism and cultural values in class, but, when the chips are down, we all feel that our values are *the* right ones.

Because one's own values are seen as the right ones, value conflicts cause extremely serious marital problems. If one person does what he thinks is right, but it conflicts with the other's values, his behavior is seen as wrong and immoral. Since he does not regard it as such, bitter disagreements are almost inevitable.

Each person feels that his position is right—not in a pragmatic, but in a moral sense. He condemns the other's position as wrong, as immoral. Since each person regards a compromise as an agreement to be immoral, a violation of his own moral beliefs, they often refuse to compromise. They may therefore spend years trying to convince each other of his immorality, but succeed only in driving themselves apart.

Unfortunately, the values which cause the most severe disagreements may not be discussed before marriage. College students enjoy discussing their beliefs about civil rights, militarism, educational policies, and other impersonal issues, but they tend to avoid the values that relate to themselves. They are afraid to expose these feelings because they would then become vulnerable to criticism or rejection. This fear causes students to know a lot about each other's attitudes on impersonal issues, but relatively little about the personal issues that affect a marriage. Governmental or educational policies are not immediately relevant to your everyday life, but disagreements about the husband and wife's role, the way money should be handled, the amount you should drink, the sort of friends you should have, and the way children should be raised can tear your marriage apart.

Because values are hard to express and even harder to measure, no rules can be given for deciding how well your values agree. I can only suggest that you discuss your personal values seriously before marrying.[17]

[17]The "Mate Analysis Questionnaire" may help you to start and to organize this discussion, but it does not go far enough. You need *many* serious, frank conversations.

Goals

Unless you have similar goals,[18] unless you want to lead the same sort of life and to occupy the same sort of social positions, you will pull in different directions and frustrate each other. Each will regard the other as an obstacle rather than a partner, a barrier which prevents him from doing what he really wants to do. You may constantly try to bring the other one over to your side, or you may simply go your separate ways, but in neither case will you have a happy marriage.

Fortunately, students are rather open about their goals. Americans, especially college students, think a lot about their careers and related issues, and they enjoy talking about their plans. It is therefore fairly easy to determine whether you want the same things *if* you listen to each other and realize that the other person probably means what he says. However, instead of listening, many students simply talk about their own plans and assume that the other person will go along with them. Since he probably cares as much about his plans as you do about yours, I suggest that you listen seriously, and, if your goals are incompatible, break up before it is too late.

Talent

It is not enough to want the same things. Both of you must also have enough talent[19] to reach your goals, an issue which very few young people consider before marriage. It seems too cold-blooded, too calculating, too inconsistent with the entire spirit of marriage. It may seem unromantic to say it, but your respective talents will have a dramatic impact upon your lives. If one of you does not have the brains or drive or social skills that the other's ambitions require, your marriage has little chance for success. The more talented one will resent the other person's holding him back, and he may even complain about

[18]Some people confuse goals with values. They overlap, but your "goals" are what you want to do and the social, economic, and professional position you want to occupy, while your "values" are your beliefs about moral issues such as honesty, marital fidelity, drinking, etc.

[19]The word "talent" is used in the broadest possible sense. It includes "brains," social skills, educational level, polish, conversational ability, and all the other things one needs to get ahead in our society.

deliberate sabotage. The other person will resent the criticism and feel (correctly) that he is not accepted or respected.

The problem is most severe if the wife's ambition is greater than the husband's talent. She may complain constantly about not having enough money, or critically compare him to more successful acquaintances, or push him into situations which he can not handle. Her behavior undermines his self-confidence, making it even harder for him to compete successfully. Her rejection and his weakened self-confidence often combine to ruin their sexual life. She thinks that he is not much of a man, and he may share her opinion and become unable to act as one. Such sexual problems further undermine their relationship.

Until fairly recently the wife's talent was not important for most men. In most occupations a wife could not help or hinder her husband very much unless she were a fool, a drunk, or something blatantly obvious. Today, the wife's talent can have an enormous impact on her husband's career, especially if he works for a large corporation. American corporations have hardly any respect for the family's privacy, and they frequently examine the wife thoroughly before hiring or promoting the husband. If the wife does not look intelligent, polished, and educated enough to fit her position in the corporate society, her husband has little chance of success.

It is, of course, a shocking violation of personal privacy and human dignity for the corporations to evaluate wives, and you may well decide to avoid that sort of environment. However, if you do intend to work in such a setting, you may as well understand the facts of life. If you marry the sweet, simple, uneducated girl you dated in high school, you are not going to go anyplace. She can, of course, try to change herself to fit the corporation's requirements, but doing so can have a devastating impact upon her. She will be out of her depth, and may even become alienated from herself because she knows she is putting on a front. This confusion and further alienation will make her uncomfortable, and she will probably blame you for her discomfort.

Since the other person's talents will have a great deal of impact on your entire life, you should carefully assess his chances to compete successfully in the world you choose to enter. If it seems that he can not compete, you will both be better off if you do not marry.

Interests

Even if you come from the same background and have similar values
and life goals, common interests are still important. You are going to
be living together for a long time, and, if you are not interested in the
same things, if you have nothing to talk about, marriage can become
a dreadful bore.

Many husbands come home at night and ask, purely as a matter
of form: "What did you do today, honey?" Then he lets his mind
wander while she prattles about things that bore him. After she
finishes her monologue, he mumbles something about his day at the
office, and they collapse in front of the television.

Now that you are in love and look forward eagerly to each meeting, such boredom may seem utterly impossible, but ask yourself:
"What do we talk about?" "What interests do we really share?" If the
answers to these questions indicate that you do not have many common interests, or, worse yet, if you are already starting to bore each
other, you have little chance of a successful marriage, and you would
be a lot better off to end the relationship.

Needs

This is the one area in which the similarity principle is often con-
tradicted. People tend to get along best who "are complementary in
their psychological needs."[20] That is, you will probably get along best
with someone whose needs "fit" yours. If you like to talk, you will get
along best with a listener, not another talker. If you tend to be dominant, you would probably fight with another dominant individual, but
get along rather well with a submissive person.

The complementarity theory does not, however, indicate that
you should marry someone whose needs are opposite to your own.
What it means is that the other person's needs must fit in with your
own so that you satisfy each other. At times, the fit is best if you are
opposites (such as talker and listener), but certain needs can be most
easily satisfied if the other person has similar needs. For example, if

[20]R. F. Winch, *Mate Selection; a Study of Complementarity of Needs.* Harper & Row,
1958.

one person is independent and the other dependent, they will frustrate each other severely; the independent person will feel trapped and the dependent person will feel abandoned. Two independent people would probably get along much better since their own independent behavior would let the other exert his independence.

Because needs are so hard to identify, and the interactions between them are so complex, it is impossible to state a simple rule here. I can only suggest that you discuss this issue as thoroughly as possible with each other, and that you use some form of premarital counseling questionnaire to explore your own and the other person's needs.

Power

Young people hardly ever think about the power aspect of the marital relationship. In fact, if a marriage counselor or other adult should raise the issue, they are likely to respond with bewilderment or indignation. "Power in marriage? Don't be ridiculous; there is no such thing." But most married people know from experience that one of them is often much more powerful than the other. He can do as he pleases and make the other bend to his wishes. The weaker person is usually resentful, but there is not much he can do (if he really is weaker).

Because of their vulnerable social and economic position, wives are usually the weaker party, but, thanks to female emancipation, they are now much freer and stronger than they have ever been. In most modern American marriages power is primarily determined by the husband's and wife's relative indifference. The more indifferent party is more powerful, and the greater the discrepancy between the importance they attach to the relationship, the more powerful the indifferent party is. He can do things that the other is afraid to do, and he can force the other to do things which are distasteful to that individual. The other has little choice but to accept his own inferior position or to lower his estimate of the importance of the relationship (a very difficult thing to do).

The obvious implication of this principle is: *you should never persuade someone to marry you, nor should you let yourself be persuaded.* A marriage should be something that both parties want. Unfortunately, many marriages occur because one person is so infatuated that he argues, pleads, begs, or "blackmails" the other. This sort of marriage can easily degenerate into thinly disguised slavery. Married people can be fantastically cruel and exploitative to each other, and the person who cares desperately for someone who is indifferent to him can be manipulated and dominated for the rest of his life.

The other person seems to be better off, but, because people lose respect for those whom they dominate and because love is impossible without respect, he may end up equally miserable and lonely. The moral is very clear: *if both people are not almost equally committed, they should not marry.*

Pleasure

Probably the best index of how you will get along after marriage is the way you get along now. A very extensive investigation of engagements and marriages indicated that the "engagement success score was found to be the best single instrument available before marriage for the prediction of marital success."[21] The reasons for this close relationship are rather obvious: the same characteristics and combinations which cause people to get along before marriage help them to get along after marriage.

Unfortunately, an astonishing number of people ignore this obvious connection. They have stormy, shallow engagements, but marry anyway. They fight all the time before marriage, but naïvely believe they will get along after marriage. They blame parents, friends, or other pressures for their problems, or rationalize that "fighting isn't so bad" because "it's so much fun to make up."

Other couples do not fight during the engagement, but they rarely talk to each other seriously. In fact, they have already begun to be bored with each other long before they get married, but their physical attraction is so strong that they don't think about what they are going to do or how they are going to live or what they are going to talk about after they marry. They simply walk blindly into a lifetime of boredom, and this boredom often turns to hatred.

Therefore, it you do not get along now, if you do not enjoy each

---

[21]Burgess and Wallin, *Engagement and Marriage.* Philadelphia: Lippincott, 1953, p. 205.

other's company now, if you do not share a lot of interests, *don't get married.*

Conclusion

The preceding analysis is based on the simple principle that you have a much better chance of a happy marriage with some types of people. From this analysis three rules emerge.

1. *Before you marry anyone, take a good hard look at him.*

Consider his background, habits, interests, values, and all the other things that have been mentioned above.[22] Then ask yourself: "Do I have a reasonable chance of a happy marriage with this person?" If the answer is no, *drop him!* Be tactful and considerate, especially if you are already engaged, but end the relationship as soon as possible. Far too many people have realized that they should not marry somebody, but have gone through with it to avoid hurting the other person, disappointing their parents, or "making a fool of themselves." They pay a terrible price for their mistaken delicacy.

2. *Never go out with anyone who would obviously not be a good mate.*

3. *As soon as it is clear that someone whom you are dating would not be a good mate, drop him.*

The reasons for rules 2 and 3 are rather obvious: It is very hard to be rational after you become emotionally involved, and you can get involved very quickly; therefore, the *only* way to be rational, the *only* safe thing to do, is to avoid involvement with unsuitable people.

These rules and the analysis on which they are based may seem cold, even cruel. They deal with human relationships in a way that may seem excessively rationalistic and calculating. These criticisms are somewhat justified, but I have seen too many miserable husbands and wives, too many divorces, and too many children from broken homes to have much faith in romantic love as a basis for picking a mate.

You may reject all or part of this analysis, but you must carefully

[22]This sort of analysis is obviously very difficult. There is a questionnaire in the appendix which both you and the other person can complete. Comparing your answers will give you some idea of your chances, and it will help you to prepare for the problems you will face if you do get married. If you are on the brink of marriage, it is probably too late for questionnaires, and I suggest you get premarital counseling. A counselor will do all the things the questionnaire tries to do, but he will do them much better.

consider the problem before it is too late. If you think rationally in the *early* stages of your relationships, if you refuse to date people with whom you have little chance for a successful marriage, you will probably end up more happily married—and you will also enjoy your dates much more.

If you let your emotions dominate you, sooner or later—perhaps before your marriage, perhaps after it—you will be torn between your reason and your emotions. You will feel strongly for someone whom you know is not right for you. Conversely, if you date only people who are potentially suitable mates, you can feel freer to "let yourself go." The net effect of rational analysis in the early stages of your relationships is therefore to increase your chances for a successful marriage *and* your freedom while you are dating.

DRUGS

"If I were asked to designate the greater evil, current use of marijuana or the impact of drug laws on the attitude of young people toward law, I would without question name the latter."[1]

The generation gap and adult hypocrisy are neatly symbolized by adult reactions to the "campus drug menace." Parents, who use sleeping pills, tranquilizers, cigarettes, and alcohol, insist that the authorities crack down and end the drug problem.

I am certainly not advocating that you smoke pot; in fact, I recommend that you avoid it and other drugs, but I think that the authorities' policies have done more harm than good. They have ignored the medical evidence that the adults' drugs are more harmful than marijuana, lied to you about the effects of marijuana, and used force to back up their ridiculous position. The net effect has been to increase both students' use of drugs and their contempt for adults.

[1]Dr. Stanley F. Yolles, Director of the National Institute of Health, testifying before the Senate Sub-Committee on Juvenile Delinquency in March 1968. Reported in the *Chicago Daily News*, Tuesday, March 11, 1969, p. 8.

In this chapter I shall attempt to present a more balanced and objective picture of the values, dangers, and reasons for using different types of drugs. The hard drugs (heroin, morphine, cocaine, etc.) will not be discussed because virtually all college students know enough to avoid them. Tobacco is also a drug, but it will also be omitted because its dangers have been adequately discussed in the popular press. I have some doubts about the evidence linking tobacco to heart disease, but the evidence relating it to other diseases, particularly lung cancer, is so strong that you are very foolish to smoke. The authorities know this, but the same papers which carry editorials about the drug menace also carry cigarette advertisements. And then your parents wonder why you say that adults are hypocrites!

THE LEGAL LOGIC

The incredibly severe penalties[2] for possessing or using marijuana and other drugs are products of the same streak of irrational Puritanism which we have encountered so frequently. The fools who make and enforce the laws neither understand nor care about the effects of their actions; they only know that drugs are bad, and that the people who use them are worse. Since drugs are sin, which all good people are against, they have followed the lead of that other glorious example of Puritanism—prohibition—with the same predictable consequences: they have raised prices, increased profits, and brought in the gangsters.

England does not have the same approach to drugs. Because they care more about controlling drugs than looking virtuous, the British authorities have removed the profit motive from hard drugs by allowing addicts to buy drugs with doctors' prescriptions. The idea horrifies Americans—How could we legalize sin? But it works: England has very little organized crime, very little violent crime,[3] less corruption of its public officials, and *less than 1%* as many addicts as we do!

American law-makers have used the same logic in their actions

[2]At the time this book goes to press there is considerable pressure for reducing the penalties for possession and use of marijuana, but the proposed penalties would still be unjustifiably severe—large fines plus months or years in jail.
[3]Many American addicts must steal to buy the high-priced drugs.

toward marijuana. Instead of legalizing a relatively harmless drug, they have subsidized the Mafia by prohibiting it. Because profits are high, marijuana is marketed aggressively, often by the same people who sell hard drugs. The law-makers, with the supreme self-confidence of the abysmally ignorant, have ignored the consequences of their actions and continued their bankrupt policies. By mixing brutal repression with unbelievable horror stories, they have succeeded only in making the gangsters richer, the cities more corrupt, the crime rate higher, and the young people more cynical and alienated.

> "If alcohol . . . were invented today . . . it
> would immediately be stringently controlled
> by law."[4]

ALCOHOL

Although most people don't regard it as one, alcohol is unquestionably a drug, and a very dangerous one. Heroin, LSD, and other hard drugs and hallucinogens have more serious *chemical* effects, but relatively few students ever use them, while alcohol has more serious *behavioral* effects and is a socially acceptable killer. It has devastating physical and psychological effects, causes sexual looseness, open aggression, and other undesirable behavior, and kills thousands of motorists each year. However, because it has been used so long and so widely, most people do not regard it as a drug, and it is much more socially acceptable than less harmful drugs such as marijuana.

Effects

The most obvious effect of alcohol is that it makes us feel good. Some people experience a slightly unpleasant burning sensation when they first drink alcohol, but the general effect upon the body is quite pleas-

[4]Peter Laurie, *Drugs: Medical, Psychological and Social Facts.* Baltimore, Md.: Pelican, 1967, p. 15.

ant. It relaxes us, makes us feel less anxious and more comfortable, pushes our worries into the background, lets us express our frustrations, and acts as a "social lubricant."

These pleasant effects have created the impression that alcohol is a stimulant, but it is really a depressant. A few drinks make people more aggressive, passionate, and talkative, but these effects are caused by alcohol's *depressant* properties—specifically, its ability to lower inhibitions. It numbs our bodies, beginning with the portions of the brain which control the higher mental processes and social inhibitions. People are therefore willing or able to express feelings which they always have, but which are normally inhibited.

Lowered inhibitions also lead to aggressive acts such as arguing, fighting, and even lynching. People often become aggressive when they drink, and heavy drinking preceded most lynchings; in fact, it was usually essential because it helped people to express their rage and inhumanity very directly. Furthermore, because antisocial, violent actions are somewhat excused if they occur while one is drunk, drinking provides a built-in justification for inhuman acts, of which lynching is only the most pronounced. Similar, but less extreme, cruelties occur every day: men criticize their wives at parties; girls say nasty things to each other; fist fights break out, but people say: "They've just had too much to drink."

In addition to its undesirable effects upon social behavior, alcohol, even in very small doses, reduces mental and physical effectiveness.

> Fine tests of discrimination, of memory, of driving skills, all show that the impairment begins with the beginning of drinking and advances steadily with the continuation of drinking.[5]

Therefore, drinking before you study, take an examination, or write a paper will probably lower your performance. Some people argue that alcohol improves their work by relaxing them, but they are usually rationalizing.

This problem is aggravated by the fact that:

> The more we drink, the more our faculties and judgement are lost, and consequently the less we appreciate this falling off of our skills. It is this which allows clearly incapable men to believe they are fit to drive. . . .

[5]Neil Kessel and Henry Walton, *Alcoholism*. Baltimore, Md.: Pelican, 1969, p. 27.

Bus drivers . . . were asked to judge whether they could get their buses between two movable posts. As they drank more and more they became less accurate, but more certain that they were right.[6]

As you have found out many times, the person who has had too much drink, often does not know it. He insists upon having another drink or, worse yet, driving home. The combination of lowered inhibitions, reduced mental and physical efficiency, and increased confidence in one's ability kills thousands of people every year.

Although alcohol does most of its damage by causing accidents, both on the highways and in other places, it also has undesirable effects upon the body, particularly if one drinks large quantities for long periods of time. It is a food, but not a particularly nourishing one. Drinking often depresses the appetite, and potato chips, peanuts, and the other foods which are normally served with it do not satisfy your body's needs. In fact, some heavy drinkers actually suffer from malnutrition.

Alcohol also directly harms the body. It is the major cause of various diseases of the liver, and it also damages the stomach and other parts of the digestive system. Large amounts of alcohol taken over long periods of time will damage the nervous system and even destroy brain cells.

These harmful effects are complicated by the fact that alcohol is an *addictive* drug: one can become physically as well as psychologically dependent upon it. The psychological dependence is the natural result of its ability to make us feel good, less anxious, less aware of our problems, more relaxed and comfortable. Furthermore, the rewards of drinking are immediate, while the costs are referred. We may say, "I will hate myself in the morning," but we keep drinking because the immediate pleasure has a much greater effect upon us than the morning hangover, the danger of driving, or the long-term effects on our health. If external circumstances are unpleasant, the relief offered by alcohol may be an even more powerful reward, making an individual psychologically dependent on it. He needs alcohol to help him to relax or to escape from his problems.

This psychological dependence combines with a physical dependence. It takes longer to develop this dependency, and it is not so

[6] *Ibid.*, pp. 27 f.

severe, but alcohol addiction is similar to heroin addiction. Therefore, if you should drink heavily for a long period of time, you may become an alcohol addict (an alcoholic).[7]

Reasons for Use

The first and most obvious reason for drinking is the pleasantness derived. Virtually every society has discovered and used alcohol, and its pleasant effects upon the mind and the body are the primary reasons for its universality.

While using marijuana, LSD, or other drugs usually tells us a great deal about the individual, using alcohol tells us more about the group to which he belongs, unless he drinks excessively. Alcohol is an inseparable part of most American subcultures, particularly the student subculture. Students from most countries have drunk fairly heavily, and American students are certainly no exception. Some reasons for this tendency are rather obvious.

Drinking is identified with adult status and is usually denied to minors. Students want adult status, and they are usually free from parental control. Drinking is therefore partially an attempt to define oneself as an adult.

Alcohol also relieves anxiety, and students are very anxious. Their status is ambiguous, and they usually do not know who they are or where they are going.

They also face rather severe frustrations: parents make irritating and contradictory demands; universities exert arbitrary pressures; economic needs are higher than financial resources, etc. Drinking blots out these frustrations, and, by lowering inhibitions, it also lets people blow off steam.

Social pressures also cause many students to drink, even if they do not want to. They may dislike the taste or effects of alcohol, but are afraid of being called a sissy or of being excluded from parties and other social events. They therefore drink "to be sociable."

These social pressures and the fact that many groups can not get together without drinking suggest that the people involved don't like

[7]The physical dependency will probably not develop unless there is also a psychological dependency.

each other very much, nor do they feel comfortable with each other. They *need* a social lubricant because they can not relate to each other without one. Without alcohol to dull their senses and to relieve their anxieties they can not put up with each other.

This need for a social lubricant, is, I think, an even more serious problem than the deaths due to drunken driving. It is not, of course, felt only by college students; your parents and other members of our society feel it as strongly as you do. The near universality of social drinking and the fact that so many events could not occur without alcohol indicate how utterly unable we are to relate to one another, how terribly trapped we are within the prisons of our individual aloneness.

Conclusion

Since I enjoy alcohol and use it as a social lubricant, it would be the height of hypocrisy for me to recommend abstaining. However, I do suggest that you look at the pattern of your drinking and analyze the causes for it, and, if you are becoming dependent upon it, I suggest that you analyze yourself more carefully, preferably with professional help.

You may feel that your current drinking is merely a temporary reaction to your current unpleasant situation, but virtually all alcoholics begin that way. Alcoholism is a terrible disorder, which *one out of every twenty* people reading this book will eventually have. In fact, some readers are already borderline or even true alcoholics. Since alcoholism is progressive and can be cured more easily in its early stages, prompt treatment may save your life.

Even if you are in no danger of becoming an alcoholic, a psychological dependency on alcohol indicates that you have problems to work on. Alcohol, by relieving your anxiety, simply removes your motivation to solve these problems, but they are not going to go away. It is therefore much more reasonable to attack the problems themselves, rather than to complicate them by creating a drinking problem.

Finally, as a matter of simple common sense, I urge you to make *prior arrangements* for someone to remain sober at parties to drive the group home. Prior arrangements are necessary because of the point made earlier: drinking reduces both your efficiency and your awareness of your inefficiency. Therefore, the only way to be safe is to agree *beforehand* that one person will abstain *completely* and drive the group home.[8] That arrangement might mean the difference between living and dying.

> "Although there are some who claim that smoking pot can cause no harm, this is bound to be a statement of faith and not an assertion of fact."[9]

MARIJUANA

Pot is really "in" on campus. Social and legal controls keep it from being used openly, but it has undoubtedly become very popular. Because it is illegal, good data are unobtainable, and estimates of its popularity vary widely: some people claim that only 5–10% of the students use it, while others estimate that at some campuses nearly all students have tried it. A Gallup poll[10] found that 36% of all students had tried marijuana, but polls on illegal behavior are unreliable. While we do not know exactly how popular marijuana is, we do know that it is becoming more popular every day.

Opinions about the effects of marijuana and the causes for its popularity are also widely divergent, and there is essentially *no* completely objective information. Everyone has an axe to grind, and everyone selects and distorts evidence to support his position. Some people regard marijuana as extremely dangerous, while others claim that it is completely harmless, but there is not an adequate base of objective research to support either conclusion

> Most scientists . . . generally agree . . . that there is no good evidence that the relatively low-potency marijuana normally available in this country is physically or psychologically harmful for most people who smoke occasionally or even fairly regularly over a relatively short period of

[8]This type of arrangement is now rather common in Sweden and other countries; the driving responsibility rotates through the group and there is no stigma about "sissiness" attached to abstaining.

[9]John Maddox, "Drugs and the Law," from *The Permissive Society: The Guardian Inquiry*, London: Panther, 1969, p. 117.

[10]*Newsweek*, December 29, 1969, p. 36.

months or even several years. On the other hand, there is no good evidence that chronic use of such relatively low-potency marijuana over long periods is not harmful.[11] With regard to the long-term hazards of marijuana, accepted scientific evidence is minimal."[12]

Because the evidence is limited and somewhat contradictory, the following discussion will be rather long, and authorities will be cited fairly frequently. Authorities do, however, have their own biases, and I have no personal experience with marijuana. You must therefore interpret this discussion very cautiously.

Physical and Psychological Effects

While marijuana's long-term effects are not clear, most scientists do agree that it has less serious effects than alcohol, a conclusion which is rejected by most policemen, judges, and legislators. Obviously, I have more confidence in the scientists, but I must note that the dangers are nearly always expressed in comparative, not absolute, terms. Marijuana may be less dangerous than alcohol, but it is *not* completely safe. In fact, as we shall see in a moment, some of the people who advocate *legalizing* pot explicitly admit that there are some dangers.

Keeping this warning in mind, we can examine marijuana's most common effects. The effects described below refer to the marijuana normally used in the United States, which is less powerful and less dangerous than hashish, a drug which comes from the same plant.

Hashish . . . is immensely more powerful than . . . marijuana. The comparison of hashish and marijuana is like that between pure alcohol and beer. . . . the mixture smoked as marijuana ordinarily contains very small quantities of the drug, and its effects are correspondingly less spectacular, less dangerous, and less harmful than those of hashish."[13]

[11]Dr. Helen H. Nowlis, Director of Drug Education Project for the National Association of Student Personnel Administrators. The project was sponsored by the U.S. Food and Drug Administration. This quotation is from *The Chicago Daily News,* Tuesday, March 11, 1969, p. 8.

[12]Dr. Stanley F. Yolles, Director of The National Institute of Health, testifying before the Senate Sub-Committee on Juvenile Delinquency in March 1968, quoted in *The Chicago Daily News,* Tuesday, March 11, 1969, p. 8.

[13]Alfred R. Lindesmith, Ph.D, "The Marijuana Problem: Myth or Reality" in David Soleman (ed.), *The Marijuana Papers.* London: Panther, 1969, p. 52.

INTOXICATION AND MIND EXPANSION   The general effects of marijuana are somewhat similar to those of alcohol—intoxication, relaxation, and euphoria. However, alcohol is a sedative, which causes sleepiness, while marijuana is a mild "mind expander." It acts primarily on the higher centers of the brain, those which affect thinking and moods, rather than those which effect reflexes and coordination. It is, then, primarily a mental rather than a physical pleasure. Although the primary effects are upon the mind, they are much less pronounced than those of LSD or the other strong hallucinogens. Mild hallucinations are quite common, but the individual usually remains in touch with external reality. In a moment we shall analyze the drug's hallucinogenic effects more thoroughly.

PASSIVITY AND INTROSPECTION   Although the user remains in touch with reality, he generally loses interest in it. He turns in upon himself and enjoys his own inner sensations.

> Psychodelic people tend to be socially passive. The psychodelic experience is by nature private, sensual, spiritual, internal, introspective. . . . contemplation . . . mediation . . . sensual openness . . . artistic and religious preoccupation.[14]

NO CRIMES OF VIOLENCE   Obviously, introspection and violent crimes are incompatible. A person contemplating his own sensory experiences is not likely to bash someone over the head. Hostile *feelings* occur, but they are nearly always expressed verbally rather than physically. Many law enforcement officers, whose beliefs are based more on antidrug prejudice than scientific facts, have claimed that marijuana causes violent crimes, but there is no evidence whatsoever in support of that position. "Psychiatrists have been unable to show an association between cannabis [marijuana] and major crime."[15]

LOWER SEX DRIVE   The reduced interest in the external world even applies to the opposite sex. Policemen and legislators have recited

---

[14]Timothy Leary, "Politics, Ethics and Meaning of Marijuana," in Soleman, *op. cit.*, p. 160.
 [15]Dr. P. A. L. Chapple, cited in Kenneth Leech and Brenda Jordan, *Drugs for Young People: Their Use and Misuse.* Oxford, England: The Religious Educational Press, 1967.

many horror stories about the sexual degeneracy caused by marijuana, but it is quite clear that these tales are figments of their own imaginations. A few people feel increased desire, but most have less interest.

> Numerous conversations with smokers of marijuana revealed only occasional instances in which there was any relation between the drug and eroticism. . . . These observations allow us to come to the conclusion that in the main marijuana was not used for direct sexual stimulation.[16]
>
> Among those who have never used hemp or seen it used by others the belief is often found that marijuana acts as a sexual stimulant or aphrodisiac. Actually its effects . . . are exactly in the opposite direction, tending to cause the user to lose interest in the opposite sex. Users more frequently than not report the absence of ideas of sex or say that "Venus herself could not tempt them when they are under the influence of this drug!"[17]

PERSONALITY STRUCTURE   While it brings out latent thoughts and emotions by reducing inhibitions, marijuana does not change the basic personality structure in any way, nor does it cause behaviors which are incompatible with one's basic personality.

NOT ADDICTIVE   Of all charges made against marijuana, the most serious is that it is addictive, but there is absolutely no evidence in support of that assertion. Addiction is a *physical* dependency upon a drug. One develops a tolerance for a drug, a physical need, which, if it is not satisfied, causes painful withdrawal symptoms. Heroin is an addictive drug, and, if used for long enough periods, so is alcohol. But the evidence clearly indicates that marijuana does not have these effects.

> Marijuana does not lead to addiction (in the medical sense) . . . its withdrawal does not lead to the horrible withdrawal symptoms of the opiates.[18]
>
> There were apparently no signs indicative of frustration in the smoker at not being able to gratify the desire for the drug. We consider this point highly significant since it is so contrary to the experience of users of other narcotics. A similar situation occurring in one addicted to

---

[16] *The Marijuana Problem in the City of New York,* Mayor LaGuardia's Committee on Marijuana, 1944. Reprinted in Soleman, *op. cit.,* pp. 302 f.

[17] Lindesmith, *op. cit.*

[18] The Mayor's Report, cited on p. 53, in Soleman, *op. cit.*

the use of morphine, cocaine, or heroin would result in a comprehensive attitude on the part of the addict to obtain the drug. If unable to secure it, there are the obvious physical and mental manifestations of frustration. This may be considered presumptive evidence that there is no true addiction in the medical sense associated with the use of marijuana.[19]

HABIT FORMING While addiction does not occur, the use of marijuana may become a habit, and there may even be some *psychological* dependence upon it. The evidence on this point is somewhat contradictory. It is clear that some people habitually get high and look forward to doing so. On the other hand, the preceding quotation about lack of frustration when pot was unavailable suggests that even psychological dependency is very limited, and two American psychiatrists have stated that "the psychic habituation to marijuana is not as strong as to tobacco or to alcohol."[20]

NO ESCALATION TO HARDER DRUGS Many people have noted that most hard drug users have used marijuana and have concluded that smoking marijuana naturally leads to using harder drugs. Since most heroin addicts have also smoked cigarettes, it would be equally "logical" to say that tobacco leads to use of harder drugs. Scientists who have examined the evidence reject both positions. The consensus of scientific opinion is that this escalation does not occur often, and when it does occur, it is not caused by the drug itself.

It is obvious that most of those who smoke marijuana do not go on to stronger drugs, and it is ridiculous and dishonest to pretend that they do.[21]

Although it is true that most heroin users have had prior experience with marijuana, it is also true that the overwhelming majority of those who try marijuana on one or more occasions never turn either to heroin or to stronger hallucinogenic agents.[22]

Use of cannabis facilitates the association with social groups and subcultures involved with more dangerous drugs such as opium or barbitu-

[19]*Ibid.*, pp. 12 f.
[20]F. Allentuck and K. M. Bowman, cited in Leech and Jordan, *op. cit.*, p. 32.
[21]Leech and Jordan, *op. cit.*, p. 34.
[22]Dr. Donald Luria, Chairman of the New York State Council on Drug Addiction, *Nightmare Drugs*. New York: Pocket Books, 1966, p. 65.

ates. Transition to the use of such drugs would be a consequence of this association rather than an inherent effect of cannabis.[23]

While the more serious charges against marijuana are not supported by the evidence, the following discussion, which is based on the same sources as the preceding paragraphs, will show that marijuana is *not* harmless.

ACCIDENTS AND IRRESPONSIBLE BEHAVIOR   Passivity, introspection, and lack of interest in the external world can result in accidents, particularly automobile accidents. A "stoned" driver is almost as dangerous as a drunk one.

ANXIETY   Although intoxicants are normally used to relieve anxiety, marijuana often *causes* feelings of anxiety.

> There are . . . two basic types of effect, one of excitation, psychic exultation and inner joyousness . . . the other a state of anxiety with fear of consequences such as death or insanity. Either one of these types of reaction may be experienced alone, but usually both are present during the intoxication. They occur in no regular sequence, but replace each other in rapid succession. These anxiety attacks often include feelings that one is in danger of dying.[24]

PHYSICAL REACTIONS   Physical reactions to marijuana range from very pleasant to decidedly unpleasant. In addition to the relaxation and euphoria, there are increases in the pulse rate, blood pressure, blood sugar, and metabolic rate as well as the following:

> Urge to urinate, increased appetite, nausea and vomiting and diarrhea . . . The alterations in the functions of the organs studied come from the effects of the drug on the central nervous system. . . . A direct action on the organs themselves was not seen.[25]
>
> Physical symptoms . . . were recorded. Of these tremor, ataxia, dizziness, a sensation of floating in space, dilation of the pupils, dryness of the throat, nausea and vomiting, urge to urinate, hunger, and a desire for sweets was the most striking. Tremor, ataxia, and dizziness were of

[23] *Bulletin of The World Health Organization*, 1965, p. 729.
[24] "The Mayor's Report, cited on p. 310, in Soleman, *op. cit.*
[25] *Ibid.*, p. 334.

the greatest frequency. These symptoms may be disturbing to the subject, and if marked enough, cause anxiety and interrupt the euphoric state.[26]

HALLUCINATIONS   Marijuana is unquestionably a hallucinogen with similar but weaker effects than LSD.

Virtually all of the phenomena associated with LSD are, or can, also be produced with cannabis.[27]

> Reports of perceiving various parts of the body as distorted, and depersonalization, or "double consciousness" are very frequent, as well as spacial and temporal distortions. Visual hallucinations, seeing faces as grotesque, increased sensitivity to sounds and merging of senses . . . are also common. . . . anxiety and paranoia reactions may also occur.[28]

Marijuana's ability to cause hallucinations is both an attraction and a danger; some users want them, but hallucinations can be very, very frightening. The high priests of the hallucinogenic cult argue that drugs can help people to cast aside their controlled, defensive ways of seeing things. They are factually correct, but casting aside defenses abruptly or seeing the things that you feel unconsciously is not always a blessing. You have built up your defenses because you *need* them; they protect you from the anxiety you would feel if you were aware of certain things. By weakening these defenses and stimulating your perception, marijuana may help you to see further and faster, but it may also make you very frightened—and this fear can create serious problems.

PSYCHOSES   Because of marijuana's direct and indirect effects, particularly its ability to lower defenses and to create anxiety, the drug occasionally causes psychotic reactions, which can be fairly permanent. The research on this point is rather weak, but:

> The conclusion seems warranted that given the potential personality make-up and the right time and environment, marijuana may bring on a true psychotic state.[29]

---

[26] *Ibid.*, p. 385.
[27] William H. McGlochlin, "Cannabis: a Reference," in Soleman, *op. cit.*, p. 445.
[28] The Mayor's Report, cited on p. 445, in Soleman, *op. cit.*
[29] *Ibid.*, p. 332.

There is a general agreement among Eastern writers that the drug plays a significant role in the precipitation of transient psychoses . . . it is clear that there is a definite associative if not causative, relationship between cannabis and psychosis.[30]

SOCIAL EFFECTS   While the physical and psychological effects of marijuana are considerably better than those of alcohol, the social effects are much worse. Legal penalties are extremely severe, and the public regards marijuana users, even occasional ones, as "dope fiends," degenerates, and perverts.

If you do try marijuana and are unlucky enough to be caught, the effects can be catastrophic. You may be denied entrance to graduate school; even if you get into graduate school, you may not be allowed to practice medicine or law; and very few major companies would give you a job with any responsibilities or opportunities.

Among college students the social effects are considerably less, primarily because pot is so much more acceptable. However, the students who accept the "dope fiend" stereotype will certainly reject and ostracize you. You may feel, of course, that you don't need people who feel that way, but they might have other worthwhile qualities or be able to make contributions to your personal development.

That is, if you smoke marijuana, you may be ostracized, or you may attempt to avoid detection by avoiding or withdrawing from relationships with people who do not use it. You may therefore become *socially* dependent upon other users and organize your life around marijuana and the rituals and groups associated with it.

The passivity and introspectiveness caused by marijuana can add to this drug-centered way of life. You may become so interested in your own sensations and in-group that you lose interest in the outside world. Given its wretched state, losing interest is rather natural, but you do have to live here, and introspection does not solve your problems. You must get a degree and make some important decisions; excessive introspection and passivity can cause you to ignore your problems, making them much more severe.

[30]McGlochlin, *op. cit.*

Reasons for Use

A wide variety of theories have been proposed to explain the popularity of marijuana, but they can be divided into four major groups: escape, defiance, pleasure, and "mind-expansion." These four reasons are not mutually exclusive: one may use pot for different reasons at different times and for several reasons at one time.

ESCAPE   A major reason for using any intoxicant is to escape from unpleasant realities, either external or psychological. Marijuana does not seem to be as common or as powerful an escape as alcohol, but some people do use it to escape. Habitual users may also have personality problems, but the evidence on this point is limited.

DEFIANCE   Many students smoke pot as an act of defiance. It is their way of defying their parents, convention, or the law. Alcohol is identified with adults, while pot is "their own thing."

PLEASURE   Not surprisingly, the advocates of legalizing marijuana minimize or ignore completely the escape and defiance motives. As far as they are concerned, marijuana is used only for pleasure or mind-expansion. I think that they overstate their case, but they have demonstrated that pleasure and mind-expansion motivate some users. How many use it for these reasons is an unanswered question.

> The use of marijuana, by and large, does not occur because the user wishes to escape from the psychological problems he cannot face. It was mostly used . . . as a casual, pleasure-giving recreational device.[31]

> The most frequent pattern of use might be termed "recreational." The drug is occasionally used for the pleasure the user finds in it, a relatively casual kind of behavior in comparison to that connected with the use of addicting drugs. . . . In using the phrase "use for pleasure," I mean to emphasize the noncompulsive and casual character of the behavior.[32]

[31]Editors' introduction to Howard S. Becker, Ph.D., "Marijuana: A Sociological Overview," p. 94, in Soleman, *op. cit.*
[32]*Ibid.,* p. 97.

They have found something pleasurable, and they take it for much the same reasons as people take a drink before dinner.[33]

MIND-EXPANSION   Dr. Timothy Leary is the most eloquent and popular advocate of the mind-expansion position. As far as he is concerned, marijuana is *useful* because it helps people to see more clearly.

It and other stimulants of sensory awareness are like corrective lenses; they bring vision into sharper focus.[34]

In general, I say that it is a good thing that more and more Americans are expanding their awareness, pulling back the veil of symbolic platitude, and confronting the many other levels of energy that are available to man.[35]

Conclusion

Medically, marijuana seems to be much safer than alcohol, but claims that it is completely harmless are based upon faith rather than evidence. There is, in fact, some evidence that it has unpleasant and harmful effects.

Furthermore, the history of drug research shows that many drugs which have been used by millions of people have later been found to be dangerous. The most obvious example is aspirin. Virtually everyone uses it, but recent research indicates that it can have harmful side effects. As one scientist put it, "If we had known anything about biochemistry, aspirin never would have been allowed on the market."[36] Calcium cyclamate is another example: it was once used by millions of Americans, but research showed that it could cause cancer, and its sale was prohibitied. If such common and apparently innocuous substances can have harmful long-term effects, the potential dangers of a drug strong enough to cause anxiety, tremors, nausea, and changes in consciousness are rather obvious.

[33]Dr. John Pollard, University of Michigan psychiatrist, quoted in *Newsweek*, December 30, 1968. (This quotation should not be construed as meaning that Dr. Pollard advocates marijuana usage.)
[34]Leary, *op. cit.*, p. 174.
[35]*Ibid.*, p. 156.
[36]Dr. Fred Forscher, personal communication.

The social effects of marijuana are unquestionably serious. It can become part of a passive, introspective way of life which prevents you from coping with external reality, can cause you to break off or to avoid certain relationships, and, if you are unlucky enough to get arrested, it can ruin your entire life. You may argue that the laws prohibiting marijuana are silly and hypocritical, but as long as law-makers, policemen, and the general public regard marijuana users as "dope fiends" and criminals, using marijuana involves enormous risks.

It therefore seems wisest to abstain, and, if you do smoke it, to do so with extreme caution (alone or in very small, very private groups). It also seems best to use it infrequently. Regular use greatly increases the chances of being caught, and it may cause you to cut off otherwise satisfying relationships or activities to reduce the risk of detection or arrest. The problem is, of course, that once you start smoking pot, you may become psychologically dependent on the drug or socially dependent upon the groups and rituals related to it, which brings us right back to the original recommendation—*don't start.*

> There is a risk that a good many trips will
> turn out to be one-way trips, with some
> form of psychosis as the end result. [37]

THE HALLUCINOGENS

Chemically LSD may be the most dangerous drug currently used by students.[38] Because it makes people introspective, relatively few people kill themselves by automobile accidents, start fights, get seduced, or have other *behavorial* problems, but the chemical effects are much more severe than those of alcohol or barbituates. Tiny doses, a small fraction of a gram, can cause relatively permanent psychological or physical damage.

In addition to being much more powerful than other drugs, LSD

[37]Maddox, *op. cit.,* p. 118.
[38]Although marijuana is a hallucinogen, LSD, mescaline psilocybin, and similar drugs are so much stronger that a separate section seemed necessary. Since LSD is the best known and apparently most powerful of the hallucinogens, I shall use the term "LSD" instead of the cumbersome, but more accurate phrase "LSD and the other hallucinogens."

exerts a very different kind of effect. In fact, these effects are so unusual that people who have taken LSD usually feel that they can not communicate their experiences clearly to nonusers. The English language, which was developed from a different set of experiences, is simply inadequate to describe this sensory and psychological experience. The science of linguistics supports their assertion: people can normally communicate with each other only in terms of experiences which they have *shared*. Some advocates of LSD usuage have therefore argued that no one should comment unless he has tried it himself.

While I agree that a nonuser such as myself can not understand the sensory experience or intense pleasure of a trip, I do not feel obliged to avoid the issue completely. I shall therefore report some of the observations and conclusions of users and scientists. However, because I can not understand the inner pleasures, but can see the more visible unpleasant effects, this discussion is probably biased against LSD. You should consider that bias when you make your own decision.

Effects

PHYSICAL EFFECTS   LSD is not a poison, nor have deaths ever been reported from overdoses. The observable physical effects are rather slight: enlarged irises, stronger reflexes, minor muscular pain, and occasional nausea. At the microscopic level the effects are much more serious: LSD can damage the chromosomes, the tiny bodies which control the inheritance of your children. We do not know what these broken chromosomes can do to your children, but deformities, blindness, and miscarriages are probable.

NEUROLOGICAL EFFECTS   LSD's neurological effects are quite complicated, and not well understood. It seems to interfere with nerve impulses in two ways: the impulses are not transmitted as efficiently within circuits, and they seem to leak from one circuit to another. The net effect is that they spread rather indiscriminantly.

SUBJECTIVE EFFECTS   This indiscriminate spreading floods one's consciousness with messages. Because your mind can handle only a few ideas or sensory impressions at one time, you normally have a series of filters which protect it by screening out most information.

For example, your eyes can see only a narrow range of light frequencies; your ears can hear only a small fraction of the sounds which reach them. You can see details and colors only with the central part of your eyes. You also have psychological filters, such as attention. If you stop concentrating on this book, you will realize that your senses have been bombarded with many messages which have been psychologically suppressed: background noises, room temperature, various odors, etc. This information was reaching your senses, but it was not getting through to you.

LSD, by causing nerve impulses to spread indiscriminately, dramatically reduces your mind's ability to filter and to select information. Some of this information comes from the senses, some from your repressed memories and feelings.

Feelings are much more intense, lights and colors seem stronger and brighter. Sounds are louder and clearer and sharper. Sensory impressions can also become confused: sounds may be seen, or lights felt. Sensations may occur without any stimulation at all—colors seen and sounds heard without any external stimulation. More elaborate hallucinations may also occur. Some people realize that these are hallucinations, but others are unable to distinguish between perceptions of reality and their own hallucinations.

Logic, habits, false-fronts, roles, and the rest of one's civilized veneer are stripped away, leaving him face-to-face with his primitive, sensual self. One also becomes aware of repressed memories and other unconscious material. Memories and feelings which have been kept buried for years are suddenly experienced.

PEAK EXPERIENCES   For some people this confrontation with their senses and unconscious feelings is extraordinarily exhilarating, a quasireligious experience which goes beyond the mundane reality of twentieth century life to a new and better world. Since I have never had this experience, I will not try to describe it. If you want more information, read Dr. Leary's books.

BAD TRIPS   On the other hand, breaking down defenses and confronting one's sensory experience can be overwhelmingly frightening. Many people are not able to handle their own sensory experiences, and relatively few people can deal with all of the things they have repressed. In fact, those things have been repressed precisely because they are frightening. You *need* your defenses, and breaking them down so that you experience all the normally suppressed or repressed thoughts, feelings, and impressions can cause very severe psychological problems, including psychoses (insanity).

Competent psychotherapists have long recognized the danger of breaking defenses down too rapidly. After a few sessions any therapist could give a patient a fairly clear description of his psychological problems, but he avoids doing so because it would only make matters worse. The patient's defenses would be overwhelmed, and he could not handle the information. Professionals therefore let their patients set a pace at which they lower their defenses and deal with the things which they have kept buried. As some psychiatrists put it: "We should never let more snakes out of the basket than we can kill at one time."

LSD lets out too many snakes, too rapidly. It acts so fast and goes so far that a person can become very confused and anxious. This confusion and anxiety normally lasts only a few hours, but these reactions occasionally have much longer-term effects.

PSYCHOSES   The most serious effects are prolonged psychotic reactions. These reactions occur more frequently when usage is unsupervised, but they have occurred even to people who took LSD under medical supervision.

> It appears that for many persons even a single dose of LSD is sufficient to produce a psychosis, especially when it is taken in unsupervised settings. The most typical symptoms seem to be paranoid delusions, schizophrenic-like hallucinations, and overwhelming fear. The majority of these psychoses have required special tranquilizer medication or hospitalization lasting from a few days to several years.[39]

SPONTANEOUS RECURRENCE   Even if one should not have a psychotic reaction, parts of the LSD experience can come back at apparently random intervals.

[39]Reginald Smart, and Karin Bateman, "Unfavorable Reactions to LSD: a Review and Analysis of the Available Case Reports," *The Canadian Medical Association Journal,* vol. 97 (Nov. 11), 1967, pp. 1214–1221.

In at least eleven cases, frightening delusions or hallucinations have reappeared weeks or months after the last ingestion of LSD and after intervals of normality. . . . A spontaneous recurrence also . . . seems to have resulted in suicide four weeks after LSD was taken.[40]

PROLONGED NONPSYCHOTIC REACTIONS   LSD has also caused a wide variety of other prolonged reactions, including acute panic, confusion, depression, and antisocial or psychopathic behavior.

Panic reactions are the most frequent non-psychotic adverse reactions to LSD. The most common features are dissociation, terror, confusion, fear of going insane and fear of not being able to return to normality.[41]

SUICIDE   Because suicides are very dramatic, the newspapers have given a great deal of publicity to the relatively few suicides which have occurred as a result of LSD. The fact that one of the suicides was Art Linkletter's daughter greatly increased this publicity. While there is clear evidence that some people have committed suicide during or after LSD episodes, the actual number of suicides seems quite small, and some investigators believe that it does not increase the suicide rate.

It is likely that LSD decreased the rate, since in such a group of subjects I would expect a higher mortality rate by suicide.[42]

Other investigators have challenged this conclusion, but the data at this time are inadequate to support either position. There is no doubt that some suicides have occurred, but we can not say whether more or less suicides would have occurred if LSD had not been taken.

HOMICIDE AND ASSAULT   Homicides and assaults are quite uncommon. The newspapers have given a great deal of publicity to the murders which have occurred under the influence of LSD, but they are certainly much rarer than murders under the influence of alcohol.

---

[40] *Ibid.*
[41] *Ibid.*
[42] Cohen, *Journal of Nervous and Mental Disorders,* vol. 130, p. 30, 1960, cited by Smart and Bateman, *op. cit.*

ADDICTION   The consensus at this time is that LSD is not addictive, nor does it cause people to escalate to harder drugs.

Reasons for Use

We really do not know why people use LSD. There are theories, of course, but they are not based upon adequate evidence.

> The present state of knowledge makes it difficult to assess the reasons for the psychodelic use of LSD. Not a single study has been made of the motivations of illicit LSD users who have not had complications. . . . Currently, we know very little of the reinforcements for taking LSD, nor do we know the personality and social needs which are served by the hallucinogens in general.[43]

The following remarks are therefore tentative.

EXPLORATION   Some people claim that LSD trips are motivated by the same exploratory drive that made the Vikings cross the Atlantic and the Americans go to the moon. According to this theory, LSD users are bold, venturesome individuals who want to explore the unknown territory within their minds, and who have the courage to face the dangers that exist there. There is no real evidence either for or against this theory.

PERSONALITY PROBLEMS   This theory is slightly more supported by the data, but the data are very limited. For example, paid volunteers for investigations of LSD have been found to have high rates of personality disturbances,[44] and people who have had unpleasant reactions to LSD often have prior personality problems, especially an inability to assume adult social and sexual roles, a tendency to use drugs to reduce tensions, a current life crisis, and a fantasy that LSD would "enable them to overcome this crisis by introjecting psychological strength."[45]

[43]Smart and Bateman, *op. cit.*
[44]H. Esecover, S. Malitz and B. Wilkins: *American Journal of Psychiatry*, 1961, vol. 117, p. 910.
[45]Glickman and Blumenfield, "Psychological Determinants of LSD Reactions," *Journal of Nervous and Mental Disease*, 1967, vol. 145, no. 1, pp. 79–83.

LSD Therapy

Not everyone who takes LSD does so for kicks; some people use it, with or without supervision, in the hope of solving some psychological problems. Their behavior is understandable, but it can actually increase their problems. We have already seen that LSD can have disastrous effects, but you should also realize that it has almost no value as a therapeutic agent. To understand why a drug with little value and serious side-effects has become so publicized as a therapeutic agent requires a brief historical analysis.

The history of LSD therapy is depressingly similar to the history of many other types of therapy: researchers begin cautiously, then get wildly, naïvely enthusiastic, and finally become disillusioned. This process has occurred with psychoanalysis, shock therapy, tranquilizers, various cancer cures, and hundreds of other therapies. At first, investigators ask: Can this method cure disease x? The first results are encouraging, causing them to try out the drug on more and more diseases. These results are also encouraging, but for very spurious reasons. The first is the well-known "placebo effect." Any form of treatment (even sugar pills) will result in a certain number of "cures." Second, investigators tend to find what they are looking for; if they are looking for cures, their patients will tend to give them the information that they want, and they will tend to distort the information they receive (usually unconsciously).

Despite the inadequacy of the early data, the "miraculous cures" of this new therapy are widely publicized. Therapists and the general public jump on the bandwagon; at last we have found *the* cure.

Meanwhile, more objective investigators have been conducting more carefully controlled studies. These studies almost invariably indicate that the therapeutic benefits are not nearly so great as they had been reported to be; research may also show that the therapy has unpleasant side-effects. When these more controlled investigations are published, the scientific community rejects the extravagant claims of the cult. Unfortunately, because of their own vested interests and lack of objectivity, the cult often continues to press its claims, and the general public, which can not evaluate the evidence, continues to believe them.

At this moment some LSD therapists are making extravagant

claims, which some people accept. But the evidence indicates that LSD therapy is no better than other methods and that it often has harmful side-effects. Therefore, if you have psychological problems, I urge you to avoid LSD therapy. There are no quick, easy cures for psychological problems, and men who offer them are dishonest and dangerous.

Conclusion

The evidence indicates that LSD can provide an exhilarating experience. It may also help some people with personality problems, but its general value as a form of therapy is very limited. Placed against these two possible benefits are enormous risks: psychosis, prolonged anxiety, chromosome damage, criminal arrest, and social ostracism. These risks are increased by the fact that even one very small doses can cause unfavorable reactions.

> No one is able to guarantee a safe dosage, a safe series of doses, or a personality which is certain to create no unfavorable reactions to LSD. Many cases have been reported in which a single, moderate dose of LSD led to a profoundly adverse reaction in an otherwise normal person.[46]

Given the limited benefits and the enormous risks, only one course of action seems prudent—*avoid LSD.*

SLEEPING PILLS AND TRANQUILIZERS

Barbiturates, which include both sleeping pills and tranquilizers,[47] are *extremely* dangerous, but most people do not regard them as part of the "drug menace." In fact, many parents who are terrified that their children may smoke pot have already become addicted to the *far* more dangerous barbiturates.

[46]Smart and Bateman, *op. cit.*
[47]The difference between sleeping pills and tranquilizers is that tranquilizers make one feel calm and relaxed, but they normally do not induce sleep, nor do they have much effect upon physical reactions. The nonprescription tranquilizers are antihistamines which usually combine relaxation with sleepiness and a general reduction in alertness and mental efficiency. The nonprescription drugs have not been shown to be dangerous unless one requires quick reflexes (such as in driving a car).

Effects

Barbiturates kill thousands of people every year. Thousands use sleeping pills to commit suicide, and thousands more die from accidental overdoses, including quite a few children who mistake the pills for candy or aspirin. Even one sleeping pill or tranquilizer can kill you if it is combined with alcohol. If they don't kill you chemically, they can dull your senses enough to cause an automobile accident. Finally, they are addictive drugs: you can become both psychologically and physically dependent upon them, and the withdrawal symptoms are at least as horrible as those caused by heroin: panic, epileptic-type convulsions, uncontrolled blood pressure and pulse rate, hallucinations, delusions, and occasionally death.

They do, of course, have some beneficial effects. Sleeping pills can preserve your health by overcoming a *situationally caused* inability to sleep, and tranquilizers can help you to cope with stressful *situations.*

Unfortunately, some doctors are so careless and irresponsible that their patients become both psychologically and physically dependent upon barbiturates. At first they use them to cope with some difficult situation, but soon they can not sleep or relax without pills. The pills create a mild physical dependency so that temporary withdrawals *cause* anxiety and insomnia, the very symptoms for which they were originally prescribed! To overcome these symptoms larger and more frequent doses may then be taken, converting an originally minor problem into a serious psychiatric and physical condition.

Reasons for Use

Since barbiturates are extremely dangerous, we must ask why they have become so popular, and why the medical profession has behaved so irresponsibly. The first reason is unquestionably ignorance. Sleeping pills and tranquilizers are not regarded as dangerous drugs, and many people become addicted to them long before they realize how dangerous they are.

Second, they solve problems for people: they let them sleep, or relax them, or enable them to deal with stresses, pressures, and anxieties. Furthermore, they provide this help without the obvious mental and physical deterioration of using alcohol.

Third, there is no social stigma attached to using barbiturates. People who would be ashamed to admit that they depended upon alcohol will openly and publicly admit that they can not sleep without a pill, or that they need a tranquilizer to get through the day. This social acceptability is caused by the general ignorance, and the fact that doctors freely prescribe barbiturates.

Finally, since physicians are the primary "pushers" of barbituates, we must ask why they behave so irresponsibly. Certainly they know how dangerous barbiturates are; they may have even lost a few patients from accidental or intentional overdoses, yet they continue to prescribe these pills as if they were prescribing chewing gum. One cause of such irresponsibility is that a number of doctors think more of their incomes than the Hippocratic oath—it would take time to diagnose and to solve their patients' problems, and it is easier and more profitable to scribble a prescription, even though the drugs do more harm than good.

Conclusion

Although there may be times that a barbiturate is temporarily useful, you should generally avoid them. Certainly, you should *never* take one unless a doctor, after a thorough examination, has prescribed it.

If you now use barbiturates regularly, I urge you to "kick the habit" before it is too late. The pills which make you feel so relaxed now are already beginning to destroy you. If you keep using them, they will finish the job.

Because such pills are an addictive drug, dropping them is far from easy. The difficulties are compounded by the fact that the problems which caused you to get started have probably not been solved. You may have both a physical and a psychological dependence. Therefore, if you are currently using barbiturates, I suggest that you seek competent medical and psychological help *immediately.* Something inside of you is so painful that you prefer oblivion to awareness. It will continue to hurt you, and drugs will slowly destroy you, unless you get help. The same advice applies to people who are not now using barbiturates, but who are tempted to begin.

Finally, when you have taken even one tranquilizer or sleeping pill, you must *completely* avoid alcohol. A drink can kill you.

PEP PILLS

Pep pills (amphetamines) are used by many students, especially for cramming sessions and big weekends. Some students also use them to overcome general tiredness and depressions.

Effects

REWARDING EFFECTS　　In addition to increasing the number of hours that a person can remain awake, pep pills increase alertness, improve performance on simple tasks, and create a feeling of euphoria and greater internal strength. Users feel "sharper," stronger, and more able to control difficult situations.

CONFORMITY AND SOCIABILITY　　Pep pills usually make people less aggressive and more sociable, cooperative, and conformist. These effects may be derived from the general sense of well-being obtained.

FATIGUE AND DEPRESSION　　Pep pills blot-out feelings of fatigue and cause the body to run more rapidly. When their effects wear off, one becomes painfully aware of how tired he really is. If the dosage has been large, or if the person has remained awake too long, he may be close to utter physical exhaustion, which can cause a rather deep depression. Despite their exhaustion, some people cannot sleep without barbiturates, which in addition to their own harmful effects, become part of an artificial cycle of stimulation and sedation.

A few pills are both amphetamines and barbiturates: they stimulate and relax you at the same time. Some students have naïvely believed that these pills offer all of the benefits and none of the risks and costs of the simpler pills, but the opposite is more nearly the case. Their immediate effect may be very pleasant, but they combine the long-term harmful effects of both types of drugs.

If large enough doses have been taken for a long enough period of time, the ensuing depression may be deep enough to cause suicide —although this is a relatively rare event.

HALLUCINATIONS　　After very heavy doses, hallucinations can occur, some of which are extremely frightening.

PSYCHOSES   These hallucinations can be part of a full-fledged psychotic reaction, even though such reactions are relatively rare and nearly always temporary.

LONG TERM PHYSICAL EFFECTS   Taking pep pills is approximately equal to running a motor at an excessively high speed without allowing for preventative maintenance. Your body is built to work at a certain speed, with regular periods of rest and recuperation. Running it faster and shortening or eliminating these recuperation periods wears it out. All the systems can be strained, but the most serious strains usually occur in the circulatory systems. Blood pressure rises, and various kinds of damage are done to the heart. Pep pills can therefore shorten your life.

Reasons for Use

Students use pep pills for three very different purposes: weight control, situational pressures, and psychological problems. Because diet pills are discussed elsewhere, we shall concentrate on the other two reasons.

Students are certainly not the only people who use pep pills to cope with situational pressures. Many housewives, soldiers, and businessmen use them for the same reason. Even physicians, especially obstetricians, use them during emergencies. The fact that so many people need pills to cope with the demands of their lives is eloquent testimony to the excessive demands of modern life.

Students are also not alone in using these pills to overcome feelings of depression, tiredness, listlessness, and so on. Many other people feel so "down" that they need drugs to get them "up." The social implications of this need are really disturbing. Something must be wrong with a society which is too depressing to face without artificial stimulation.

Conclusion

Because occasional and habitual uses of pep pills have considerably different implications, I shall comment separately about each type.

TEMPORARY USE   While I think it is unfortunate that we place such heavy demands upon students that they need drugs to cope with them, I do not feel that occasional use of pep pills is particularly dangerous —*if the doses are extremely limited.* Under no circumstances should you exceed the manufacturers suggested maximum dosage, nor should you use the pills for more than 24 hours.

The danger is, of course, that you may slowly change your definition of "emergency" so that you are using the pills more often, perhaps with increasingly larger doses. I therefore suggest that you avoid them completely or use them only for genuine emergencies. Tiredness is a message from your body which only a fool will ignore.

HABITUAL USE   It is even more foolish to ignore repeated messages such as depressions, general tiredness, and similar reactions. These feelings indicate that you have some sort of physical or psychological problems. You may, for example, be anemic, or have a thyroid deficiency; you may also have some fairly significant psychological problems. Pep pills, by relieving your symptoms temporarily, divert attention from the real problems. Furthermore, when their effects wear off, you will feel even more depressed or tired. You may then take more pills, further aggravating the situation. Therefore, if you are habitually using pills, or are tempted to do so because you feel depressed or tired, see a physician.[48]

DIET PILLS

Many students use diet pills, but relatively few students would regard them as a drug. They just "eat candy," or "chew gum," or swallow a pill to reduce their appetite, without realizing that the drugs involved often have serious physical and psychological side effects. Many diet pills are chemically related to pep pills, and all types of diet pills have been linked to physiological and psychological problems—including depression, excitability, and insomnia. The evidence also indicates that they are not very valuable for weight control: people

[48]You should start with your physician because physical problems are usually rather easy to diagnose and to correct. If a physical examination discloses no organic cause, you can then see a psychologist or psychiatrist.

who take them generally do not lose weight. Since these agents have little measurable value and potentially serious side-effects, *I urge you not to take any form of diet pills—even if they are prescribed by a physician.*[49]

CLOSING COMMENTS

The preceding discussion clearly indicates that I am opposed to using nearly all drugs—tobacco, alcohol, marijuana, LSD, pep pills, and barbiturates. My reasons are pragmatic. not moralistic. Drugs rarely solve problems, and they often create more serious ones.

Any drug which is powerful enough to change your mood or consciousness or appetite is powerful enough to hurt you, perhaps permanently. Furthermore, drugs which are distributed illegally are often manufactured very carelessly; sanitary facilities and quality control are almost nonexistent. You would not eat black-market meat, why take a chance with black-market drugs?

Even if the drug is not contaminated, the history of drug research has shown—again and again and again—that apparently innocuous drugs can have serious or even fatal side-effects. Calcium cyclamate can cause cancer; antihistamines cause drowsiness that leads to automobile accidents; birth control pills have killed over 250 people.

Unfortunately, most Americans of all ages have childishly naïve conceptions of drugs. Drugs are the all-purpose cure, the immediate, inexpensive relief, and people rarely think of their long-term effects. For your entire life you have lived in a drug-oriented society. The same short-sightedness which has made us pollute our air and water is causing us to pollute our bodies. A trip to the doctor usually means pills or a shot. Your medicine cabinet is stuffed full of pills. You have routinely taken aspirin for headaches, antihistamines for colds, and vitamin pills for real or imagined dietary deficiencies.[50]

Now that you are in college and face psychological problems, it

[49]As many parts of this book clearly indicate, I believe in leaving most medical issues to physicians, but here I must make an exception. One reason is that several investigations have revealed that doctors have earned fantastic amounts of money by prescribing worthless and harmful diet-control pills.

[50]Many nutrition specialists believe that fewer middle-class Americans suffer from vitamin deficiencies than overdoses (which can have serious side effects), and nearly all nutrition specialists are opposed to using vitamin pills routinely.

is natural to look for chemical relief. But that relief is very temporary and very costly. Pain is useful: it tells you that something is wrong inside of you, and it motivates you to do something about it. If you remove the pain chemically, you lose that information and motivation. The pain goes away, but the problem persists, and it probably becomes more serious.

The real drug problem in America is not marijuana, LSD, alcohol, or tranquilizers, nor is it confined to college campuses. It is a way of life which is so unsatisfying and frightening that many people need drugs, and a philosophy which ignores these drugs' long-term effects.

Therefore, if you feel a need for drugs, if you are lonely, depressed, and miserable, if you can't study or sleep, get to work on your problems and leave drugs to the weaklings.

LEARNING

*"What does it all *mean?*"*

Most students cannot answer that question, and many do not even try. They are so busy responding to examination and grading pressures that they never have a chance to think about meaning. My purpose here is to outline a system which will ease the pressures and give you a chance to think independently about your school subjects and life in general.[1]

THE ECONOMICS OF LEARNING

The system outlined here is based on two social sciences—psychology and economics. The relationship between psychology and learning is quite obvious, but you may be somewhat surprised by the reference to economics. Economics is, however, relevant whenever one considers the distribution of scarce resources, and there is no scarcer re-

[1]This chapter will not discuss many of the typical subjects such as the need for good lighting, quiet, regular study hours, or mental discipline. You have heard that song before, and you did not pay much attention to it.

source than time. There is absolutely no way for you to increase the number of hours in your day, so you must learn how to get the most out of the ones that you have.

Most students use their time uneconomically. They spend 10 or 12 hours a week in lectures, but learn very little there. They waste countless hours by reading slowly and writing in longhand. They take extensive, but unnecessary, notes. They underline their books even though underlining is a slow and inefficient process. That is, they get a poor return on the time they invest.

Most students realize vaguely that time is convertible into money, but they waste $10 worth of time for every dollar they save. They go to the library and waste hours trying to get books that they could buy for a few dollars. They sit in lectures instead of buying commercial notes. They copy material that they could easily Xerox. When they do these things, they are effectively selling their time for a lower rate than they could get on the open market. The terms of the money/time trade are so favorable to them that they should work a few additional hours each week and use that money to save twice as much time.

They also let short-term considerations cause them to pass up investments which could pay fabulous returns. If a businessman were offered a risk-free investment which returned several hundred percent in one year, he would jump at the chance, but students regularly turn down exactly that sort of investment. They feel that they do not have the time to learn speedreading, shorthand, typing, and many other skills, even though these skills would save many times their investment in a few months.

Return on investment and other principles are used by economists to make cost-benefit analyses. For each possible alternative they try to quantify all the factors and then select the alternative which yields the best benefit/cost ratio. This approach is brutally rational; all alternatives are evaluated in terms of this benefit/cost ratio, and the best alternative is selected, even if it violates tradition or habits. Obviously, I cannot perform such sophisticated analyses here, but my general approach is based on the same logic and brutal rationality. Study habits and academic traditions are therefore analyzed and actions are proposed in terms of only one criterion: *maximizing the return you get on your money and time investments.*

THE PSYCHOLOGY OF LEARNING

To get this maximum return, we shall have to use a few psychological principles. As we saw in Chapter 3, psychologists have conducted extensive research on learning, but their work has had virtually no impact on educational policies. Most professors do not know much about teaching or learning. You must therefore compensate for our incompetence by your own competence. *Since we do not know how to teach, you must learn how to learn.*

Most of these psychological principles will be described in the parts of the discussion to which they refer, but two principles, which refer to virtually all learning, will be briefly discussed here and then elaborated later. First, learning is an *active* process. You learn best by doing things. Some of these activities are physical and visible, such as writing papers and asking questions, but the mental ones are at least as important.

A passive approach to books or lectures is much less efficient than an active one in which you ask and answer mental questions, challenge the author, and relate the material to your own experience and other subjects. The following discussion will therefore emphasize ways to take an active role in situations to which most people respond passively.

Second, meaningful learning is much faster and more efficient than rote learning. If you understand what an author or lecturer is trying to do, and the way that he is attempting to do it, you will learn much faster and retain much longer. Academic pressures, especially multiple-choice examinations, pop quizzes, and the obsession with terms and definitions, emphasize rote learning, but there are ways to counteract this emphasis. So the following discussion will stress ways to grasp and to retain the two central elements of meaningful learning: *purpose* and *organization.*

IF YOU DON'T LIKE IT, DON'T DO IT

Most students waste their time on trivial, meaningless tasks because the system is so authoritarian and because they have been conditioned to take a passive role. You cannot afford to do that. Passivity reduces the amount you learn in class, and it also prevents you from learning who you are and what you enjoy doing. You must therefore expand your freedom to choose your own tasks and approach. You may feel trapped by the system, but, if you know how to operate, you can avoid lots of odious, silly tasks and greatly increase your independence.

First, whenever possible avoid the authoritarian, incompetent professors who demand that everyone does the same thing. From a distance they may all look like that to you, but, if you approach them as individuals, you will find that many professors hate assembly-line education as much as you do. They are trapped on the same treadmill as you are, and will do whatever they can to let you off it. Some will waive examinations and let you write papers; others will agree to let you read independently and take a separate final; others will supervise independent research projects.

Second, regardless of the professor you have, ask for opportunities to work on projects or subjects that you enjoy. If they think you are sincerely interested in learning, a surprising number of professors will let you make minor changes in your work-load (such as substituting a paper for an examination or taking an oral rather than a written examination).

Third, become so efficient at learning that you can satisfy the basic requirements in only a few hours a week. If you cut all lectures, learn speedreading, shorthand, and typing, and master the note-taking and study systems presented here, you can control all but 12 to 15 hours per week.

Fourth, budget your study time wisely. Don't work equally hard on all courses. Select the ones which are most interesting or offer the best grade increase for the time you invest. That is, if you need or want a certain grade point average, work out the grade mix that satisfies your intrinsic interests or that maximizes the return on your invested time. If you need a "B" average and like history but dislike math, don't shoot for a "B" in each course; settle for a "C" in math, but try for an "A" in history. You will therefore spend most of your time on the subjects you like best, without hurting your overall average. If you have "C's" at midterm in two courses which do not interest you, and have to raise one to a "B," don't waste your time trying to raise both because you will probably end up with a "C+" in each course, a grade which does not help you. Instead, decide which one is easier or more interesting, then concentrate on it and write-off the other one.

Some of these specific suggestions and the study system and philosophy on which they are based will offend some people. Many professors will feel that it is immoral to tell students to cut lectures or to write-off courses, and some students will agree with the professors' position. The professors' position is consistent with the Protestant Ethic and academic authoritarianism, but it is based on force, not morality. Having unilaterally established the rules for the game, they say: "Anyone who doesn't follow these rules is lazy, irresponsible, and immoral."

If one begins with the assumption that students should passively follow the professors' rules, then my position is clearly immoral, and so is anyone who endorses it. However, if we assume that you are a sovereign human being who has the right to make his own decisions, if we look at the overwhelming evidence that coercion interferes with learning, and if we examine the utter inadequacy of the teaching system, my position may be justified.

Since there are no moral absolutes, you will have to decide for yourself whether you should break the professors' rules, but I hope that you have the courage and independence to do so.[2]

THE TOOL SKILLS

Speed reading, typing, and shorthand[3] can dramatically increase your learning efficiency. Many people can read several thousand words per minute with equal or better comprehension than you have. Typing is several times faster than writing by hand, and it is also easier to read, to review, and to correct. Shorthand is even faster than typing, and, because of its speed, you can listen to what a lecture means, instead of frantically scribbling longhand notes. Shorthand also helps you to write papers; instead of losing your thoughts as you try to get them

[2]Please note that I am not advocating rebellion or demonstrations; I am simply saying that you should exert your independence by working on tasks which pay off in either enjoyment or grades.

[3]A fourth tool skill, using the library, is not discussed here because so much written material is available about the subject. You should certainly ask your librarian for information and study it carefully. If you really learn how to use a library, you will save a great deal of time and learn much more efficiently—for the rest of your life.

on paper, you can let them flow freely, jot them down in shorthand, and then revise them later.

Given the extreme value of these three skills, I regard it as criminally irresponsible for the academic establishment to refuse to teach them. It violates their delicate conception of academic respectability to teach something useful, and you suffer. These skills can all be learned easily and quickly. You may be reluctant to add something to your already busy schedule, but the increase in your efficiency will save you hundreds of hours for every hour you invest.

Speed Reading

Speed reading is the hardest skill to learn. You have practiced the wrong habits for so long that you can not learn the right ones without outside help and discipline. The speed-reading methods will make you feel so uncomfortable that you will probably revert to your old, inefficient habits. I therefore suggest that you avoid reading improvement books and the courses run by most universities. The books cannot provide the necessary discipline, and most university courses are run by academic hacks who do not know how to read.

I dislike giving a commercial endorsement, but I have little choice. The hand-pacing method is so far superior to any other system that I suggest you pay for a course from any one of the commercial organizations which use it. One organization claims to have the exclusive rights to this method, but several other companies and a few universities offer very similar courses. You should not pay for a commercial course unless there is a guaranteed refund if you do not triple your reading speed. The good courses routinely contain that guarantee.

The method itself is quite simple, but it is so uncomfortable at first that very few people can learn it on their own. In fact, a large percentage of the people who pay for these courses feel so uncomfortable that they do not do their homework. They therefore learn the simple theory, but do not improve their reading very much. Because the course and homework are time-consuming and exhausting, I suggest that you take the course during the summer or the first part of a semester. Then the course will not have to compete with your examinations, and you will be freer to learn how to read.

Typing

Typing is considerably easier to learn. It is a fairly simple skill, which simply requires practice. A great advantage is that after a few hours of practice you will be able to type more quickly than you can write —*if* you don't worry about making mistakes.

Typing teachers stress neatness, but you will learn and type much faster if you ignore that. Just type everything that does not have to be too neat. Then you can move quickly by ignoring errors and concentrating on speed. If you make a mistake, do *not* erase it or even strike over it. Just type the word properly and keep moving. When you review and revise your material, you can cross out the mistakes. Your paper won't be neat, but it will be done. Naturally, final drafts should be done by a professional typist because she can do a neat job more cheaply than you can (unless you take the time to become highly proficient).

You should purchase an electric typewriter with automatic carriage return (possibly a used one) because it will be much easier to learn and you will be able to type much more quickly. The greater speed for both learning and typing will repay the difference in your initial investment within a few months.

Many people start to learn typing but drop it because they feel so uncomfortable and unnatural. The typewriter acts as a barrier to the free flow of thought; they have to spend so much time thinking about typing that they cannot think of what they are trying to write. This is a very natural problem, but one which you will overcome quite quickly if you stick with it. In fact, after you have learned how to type, you will realize that the time it takes to write things in longhand is an even greater barrier to thinking.

Shorthand

Some shorthand systems are quite easy to learn. Gregg and Pitman, the traditional systems, are very difficult, but speed-writing and various notehand systems can be learned in 10 to 20 hours. Furthermore, they start saving you time as soon as you begin. You therefore have virtually no transition costs, and you start getting a benefit immediately. I therefore suggest that you go to a bookstore *immediately* and buy one of the paperback books on speed writing, notehand, or any other simple shorthand system. It will cost you about $1, an amount you will get back ten times over in a week.

If you learn these three skills, you are well on your way to becoming an efficient learner. They will reduce the time you spend on drudgery, make learning more enjoyable, improve the quality of your writing, raise your examination grades, and give you the freedom you need to educate yourself.

LECTURES

There is only one intelligent response to lectures: *don't go*.

Why should you waste your precious time listening to a man parrot what is in various books? Chapter 3 showed that lectures are an extraordinarily inefficient way to transmit information, and there is no rational reason for you to be a party to this inefficiency. Your time is too precious to waste; you should therefore avoid lectures whenever possible.

At some universities there are organizations which take and sell lecture notes which are much better than the ones you could take. The people who take them are trained, often have shorthand skills, and the notes are typed and organized. The cost of these notes is so much less than the value of the time saved that you should buy the notes and avoid the lectures.

If commercial notes are not available, you and your colleagues should form a note-taking pool in which one person takes the notes and makes them available to the group. You can pay someone to take notes for you, or you can work out a rotation system in which each of you attends one-fifth or one-eighth or one-tenth of the lectures.

If you avoid lectures but make arrangements for notes to be taken, you will miss nothing important, nor will you damage your grades. But you will release an enormous amount of time for more worthwhile activities. Unfortunately, most students do not have the nerve to cut their lectures. They know that they will not learn very much, but they go anyway. They may hope to improve their grades, or they may just be used to sitting in class, but they waste their time sitting there while the professor wastes his time lecturing. Furthermore, some schools actually have required attendance, a carry-over from the kindergarten.

Inasmuch as most students will attend lectures, I feel obliged to make a few suggestions about ways to get more out of them. The principles for listening to a lecture are the same as those for reading a book. You must concentrate, not on the details, but on the lecturer's purpose, logic, and organization. *What* is he trying to do and *how* is he trying to do it? The only way you can answer these questions is to be an *active* listener, one who uses his mind more than his notebook. Instead of scribbling frantically, keep asking: What is he trying to do? How is he trying to do it? What does this particular remark mean? How does it fit with what else he has said?[4]

It will be much easier to answer these questions if you follow a few simple rules.

1. *Concentrate on his opening remarks.* Most lecturers will tell you what they intend to say, and many will give an organized overview of the lecture. These opening remarks set the stage for everything that follows, and, if you do not understand them, you probably will not understand anything else.

2. *When the lecturer gets bogged down in details, step back.* Instead of trying to follow the details, ask: What do these details mean? Why is he giving these examples? Most important of all, try to relate the details and examples to his original purpose and overview. He generally has a reason for almost everything he says, and you must grasp that reason.

3. *Be alert for words which refer directly to the* organization *of his presentation.* Words such as "first," "a contradictory theory," "therefore," "a major development," are similar to subtitles. They tell you where you are or where you are going.

4. *When he says phrases such as "for example," or "in other words," stop taking notes.* He is deliberately telling you that he has stopped saying new things and is trying to clarify what he has already said. You should therefore check his example or rephrasing against your earlier understanding. Are they consistent? If not, you are confused, and you must reduce your confusion as soon as possible.

5. *Look for the nonverbal communications.* The *sole* advantage of lectures over books is that the speaker can use nonverbal techniques

[4]Obviously, shorthand helps you to understand his meaning because you do not have to spend so much time scribbling.

to emphasize points. Most lecturers speak more loudly, or slow down, or repeat the points which they regard as most important. If you notice these changes, you will get a much clearer understanding of his purpose and organization. (You will also get some ideas about the examination.)

6. *Take only outline notes.* Obviously you can not do any of the things suggested above, if you are frantically scribbling notes, even if the notes are in shorthand. Shorthand helps immensely, of course, but it is no substitute for thinking or active listening. Your notes should therefore be in outline[5] rather than sentence form and should include *only* the lecturer's purposes, major points, and organization. The rest you can leave to the mindless drudges who, because they cannot discriminate the important points from the trivial details, must try to imitate medieval scribes.

7. *Write a commentary.* In addition to his points you should write down your comments and questions. What do *you* think? Where have you gotten confused? What questions should you ask? By making these comments you are involving yourself in what he is saying instead of merely listening passively.

8. *Ask questions!* Whenever you do not understand anything, ask the lecturer for clarification. Most lecturers welcome questions *if* they are not challenges or attempts to show off. Questions give us feedback, which we need as much as you do. If you can not ask questions during a lecture, see the lecturer as soon as it is over, but you should not leave the room until you understand what he meant. A minute or two right after class can save you an hour later.

9. *Review and revise your notes as soon as possible.* A quick glance through your notes before the next class will increase your understanding of both the notes and the next lecture. If possible, meet regularly with someone else and compare and discuss your notes. Why did he get a different impression than you did? Whether you meet with someone or not, regular reviews save ten times your investment. If you wait until the end of the term, you may not understand your own notes. A few minutes' revision while your memory is fresh will therefore accomplish more than an hour's study later on.

---

[5]Subtitles, Roman numerals, and underlining will make your notes much clearer.

STUDYING

Obviously, studying is an important part of learning, but most students do not understand or apply the basic principles of learning when they study. They spend so much time on the details that they lose sight of the forest for the trees. They waste hours underlining books, and often end up more confused than if they had not done any underlining at all. They cram so hard that they get fatigued and confused. The system described here can increase your efficiency so that you study less, but learn more and get better grades.

Whole Versus Part

Reading an entire book, chapter, or article at one time is much more efficient than reading it a bit at a time because the overall structure will be clearer, and this structure will help you to understand and to retain the details. This point can be clarified by looking at the way that professionals build houses. If they did it the way that many students study, they would be working on the cabinets and wall paper before they finished putting on the roof. But, because they know better, they build the framework first and then work their way down to the details. When the framework is finished, the details fall naturally into place. Good readers do the same. They look for the organization when they read, giving their work unity and direction. Then, because it holds together and makes sense, it is easier to understand and to retain.

Your understanding of the structure will be clearer if you take advantage of the author's attempts to help you. Nearly all books contain a preface, foreword, or introduction in which the author says what he is going to do and how he is going to do it. This material clarifies the meaning of everything you read and should *always* be read, even if you have only been assigned one or two chapters of the book. You should also spend a few minutes analyzing the table of contents. It is the clearest statement of his organization that you can find. Within chapters or articles you should begin by surveying all the subtitles, *before* you read a single word. They tell you how the material is organized.

After the subtitles have been read, you should rapidly skim the entire chapter. Do not worry about not understanding all the details.

They will come later. Now your task is to clarify the overall purpose and approach. As you skim, you should underline the important points, using the system which will be described in a later section.

Once you have a picture of the entire chapter, you can read more slowly and work on the details. You will find that the time that you have spent on the organization will make it much easier to understand and to retain these details. Conversely, if you begin by concentrating on the details, you will become confused and understand neither the overall organization nor the details.[6]

Active Involvement

Virtually all students spend too much time passively reading and not enough time doing things which involve them in the material. They read and reread books and their lecture notes instead of taking more active roles. Some students go a step beyond reading, by writing notes or reciting passages aloud, but doing so involves physical rather than mental activity. Their hands write down notes, or their mouths say things, but their minds are not involved.

It is far better to *close your book and to open your mind.* Many textbooks try to involve you actively by listing discussion questions at the end of each chapter, but most students ignore them. Since these questions usually refer to the important issues, I suggest that you routinely try to answer them and then check your answers against the text. You will therefore involve yourself actively and get feedback. If there are no discussion questions, try to reconstruct what the author said—not the words themselves, but his purpose and organization. The best way to do this is to explain his message to another person.[7]

After you have explained his general meaning, criticize his position and approach. Is his logic sound? Is his evidence adequate? Could he have expressed himself more clearly? How? Then try to use his ideas in some other situation. Do they apply? Why or why not? Finally, try to build a case against him. Can you punch holes in his argument? Lawyers, who must do this for a living, are among the most

[6]This brief discussion is much less useful than a reading course, which stresses the importance of concentrating on purpose and organization.

[7]Any professor will tell you that lecturing about books helps him to understand them.

thorough readers in the world, and this technique can clarify a man's meaning more than anything you can do.[8]

As you are doing these things you will naturally have to refer to the book or your notes from time to time. You will therefore get feedback on your understanding. But, once you have checked out your understanding, close that book! Don't just continue reading. Get back to the activity/feedback cycle by explaining, criticizing, and making arguments.

The general consensus of specialists in learning is that *you will learn most efficiently if the book is closed more often than it is open.* Some even suggest spending *twice* as much time on recitation, paraphrasing, arguing, and other activities as you spend "studying."

Study Schedules

So many students ignore the frequent warnings not to cram, that I am reluctant to add my voice to those of the "anticrammers," but the evidence is so clear that I have no choice. Reviewing extensively before examinations will improve your grades, but reviewing is very different from trying to learn new material. If you leave some of your reading until the end of the term, it will interfere with your review and lower your grades.

Even more important, if you try to do all of your studying immediately before the exam instead of spacing it out over the weeks, you will get a much lower return on your invested study hours. You must therefore study more hours to learn as much or to get the same grades. The evidence in support of that statement is literally overwhelming; psychologists have conducted hundreds of investigations on what we call the "massed versus distributed practice issue." These studies unequivocally support the conclusion that distributed practice is more efficient. At least three factors contribute to this greater efficiency.

The first and most obvious factor is closely related to physical fatique. If you try to do one hundred push-ups within 20 minutes, your body will become so tired that it can not respond. Approximately the

[8]Note that these activities are essentially the ones you must do on your examinations, which are supposed to be learning as well as disciplinary activities. Since you are going to be graded on your ability to do these things, it makes sense to practice them.

same process occurs when you study too long or too intensively; your mind gets so tired[9] that it can not absorb material very effectively.

Second, if you space out your studies, the material you study will automatically be associated with other things that you hear or read. These associations will increase your understanding, and make it easier to retain what you have read. For example, if you were required to study Marx for an economics course and read the assigned readings early in the term, you would encounter dozens of associations before the final examination. Newspaper accounts of Russian-Chinese disagreements, the changes in attitudes of European socialist parties, and the speeches of student militants would add to material you would automatically encounter in your sociology and philosophy classes, and be further strengthened by remarks in informal conversations. Then, when you take the final examination, Marx would not be just some funny name that you read in an economics text.

Marx is, of course, a rather obvious example because so much has been written about him. But the same general principle applies to almost everything you will study, even such esoteric subjects as mathematics and physics. The material you learn in any course is related to the other things you read and talk about, and the more you spreadout your reading, the clearer these associations will become, and the less time you will have to spend on formal study. Even more important, by spacing your study and allowing the natural associations to develop, your education becomes more closely related to the rest of your life. Instead of dividing your life into studying and "important things," you can integrate the two, so that your life has more unity.

Third, these associations, in addition to clarifying the meaning of what you have read, cause informal, spontaneous practice. By reminding you of what you have read, they make it easier for you to recall it on examinations.

Because of Points 2 and 3, you will reduce your study time significantly if you *always read material before lectures and class discussions.* The class discussion will build up your associations and remind you of what you have read. You will also be able to participate in discussion, and discussions cause *active* learning. An hour's studying

---

[9]The mind (or the brain) does not, of course, get tired in the same sense as the muscles do, but the distinctions between physical fatique and mental inefficiency need not concern us here.

before class will improve your learning and grades more than two hours studying after class. Furthermore, if you read several weeks ahead of the class schedule, and then review each topic immediately before it is discussed in class, your efficiency will be even higher. The organization of the material will become clearer; you will know where you are going; you will get more reminders, causing you to learn *much* more efficiently; and you will more favorably impress professors!

Underlining Books

Many students underline their books,[10] but very few of them know how to do it. They underline anything that looks important, and some students even underline one-quarter or one-third of a book.

This lack of selectivity indicates an inability to read well. An efficient reader does not try to retain everything because he knows that trying to do so would only confuse him. He concentrates on the author's *purpose* and *organization* because, if they are understood, the details fit naturally into place and are easily recalled.

The idiotic emphasis on multiple-choice exams is another reason that so many students read poorly and underline excessively. By measuring your ability to recall trivia, these examinations reinforce poor reading habits and excessive underlining. You have been taking multiple-choice exams for so long that you are probably much better at regurgitating trivia than at understanding the important points.

A speed reading course will help you to separate the wheat from the chaff, and a good underlining system should help you to recall the author's major points. An efficient system should also minimize the time spent on underlining. Underlining is a *very* slow process and the time you spend drawing those lines can be invested much more profitably. The following system reduces the amount of time spent underlining and clarifies the author's purpose and organization.

The core of this system is that a few symbols have different weights and meanings. The great disadvantage of underlining is that it is utterly uniform; as you review the book for an examination you can not tell whether an underlined sentence or paragraph is crucially important or a trivial detail. When you use different symbols for items

[10]This system should also be used for underlining lecture and class notes.

of different importance, the central points stand out, and you can understand the way the article is structured. Furthermore, in your final review, the one you do just before you enter the examination room, you can cover *all* of the important points.

It really does not matter what symbols you use just as long as each symbol has a different meaning, and they are arranged in a hierarchy of importance. However, to simplify matters, I will describe the symbols I use and the meaning and weight of each one.

The basic symbol is a vertical line with "hooks" at each end, as shown in the right margin. This symbol simply means that an idea is important enough to be reviewed. All material to be reviewed is marked by this symbol, and the more important ideas get additional symbols as well. This particular symbol was chosen because the "hooks" indicate the beginning and end of the important idea, and it can be made so easily that it has hardly any effect on reading speed and comprehension.

If an idea, sentence, or paragraph is somewhat more important than those which are marked with a plain line, place one or more check marks (✔) in the margin. The more check marks, the more important it is.

If an idea is still more important, place one or more "x's" in the margin.

If an idea is so important that you can not afford to forget it, write "VI" ("Very Important") in the margin.

If an idea is crucially significant, write "CS" in the margin. The "CS" material are the central ideas.

If a summary is presented, mark " Σ " in the margin. " Σ " is the mathematical symbol for summary. The summaries are about as important as the "CS" ideas because they provide an overview of the author's main points and general organization.

If you do not understand something, do not spend too much time on it. Simply put a "?" in the margin and keep moving. Later material will probably clarify the issue. If it does not, you can try to work it out yourself or ask the professor.

If something appears dubious or questionable, put a " *?* " in the margin. If later material does not resolve your doubts, ask the professor.

Other marginal notes should also be made such as "disagrees with page 7," "seems biased in favor of. . . . ," "evidence appears weak." Making these notes is a part of the active reading process. The notes will also provide material for class discussions and facilitate reviews.

Underlining should be saved for identification purposes. One word, three words, or perhaps an entire sentence should be underlined to help you to understand exactly where you are. Underlining a name or a statement such as "my purpose is" will force these particular words into your consciousness, and clarify the material which follows it. For example, if you were reading a book about the Arab-Israeli conflict, and the author were expressing the positions of both sides, underline words such as *"The Jewish position"* or *"The Arabs' central argument."* Then they will stand out from the page, and you can readily understand exactly what is happening.One additional type of marking is used. If an author says "there are five factors influencing this situation," or "there are three points to be remembered," underline that statement, and place the numerals "1, 2, 3," in the margin at the proper places. You can then rapidly review the structure of his position instead of getting bogged down in the details. Incidentally, you will often find that you have placed more or less numbers than the author did. You may have written the numbers "1," "2," and "3" before he says "my third point is. . . ." The discrepancy between your marginal markings and his comments warns you that you are not following him, and you can then correct your misunderstanding.

After you have read the entire book or article, you will have a much better understanding of the author's purpose and approach, and your marginal markings should reflect this clearer understanding. Go through the material again and make the necessary changes. If a question has been answered or a doubt resolved, cross out the "?" or "*?*." If an idea which you thought was crucially significant appears to be somewhat less important, change "CS" to "VI."

In addition to underlining key words and marking symbols in the margin, fold down the corners of the pages which contain material marked "VI," "CS," or "Σ." When you review the book, the very first thing to do is to go to the folded pages to clarify the organization.

When you first try to apply this system or one based upon similar principles, you may feel rather uncomfortable; you do not know which symbols to mark, and it seems so much easier and more natural to underline or to use the same marking for everything. Your discomfort is a sign of how poorly you have been trained. Because you can not separate important and unimportant points, you feel uncomfortable with a system that forces you to make these distinctions. Since developing this ability will help you to pass examinations and is also much more important than your grades, I am especially emphatic in my recommendation that people who feel uncomfortable use this sort of system. In fact, the more uncomfortable you feel, the more you need a system like this. You need some form of discipline to help you to select and to organize the important ideas.

Library Books

A significant number of students underline library books, and a few even steal books or rip out pages. These practices are very inconsiderate—and quite unnecessary. I doubt very much that I can change anyone's morals, but showing how these actions are unnecessary may cut down on these practices, and it will certainly help other people to use the library more efficiently.

Far too many students do not use library books efficiently. They spend hours copying notes, usually in longhand, an incredibly wasteful practise. Why in the world should you spend precious hours trying to imitate a Xerox machine? If you spend one hour copying and making notes of an article that you can Xerox for 80 cents, you are working for 80 cents an hour. Is that all your time is worth?

There are, however, situations in which Xeroxing is too expensive. You obviously can not afford to Xerox an entire book, and it may *seem* cheaper to make notes than to do anything else. Frequently, it is more economical to buy a book than it is to make notes on it. If a book costs $6, and you spend six hours walking to the library, checking it out, and writing notes, you are working for $1 an hour, and you're not even getting that much *value* because your notes are not as good as the book. I therefore suggest that you buy most of the books that you need (particularly if you can get paperback editions or used copies).

If it is not economical to buy the book or to Xerox the pages you need, there is still a much better system than taking notes. Simply write down the page numbers and the place on the page where the important ideas occur. For example, if important ideas are on the top of page 41, the middle of page 52, and the bottom of page 56, just write down 41′, 52-, and 56,. If a book has two columns per page, note the column as "L" or "R." For example, an important idea in the middle of the right column on page 96 would be marked 96R - You can then review the book almost as rapidly as you could review notes, without investing so much time in note taking. Furthermore, if you use essentially the same system with these page numbers as you do with your own books, you can structure the book more effectively than you can by writing notes.

The underlining symbols provide you with a simple system for indicating the importance of various page numbers. A page number and place has about the same weight as the vertical line, and check marks, crosses, "VI," "CS," and " Σ " have exactly the same meaning. "1-5" means that five important points are listed. Purpose statements and marginal comments are simply marked next to the page numbers. Pages which would be folded if the book were your own are circled. You might also Xerox the circled pages to save trips to the library.

If you use this system and the underlining system on which it is based, you will dramatically reduce your note-taking and studying time, but improve both your understanding and your grades.

Mnemonics

Many students use mnemonic devices, but they usually do more harm than good. A formula, code, or poem may help you to remember a few details, but forcing material into an artificial structure will obscure its inherent logical structure. Since this logical structure is easier to retain and helps you to relate this material to the other things that you have learned, it is far better to concentrate on it and leave the mnemonics alone.

There is, however, one situation in which mnemonics are justified. Some professors, particularly ones with large lecture courses, insist that you memorize many terms and definitions. They are wasting your time, of course, but, since they have the power to insist that you learn these things, and since terms and definitions are rarely related logically to anything, you should use any form of organization, even an artificial one, to help you to satisfy the examination requirements. Once the examination is over, you will forget everything, but a professor who wastes your time with terms and definitions deserves to be forgotten.

The Ponies

Most professors, including this one, despise the ponies (outlines, study guides, plot descriptions, etc.). I wish students would read books and make their own interpretations. But we must be realistic. As long as the grading pressures are there, you have to respond to them, and the ponies do save a lot of time. Furthermore, there is really not that much difference between a pony and the average textbook: neither has any style or literary merit, and the ponies are often better organized and easier to use.

Since you will be required to take many courses and to read many books which do not interest you, you might as well use the ponies for those courses and save your time for the subjects in which you are really interested. That is, if all you want out of a course is a grade, you can get that grade more easily by using the ponies and ignoring the other readings.

In addition to saving time, using the ponies is actually an act of independence and maturity, a sign that you can make your own decision about what you will read and ignore.

On the other hand, if you use the ponies in courses that you like, you are cheating yourself and behaving immaturely. Grading pressures are dominating you so completely that you have lost control of your own life.

Reviewing for exams

If you use the system described earlier, reviewing for exams is easy. First look at the preface and table of contents and review the folded or circled pages to get an overview; then look at all the pages and ideas which are marked; then review again but drop out the material which does not have at least a check mark, then review again and drop out the crosses; then drop out the "VI's." This way you will spend more time on the more important ideas and move progressively from the structure to the details and then back to the structure. Then, when you take the examination, the entire structure will be clear in your mind and the details will fit in easily.

In addition to concentrating on organization, your review should concentrate on the material you do *not* know. Most students understand the principle, but do not apply it very well. They may devote more time to the subjects or books which they do not understand clearly, but they still waste a lot of time reviewing material that they already know. They read their books from start to finish and spend about as much time on each page or chapter whether they understand it or not. Since it is much more efficient to spend your time on material you do not understand, you should *check-off* the material which does not require further study. The simplest way to do this is to mark "o.k." next to all material which you understand well enough. Then, on your next review, you can skip that material, or scan it quickly. Your time will therefore be invested in studying the material you do not understand.

This reviewing should be done *immediately* before you take the examination. Lots of people say that the most important thing to do is to get a good night's sleep, but their advice is only half true. Mental alertness does help, but the research on learning and forgetting clearly indicates that people forget things very rapidly. In fact, much of what you read is forgotten within a few *minutes.* You can therefore dramatically improve your examination grades by the simple expedient of a "last-minute review." The LMR should cover *only* the summaries, and the points which are marked "CS" and "VI," and it should occur at the *last* possible minute. If the exam begins at 9 o'clock, at 8:59 you should be working on this last-minute review. If you review during those last few minutes, you will probably get a higher grade than if you did the same amount of work two hours before the exam, and a much better grade than if you reviewed the evening before. Since the same time investment pays higher dividends, you should always make an LMR.

FEEDBACK LOOPS

The suggestions for increasing your active involvement were based on the principle that people learn best by doing things and then getting feedback on their performance. Here we shall discuss other ways to get feedback. Ideally, your professors would provide usable feedback, but most professors give you little more than grades—which do not help very much. Since the system does not provide you with the feedback you need, you must create your own feedback loops.

Fortunately, it is rather easy to make arrangements with your professors and classmates to get feedback. Most professors like their subjects and enjoy helping students to learn them. In fact, most of our satisfaction as teachers comes from the few students who are genuinely interested in learning. Therefore, if you approach us properly, you will find that we are eager to give you useful feedback. However, you will get it only if we feel that you are really interested in learning rather than in getting certain grades. Most students do not give us that impression; they begin conversations by asking why they received a certain grade, which immediately puts us on the defensive. Instead of trying to help them to learn, we try to justify the grade or to end the conversation.

In addition in approaching us in a nonthreatening way, you should ask fairly specific questions, preferably in terms of alternatives. General questions often look like challenges, and feedback is more useful when it is specific. Don't ask: "What is wrong with this paper?" That question is too general, and it may give the impression that you are challenging the professor or the grade. Say: "I thought of organizing the paper this way, but decided on that way. Which do you think would have been better?" "Why?" When you approach a professor that way, he realizes that you are not challenging him, nor are you asking him to write the paper. He also realizes that you have done some thinking about it. He may say that neither approach is proper, but he will respect your inquiry and try to help you.

A more organized approach is to use special footnotes ("a, b, c,. . . ." rather than "1, 2, 3,. . . .") which refer to questions about writing. For example, if you were unsure that a particular example was appropriate, give the example and place a footnote after it. The footnote would be a question: "Do you think this example is appropriate?" If you explain to the professor what you are trying to do and get his agreement to answer such questions, they can dramatically improve your writing. Some professors will refuse to give you the time, of course, but a surprising number will agree if they think you are seriously trying to learn.

If you have to write a long paper, you should get feedback on the outline and general approach. There is not much sense in working on the details if the basic idea and approach are inadequate. Furthermore, when the paper is in outline form, its purpose and organization can be seen more easily. If they are not clear, it is best to clarify them before you start on the details.

Professors are certainly not the only source of feedback, nor are they suitable for all purposes. They can give you feedback *after* an exam, paper, or outline has been submitted, but you often need feedback beforehand. This type of feedback should come from your classmates. Before you type up the final draft of any paper, have someone read it critically. Ask him for *specific* criticisms and suggestions for improvements. Virtually every professor and professional author asks his colleagues for this sort of feedback. These criticisms will improve the paper itself, help you to understand the subject, and improve your writing.

The same principle holds true before examinations. Most of your studying should be done independently, but a day or two before the exam you can work with someone else. The lowest-level form of mutual study is to have one person recite while the other checks his understanding against the textbook. This type of activity involves two important learning principles, *active recall* and *feedback*, but it is not nearly so efficient as a discussion of the purpose and organization of the material you have read. It is much better to leave mindless regurgitation to the drones and to try to explain the purpose and organization to each other. You will then be concentrating on the essentials and both parties will use active recall and receive feedback.[11]

WRITING PAPERS

The ability to write clearly and well is the *most* valuable thing that you can learn in college, far more important than any course you will ever take, but many students do not realize its importance. They complain when professors criticize their writing and say: "I don't need to know how to write. I'm going to be a doctor, engineer, lawyer, or business-

---

[11]Mutual study sessions often degenerate into guessing games about the examination. Since you probably cannot out-guess the professor, you will get a better return on the time you invest by focusing on the material itself.

man. My secretary can do the writing; I'll have the ideas, and that is what counts." This reasoning is ridiculous. Ideas rarely accomplish anything until they are communicated. If you can not communicate them, they will never have any impact on anyone. Your ideas may be brilliant, but, if you don't learn how to communicate them,[12] you are going to be another "forgotten genius," sitting in a corner, talking to yourself.

Furthermore, if you can't communicate your ideas to someone else, you do not understand them yourself. You may say: "I understand this, but I just can't put it into words," but language and thought are inseparable, and your inability to put your ideas into words indicates that you do not understand them. If you doubt that assertion, try to think of any complex idea without using some language.[13]

This relationship between language and thought is the primary reason that professors assign papers. We do not expect you to discover anything new; we just hope that the discipline of writing will help you to learn more about the subject.[14] The same reasoning causes us to give low grades for papers or examination essays with lots of ideas but poor writing. We feel that poor writing is a sign of poor thinking.

Since writing well is an indispensable part of learning which will also have an immense impact on your grades and entire career, *you are a fool not to work on your writing.*

The following discussion will show you how to improve your writing. Instead of discussing the usual grammatical topics, it outlines a *procedure* for writing papers, a method which will automatically improve your writing.

Creation Versus Criticism

A good paper needs both creativity and critical thinking, but they interfere with each other.[15] Critical thinking inhibits the free flow of

[12]Obviously, communications can be spoken as well as written. The ability to speak clearly is therefore the second most valuable skill you can develop.
[13]Mathematics, music, and other art forms are also languages.
[14]A few professors also hope to develop your ability to write well.
[15]Some people feel that they do not interfere with each other, but the evidence on this point is quite clear. Brainstorming and other techniques in which critical thinking is suspended cause great increases in the number and quality of proposed ideas.

ideas, and the creative mood can override legitimate critical objections. Since they are both necessary, but mutually inhibitory, you should work on one at a time. First you write down a lot of ideas without worrying very much about how well they are stated or whether they fit together. Then you organize, revise, and polish this raw material to form a finished work. As you move from topic to topic or from first to second drafts, this phase sequence can be repeated several times, but the creative phase should always come first.

Many students do not separate their activities into phases, and their papers show it. Some hand in papers which are little more than a series of disorganized, poorly expressed ideas. Others are so critical that they cannot get started. When they do get started, they can't get enough ideas. Their papers are therefore late, narrow, and unoriginal.

It is not easy to separate these two activities. Doing so violates some of your most basic attitudes and habits. It is especially hard to suspend your critical judgment because all of us are inhibited. We don't like to let our minds run free. But you can overcome your inhibitions by "free associating." Just write down[16] whatever crosses your mind, no matter how silly or irrelevant it seems. Your mind does *not* wander randomly; there is a method in its madness and a reason for every thought that enters it. If you just let it go, and follow it wherever it goes, you will be astonished at the originality and creativity that you have buried inside of you. You will also end up with far more ideas than you need and solve that terrible problem of getting started.

When you feel that you have enough ideas, and they seem to be falling into a pattern, you can become critical. Review *everything* you have written, decide upon your *exact* purpose, and construct a *skeleton* outline. This skeleton outline should indicate simply the interrelationships between the ideas you intend to express. You just want an overview of your purpose and organization.

Then slip back into a creative phase by writing a *rapid* first draft. This draft should follow the skeleton outline, but little attention should be paid to the niceties of grammar, phrasing, etc. The purpose here

---

[16]Shorthand is extremely valuable here because it is faster and easier. Dictaphones or tape recorders are even better because talking is so much faster and more natural.

is simply to put some meat on the skeleton. Do not devote too much attention to polishing any one paragraph or section because, when you revise the paper, you may find that this section should be omitted or changed drastically.

Once you have written a rough draft, become as critical as possible about grammar, choice of words, etc. Shorthand is also valuable here because it reduces the amount of investment that you have in any one sentence or paragraph; because it did not take so long to write it, you do not mind revising it, and you can do so quickly. The revision process will go more smoothly if you write or type all of your drafts double or triple spaced. You will then have enough room to insert other words, new sentences, etc. If you do not have enough space for some revisions, simply mark "Insert A, B . . ." at the proper place and use a separate sheet of paper. Virtually all professional writers use this system, and it will not confuse any good typist.

After the first draft has been extensively revised, you must make a decision. If it looks good enough and is not extremely important, you can simply get the paper into the proper form for the typist or final reader.[17] However, if it is an extremely important paper (such as a thesis or research report), it is probably best to put the material aside for a week, and then come back and revise it again. You will become more objective and see many flaws that can more easily be corrected.

Obviously, examination questions can not be revised so extensively, but the creative and critical phases can still be somewhat separated, and the basic approach should still be the same. Briefly free-associate, preferably as soon as you get the examination (but be selective in what you write down). Then, as you are working on other questions, write down any other related ideas that cross your mind. When you finally have to write the actual answer, your raw material will be all ready and it will be much more complete than it would be if you had waited until the last minute. Scan the raw material and free-associate as you do so. Make a skeleton outline, and then write your answer, double spaced. Even if you have to write less than you want, leave some time for revision. A minute or two's revision can

---

[17]If you have written it in shorthand and do not type very well, the fastest thing to do is dictate it while she types it.

mean 10, 20, or even 30 points on essay examinations. You will see omissions, illogical statements, contradictions, etc., that can easily be corrected.[18]

You may feel that this system, with its emphasis upon organization and revision, will take too much time, especially for essay examinations, but I assure you that it does not. In fact, because the critical and creative attitudes inhibit each other, it is much faster and more efficient than any other system for writing *organized,* well-written essays. Obviously, it is not so fast as scrawling out a series of loosely related ideas, but such a paper is not an acceptable essay. Now that we have outlined the basic procedure, let us look at three elements of good writing: purpose, organization, and grammar.

Purpose

The single most important part of any essay is its purpose. *Everything* should be subordinate to that purpose; if an idea, a paragraph, a sentence, or even a word does not contribute to that purpose, it does not belong there.

Because everything is subordinate to purpose, the first thing you must do in your first critical phase is to decide *exactly* what you intend to do. Then you must communicate this purpose to your reader in the clearest, most explicit way, preferably by saying: "My purpose is. . . ." In your later revisions, you should constantly ask: Does this idea, paragraph, sentence, or example, contribute to my purpose? If not, drop it.

Far too many students do not follow that rule. Their essays become rambling discourses about the world in general. They try to impress the professor with their knowledge or the amount of energy they have spent writing the paper, but nearly all professors mark *down* for irrelevant remarks. We want to know your purpose and the way you try to achieve it, and padding confuses and irritates us. Later audiences (such as your bosses) will have even more damaging reactions: they will simply ignore your memos and reports.

---

[18]Techniques for answering essay questions will be discussed more completely in a moment.

Organization

A paper's second most important characteristic is its organization. An essay is not a list of ideas; it is an organized statement with a beginning, a middle, and an end, and your reader should always know where he is. Furthermore, all of your ideas are not equally important; some are subordinate to others, and you must clearly communicate that subordination and the overall logical structure of your position.

The most common reason for failing to communicate this structure is that the writer does not know it himself. Since he is not sure of the way his ideas fit together, he can not communicate their logical structure to anyone else. Many students do not want to confront their own confusion; doing so would make them uncomfortable. They therefore refuse to take the obvious step of writing a preliminary outline. Instead of using an outline to expose and to reduce their confusion, they try to cover it up with a pile of words. Unfortunately, instead of covering their confusion, they simply pass it on to the reader.

Since organization is so crucially important, I urge you to make an outline for everything you write, even examination essays. Without one you are almost certain to wander, and readers are not willing to wander with you.

SUBTITLES   Once you have a clear organization in your own mind, you must *explicitly* communicate it to your reader. Let him know where you are and where you are going. The best way to do this is to use weighted subtitles. The reader can then understand the overall structure and the way each idea fits. Most books and articles use different kinds of print for different weights, and you should use a similar system. For even greater clarity you can use the typical outline headings such as Roman numerals, capital letters, regular numerals, and small letters. If you use the subtitles in all of your papers, they will be easier to write and much easier to read.

EXAMINATIONS   In examination essays the subtitles should be less elaborate, but they should still be used to mark off the major divisions of the paper. The more clearly the reader can understand your organization, the easier it is for him to follow you, and the more he will like your paper.

BASIC FORM   You should also use the basic expository form whenever possible. This form is based upon the simple principle that people can follow your argument most easily if you start with an overview, then give them the detailed statement, then pull the threads together in a final summary. This principle applies not only to the paper as a whole, but to every major division within the paper. Each major idea should be stated simply, then discussed in detail, and then summarized.

THE 2, 1, 3, RULE   On highly polished papers this same general principle is even applied to paragraphs and to sentences. Many writers use the "2, 1, 3 rule." They know that people remember most clearly the last thing they have read, then the first thing, and then that great undifferentiated mass in the middle. They therefore put the most important ideas at the end of a sentence or paragraph, the second most important at the beginning, and the least important in the middle. If you open almost any book on your shelf, you will find that the great majority of chapters, subsections, and perhaps even paragraphs are written in that general way. Obviously, you can not apply this rule on essay examinations, but it can improve your writing dramatically on papers which you have time to polish.

Grammar and Spelling

When most students think of good writing, they think of grammar and spelling. A well-written paper is one with few grammatical errors or misspelled words. This misconception is, I think, an indication of how poor a job we have done at teaching you to write. Grammar and spelling are simply the *minimal* elements of writing, which should be so automatic to you that they need not be discussed.

Good grammar and spelling do not necessarily help you to communicate; they simply prevent you from making a fool of yourself. If you misspell words and make grammatical errors, you will create a very negative impression, but good grammar and spelling have less impact upon your ability to communicate your ideas. Therefore relatively little time should be devoted to them at first; they should be virtually ignored until the final draft. That is, since earlier drafts and revisions are concerned with the essentials, you should not let confusion about spelling or grammar interfere with your basic task. Later, when you have the ideas clearly expressed, you can polish the paper to get rid of the rough spots.

Summary

Writing a paper or answering an essay question involves many of the principles of learning that we have already discussed. It is an active process; the emphasis is upon purpose and organization; your paper can be read, reviewed, and criticized, which provides feedback. Note, however, that these principles of learning are most closely applied when you follow the system outlined above. If you simply write down everything that comes into your mind, you are doing little more than passive regurgitation. But, if you express the ideas, abstract a central principle or purpose, organize it, draft an answer, and then critically revise it, you will understand the logical structure of your own paper and provide your own feedback. This approach to writing therefore increases your knowledge, dramatically improves your grades, and develops your most important skills.

Writing has been discussed at some length because it is more important than anything else you will ever learn. It is important in itself, because it helps you to build your grades, and because it helps you to learn and to think clearly. *If you do not learn how to write, you will probably never learn how to think.*

TAKING EXAMINATIONS

No matter how well you have prepared, the proper examination technique can increase your grades. Time is at a premium and must be used wisely. Everyone feels these time pressures, but most students do not make an intelligent response to them. They simply pick up the examination and start answering questions. They act like the motorist who does not know where he is going, but keeps the gas pedal on the floor. He may not go in the right direction, but he makes excellent time. Since the goal is not to exert the maximum effort, but to get the best possible grade, you can not afford to rush blindly. The following suggestions will help you to improve your grades by using your time more effectively.

The Instructions

Countless points are lost by failure to read the instructions carefully. Students leave out questions, or answer the wrong ones, or provide irrelevant information. You should therefore *read the instructions* very *carefully and underline the key words.*

How many questions must you answer? Which questions? *Exactly* what are you supposed to do for each question? The minute or two it takes to answer these questions can increase your grade substantially.

Multiple-choice Questions

Most students carelessly invest their time on multiple-choice examinations. Some do not finish because they spend too much time on the hard questions, and not many students have a system for taking advantage of the associations between questions.

You can improve your grade by going through the examination rapidly and answering all the easy questions. If you do not know an answer, simply place a check mark (✓) in the margin and *keep moving.* Later questions may help you to remember the answer, and you can not afford to spend so much time on the hard questions that you omit or rush through the easy ones. If an answer to an earlier question should come to you, go back to it immediately because it could easily slip your mind again.

After you have answered all the easy questions, start again on the checked ones. If you are now sure that you know the answer, mark it down and cross out the check mark. If you are not sure, don't spend too much time on it. Put down the best answer you can,[19] but leave the check mark alone and move on to the questions which offer better

[19]Unless the professor subtracts severely for wrong answers, you should never leave a question blank. Even if he subtracts one-fourth or one-fifth of a point for wrong answers to discourage guessing, you should still answer virtually every question because you can usually eliminate one or two alternatives.

possibilities. If you have time, you can come back later, but you must always invest your time in the questions which offer the best possibilities, and you must take maximum advantage of the associations between questions.

After you have tried all of the checked questions, review the entire examination. The associations between questions will help you to recognize incorrect answers, and reviewing may suggest answers for the questions which are still checked.

If you have any time left after the review, get back to work on the checked questions. The rest of your work is done, so your time can most profitably be spent on the answers which are most likely to be incorrect.

Essay Questions

No matter how you do it, make sure that you answer all the questions. Far too many students work so long on one or two questions that they do not complete their examinations. Doing so is extremely costly because they gain one or two points for their excellent answers and lose 5, 10, or 20 points for the ones they omit. Two half-answers will nearly always get more points than one complete answer.

Four simple rules can help you to answer all the questions. First, scan the entire examination before answering any questions. See how many questions there are, the points allotted to each, and jot down free-associations. Then decide on a tentative budget. The time allotted to each question or part of the examination should be roughly proportional to its points. If one essay is worth 10 points, and another is worth 20, approximately twice as much time should be spent on the 20-point question.

Second, you should devote somewhat less time than their points would indicate to easy questions and somewhat more time to the hard ones. The additional investment in the hard questions will provide more points. You will get a rather good grade on the easy questions anyway, and the points gained on the hard questions will more than compensate for the few that are lost on the easy ones. Many students follow exactly the opposite principle. They spend most of the time on the easier questions because they feel more comfortable and because they hope to write at least one excellent answer. They pick up one or two additional points on easy questions, but lose five or ten times that many on the hard ones.

Third, avoid unnecessary details. This point has already been considered in the discussion of writing papers, but it is especially important on examinations. Unnecessary details and overly long answers *do not* get higher grades; in fact, by confusing and irritating the reader, they often result in lower grades on that answer, and the time you spend on them also costs you points on the other questions.

Fourth, if you should get behind schedule, write *complete* outline answers, instead of incomplete detailed essays. A complete outline shows the examiner that you understand the major points while a detailed beginning tells him very little except that you have organized neither your time nor your thoughts.

RECALL AND ORGANIZATION   The same logic that suggests that the review should occur at the last possible minute suggests that immediately after reading the instructions you should scan all the essay questions, and write down the major points. You will then reduce the amount you forget between the review and answering the questions. In fact, if you have done a last-minute review and begin your exam this way, there is a lapse of only a few minutes between the time that you read your notes and the time you write them down again. You will therefore have virtually all of the important points written down before you have a chance to forget them.

On the other hand, if you answer the questions one at a time, you will have a much longer delay between review and examination, and the answers to your other questions will interfere with your recall. The evidence is clear that the longer the delay between reading and recall and the greater the amount of material between them, the greater the amount of forgetting.

This procedure also increases the amount of time you have to answer the questions. You will have the entire examination period to remember the answers instead of the few minutes you spend on each question. The other questions will also remind you of additional points which you can easily write down.

This system also separates the "creative"[20] from the critical phase.

[20]In examinations the "creative" phase is usually more concerned with recall than creation, but the same general principles apply.

Your ideas will come more easily; you will have more of them; and you can organize them into a good answer.

CHOICE QUESTIONS   Usually, because one of the questions is easier for you, the choice presents no problem. When your preliminary scanning suggests that you are equally prepared for two or more questions, the best thing to do is to free-associate briefly about each one of them, then turn your attention to the rest of the exam.

As you work on the other questions, write down any ideas which are related to the choice questions. When you have to make your decision, you will probably find that you have more ideas and can give a better answer to one of the questions.

IMAGE AND SUBSTANCE   Marshall McLuhan has undeservedly received credit for an idea that the Gestalt psychologists proposed over 50 years ago:[21] people do not absorb information bit by bit and then add it up to decide what it means; they get a total impression *immediately* and interpret later information to fit this impression.

You can therefore increase your grades by a few simple steps which create the right impression. An organized introduction and clear structure for essay questions obviously help; they show that you know where you are going and help the reader to follow you. But details such as grammar, spelling, and even penmanship can add to that impression. If your paper *looks* good and reads easily, the examiner will grade it somewhat higher.

Many students argue that professors should ignore writing, grammar, spelling, and punctuation and concentrate only on the reported facts. Perhaps we should, but we can't. We are human, and all humans are influenced by essentially irrelevant details, whether they like it or not. For example, you dislike some people for reasons which have nothing to do with their basic character—such as pimples, dirty fingernails, or an irritating voice. Since details *inevitably* contribute to the examiner's impression and grade, you should write clearly and be careful about spelling, punctuation, etc.[22]

---

[21]McLuhan did, however, make an original contribution by relating this idea to the impact of different media.

[22]You should therefore never leave early. A review will undoubtedly improve your paper, and, if you have time after your review, do it again.

Panic

A few people panic during examinations. They know the answers, but are so anxious that they can not remember or write them down clearly. This anxiety indicates rather severe problems which tranquilizers or alcohol will not solve. However, your immediate need is to survive. Failing your examinations will harm your future and aggravate your problems; you should therefore take a tranquilizer immediately before examinations. Tranquilizers are better than alcohol because they calm you without having much effect on mental efficiency, while alcohol tends to put you to sleep.[23]

---

[23]Since neither tranquilizers nor alcohol will solve your problems, and since dependence on either will create even more serious problems, anyone who panics on examinations should seek professional help.

MISCELLANEOUS ISSUES

In the preceding chapters we have discussed several issues at some length. Here we shall briefly touch a few other issues.

PARENTS

One of the most important and difficult tasks of your college years is developing a new relationship with your parents. You both know that your relationship must change, but neither of you knows how to make the necessary changes. Your parents vacillate between overcontrolling and rejection. One minute they treat you like a child, then, when you insist upon being independent, they completely abdicate their responsibilities and say "go ahead you damned fool, but don't cry on my shoulder when it's over." You vacillate between dependence and counterdependence; sometimes you reject everything they stand for, and do so in the most insulting possible way and sometimes you depend abjectly on their financial or psychological strength.

Some of this vacillation is unavoidable because no one can be completely rational about an emotional issue. Everyone is frightened by all of the alternatives and confused about his motives. You want greater freedom, but are afraid of it. Your parents are proud that you are growing up, but they want to keep you small and close to them.

While some vacillation and conflict is unavoidable, in many families there is nothing else. Instead of mutual, rational efforts to solve a common problem, each side vacillates between trying to force the other to accept its viewpoint, or giving up because the other "is hopeless." Parents use their checkbooks, moral authority, threats, and so on to dominate the children, and the children reject everything their parents say without seriously considering it. In their obsession with "winning," or their despair when victory seems impossible, both sides forget that they are stuck with each other, and must therefore work out a *mutually* satisfactory arrangement.

Since you are stuck with each other, you might as well accept the fact and start working together on your common problems. "A Note to Parents" in the appendices contains several rules which could help your parents to get along better with you; you might find it useful to have your parents read it.

However, they are not the only ones who must work to improve your relationship, nor do all of these suggestions refer only to them. They should try to understand you; they should avoid lecturing; they should show respect and let you make your own mistakes. *But so should you.* Far too many children feel that the entire burden of improving the relationship rests on the parents, and they communicate the same arrogance and disrespect to their parents that their parents communicate to them. They tell their parents what the "real truth" is about America, criticize their values, lecture to them about morality and politics, and treat them with general contempt. This behavior is, of course, often stimulated by similar behavior from the parents, but whatever its causes, it creates defensiveness and closed minds rather than mutual respect and tolerance.

Since ways to improve personal relationships have been discussed in many other chapters, there is no need for a long list of rules for getting along with your parents; you should simply realize that the basic rule for getting along with them is exactly the same as the rule for getting along with other people: *people act toward others the way that others act toward them.* If you fight, they will fight. If you listen to them, they will listen to you. If you communicate arrogance, they will return it—with interest. If you show them respect, they will show you respect. So, if you want to work out a new and more adult relationship with your parents, *give them the same respect, tolerance, and understanding that you demand for yourself.*

FRATERNITIES AND SORORITIES

Fraternities and sororities are perhaps the most overrated and over-criticized campus organizations. To some people they are absolutely essential, the only place in which one can find genuine friendship and warmth on our alienated, impersonal, campuses. Adherents also claim that they fulfill a vital educational role by helping students to develop social skills, etc. Critics often regard them as an unmitigated evil, a breeding ground for superficial, reactionary, conformist, racist thinking. The truth is, of course, somewhere between these two extremes.

Such organizations do offer some very substantial benefits, including social support at a difficult time, a chance for close personal relationships, a place to go for dates, training in social graces, and, perhaps, an introduction to valuable people after you graduate. These benefits can be quite worthwhile, but they are not so overwhelmingly important as many people think they are, and they often come at a fairly high price.

Fraternities and sororities generally do require a greater degree of conformity than less formal organizations.[1] There is also the problem of snobbishness and perhaps racism, although many fraternities are much more truly integrated than other campus organizations.[2] Belonging to a fraternity or sorority will also somewhat limit your circle of friends. You will be expected to associate primarily with members of your own and closely related organizations. You may

[1]However, they require much less conformity than most political organizations, particularly revolutionary ones, and the revolutionaries are their most strident critics.
[2]A brother is a brother, regardless of the color of his skin, and he is accepted at all types of activities.

therefore live in a rather homogeneous social environment. This homogeneity may make you feel more comfortable and secure, but it can interfere with your education.

Because so much has been written both pro and con about fraternities and sororities, I see little value in discussing these issues further, but I would like to make one point. As everyone knows, there is a status hierarchy among fraternities and sororities. Some of them have "the best" students, while the others must settle for "the left-overs." This status hierarchy is, I think, one of their most objectionable features. It causes people to choose friends not on the basis of common interests and values, but in the hope of increasing their own status. Since you have the rest of your life to worry about status struggles, I urge you to minimize status as a factor in your decision. Whether you rush or not, concentrate on finding people whose company you enjoy.

FOREIGN TRAVEL

Foreign travel can make an enormous contribution to your education, particularly if you live abroad for an extensive period. A three-week guided tour through six countries may be a lot of fun, but it can't do very much for you. You will just walk around with a bunch of Americans and see some pretty sights. The real educational value comes from living in a foreign country.

I have spent about three years abroad, and they have been my most valuable educational experience. They have given me a perspective which I could not have gotten any other way. I dislike police brutality, but after nine months in Spain, where the police routinely carry submachine guns, where cars are routinely stopped and searched, where criticizing the government is a felony, and where suspects are pistol-whipped, I know that charges that America is a Police State are utter nonsense.

After seeing the Catholics and Protestants beat each other up in Ireland, living with the Flemish-Walloon conflicts in Belgium, and talking to Scottish Nationalists and Communist revolutionaries, I know that America's racial problems are far from unique, that they are a natural by-product of man's need to hate someone, and that this need is so basic that none of our social policies will eliminate racial hatreds.[3]

After seeing the way that European professionals must submit to petty tyrannies, I knew how lucky we are to be able to change jobs. After waiting months to get a telephone in Belgium and wasting fruitless days trying to get a work permit from the German bureaucratic labyrinth, I realized how extraordinarily efficient America really is.

But the experience which had the most impact on me did not involve revolutionaries, professionals, or bureaucratics; it was a simple walk at night on which I suddenly realized that I was not afraid. Years in American cities had made fear into a natural part of my life, as inescapable as my glasses and graying hair. I kept a watchdog, never walked alone at night, and automatically avoided dark streets. But, after seeing unescorted ladies walk casually along dark streets in London, Madrid, and Brussels, I slowly stopped being afraid and realized that fear is not a natural part of urban life, that some terrible flaws in American character and society have caused an unpredecented level of violence and a passive acceptance of an intolerable situation.

Any of these understandings could come from reading, of course, but the knowledge would not be the same, nor would it have the same impact. You have to live it to believe it. You have to walk down the streets by yourself at night and realize, almost in amazement, that you have forgotten to be afraid, that months of living in a nonviolent society have finally overcome the fear that Americans regard as natural. You have to realize how precious American freedoms are by living with people who don't have them. Then you can come to terms with this great big beautiful, ugly, wealthy, poor, violent, charitable country of ours. You will understand both its strength and its weaknesses, and this understanding will protect you from adolescent excesses of enthusiasm and depression. You will never again be so sure that America is right—or wrong—and you will learn to love this country as it really is.

Therefore, if you have to borrow the money, work your way across, join a junior-year-abroad program, or whatever, *go and stay as long as you can.*

---

[3]These policies will correct some intolerable social abuses, but I doubt that they will substantially change the way blacks and whites feel about each other.

MONEY

Enough has been written about the principles and values of budgeting to make an extended discussion unnecessary, but I would like to make one rather neglected point. It may seem foolish and irrelevant to you now because you have so little money, but I suggest that you try to develop the habit of saving money, even if you have to do without certain things.

The actual amount saved is almost irrelevant, but the habit itself is extremely important. If you don't develop that habit soon, you may be a slave to money for the rest of your life. Lots of people now earn the sort of money that you dream about—25, 40, even 80 thousand dollars per year—but must struggle constantly to earn even more because they spend more than they earn. They live on an eternal treadmill, constantly trying to increase their incomes, but no increase is enough to cover their spending habits. They are therefore as dominated by money as you are now. Since freedom is more important than goods, you should develop the saving habit.

THE DRAFT

The draft laws change much too rapidly and randomly to give detailed advice, but a few general principles may help you. The following comments refer to conditions in effect when this book goes to press; before taking any action you should make sure that the laws have not changed.

Appeals

Almost any action taken by a draft board can be appealed, and appeals can use up enough time to allow you to finish certain programs. Furthermore, this crazy war can't go on forever, and the longer you stay out of service, the better your chances of avoiding actual combat duty.

There are three levels of routine appeal (local board, state board, and state director); you can also appeal to the National Director, your congressmen, the President, and, most important, the courts. These appeals can use up *at least* 4 months, and, if the bureaucratic and judicial machinery grinds slowly, they can use up years.

You normally have 30 days to file an appeal of any actions, and hearings on your appeal can take as much as two to three months to schedule. Therefore, if you are classified 1A, wait 29 days before filing your appeal. It will take them a minimum of a week or two to hear your appeal and to make a decision. It is more likely to take a month or more. If the decision of the local board is unfavorable, you have another 30 days to appeal to the state board. Wait 29 days, then file your appeal. State boards are even less efficient than local boards, and it may take them months to schedule a hearing. They can not draft you during either of these 30 day periods or while you have an appeal pending to the state or local boards.

Once the first two levels of appeal are exhausted, you are draftable, but you can still appeal to the state director. Your chances here are very limited.

If you are willing to spend the money, and have a reasonably good chance of deferment, appeal to the courts. Normally, your lawyer can get an injunction against your being drafted while the appeal is being considered. Since American courts are notoriously slow, it may take them *years* to make a final decision.

Note that the above recommendations refer to appeals of your *classification*, not to the decision to draft you. It is far better to fight over the classification than over the actual call-up. Once you have officially received your notice to report for induction, the game changes drastically. You become liable to severe criminal penalties if you do not report, and the courts are much harsher on people who resist the draft than on those who object to their draft classifications.[4]

Medical Examination

You can request a medical examination while you are in *any* classification, and if the results indicate that you are physically unfit for service, your classification will be changed. It does not, however, do you much good to have the army doctors examine you if you have no reason to expect that you will get a medical deferment. The draft physical is one of America's sloppiest and least competent medical examinations. The

---

[4]They also tend to act more rapidly on cases involving refusal to be inducted.

doctors know that their job is primarily to pass you, not to conduct a thorough or objective physical examination. Therefore, if you are trying to avoid the draft, you must get a very thorough physical examination from your own physician,[5] and then make the results of this examination known to the official doctors. If your private examination indicates that you have some medical condition which should result in deferment, the official doctors have no choice; they must examine you on this specific point.

If you get a thorough physical from a clinic which specializes in physical examinations, you may well find that you have some condition which justifies a deferment. For example, there are at least one million unknown diabetics in the United States. The routine blood test conducted by the army doctors will not disclose a minor diabetic tendency, but a glucose tolerance test will show it clearly. Once your physician indicates that your glucose tolerance test is positive, the army doctors must conduct their own tests. If these tests are positive, they must defer you.

Millions of people suffer from allergies, some of which are severe enough to cause deferment, but the army doctors will not find them without your help. A thorough X-ray examination of your entire body, particularly your spinal column, may reveal some problem that justifies deferment—such as a shallow hip socket or misaligned vertebrae.

This sort of physical examination can be quite expensive, but, if you are firmly set on avoiding the draft, it may provide you with a legal way to do so. And, if you are a secret diabetic, or have some equally serious problem, it can save your life.

The ROTC and the National Guard

If your primary consideration is completing your education rather than completely avoiding the draft, both the ROTC and the National Guard can solve your problem. The price is high, but they will allow you to finish your education. One warning is essential: if you join either organization, but fail to attend meetings, you may be drafted immediately.

---

[5]Most private doctors do not have the facilities to conduct a truly adequate examination; you should go to a large hospital.

The Wild Schemes

The above suggestions are just the beginning. Several books have been written about draft avoidance, but conditions change too rapidly to recommend any one of them, and many of them contain ideas which are almost insane. You can avoid the draft by making homosexual overtures toward an enlisting officer, wetting your bed, masturbating openly, and so on, but these actions and your psychiatric rejection or discharge will stick with you for the rest of your life. Therefore, if you do not have a legitimate reason for avoiding military service, you will be far better off to accept it. It will be an unpleasant and wasted period, but you probably will not see combat, and, when your service is over, you can resume normal life.

Enlisting

Some people have such a negative image of draftees and the army that they enlist in one of the other services to avoid the draft.[6] Since there is very little difference between the services, I think enlistments are very foolish. The army, navy, Marine Corps, and Air Force spend millions on creating distinct images, but they are about as different as a Chesterfield and a Lucky Strike. So ignore the propaganda and take the shortest possible period of enlistment.

Many other students enlist because they hope to get a special school or assignment. Since military schools are trade-oriented, they have almost no value for college graduates. Therefore, if you intend to get a degree or already have one, you will be paying a high price for worthless training. However, if you do not expect to finish your degree, military schools can be quite valuable, particularly in technical fields such as electronics.

Even if you want a particular school or assignment, enlistment is probably *not* the best strategy. You would give up one or more additional years of your life without knowing what military life is all about. It is much more reasonable to defer your decision until after you have been drafted and found out what military life is like. Then, if you enjoy it, or feel that an additional year or two is a reasonable invest-

[6]I did it—and it was the stupidest thing I ever did.

ment for a particular school or assignment, you can "ship over" (change from a short to a longer period of service). You will normally receive *greater* inducements for shipping over than you would for enlisting directly: they will give you the school or assignment you want, plus, perhaps, some form of cash settlement.

THE BUREAUCRATS

Academic bureaucrats are among the world's most incompetent, obnoxious people. Registrars, admissions directors, business managers, and most other administrators work in academia because they do not have enough talent or ambition to get into private industry. They don't get paid much money, but they don't have to work very hard or to use much intelligence.

They also enjoy the power they have over students. In the academic pecking order, students are below the janitors, and academic bureaucrats enjoy treating their mental superiors as if they were incompetent children. The secretaries and other low-level personnel are especially obnoxious. Most of them couldn't get through college themselves, but they lord it over the students.

These people can make your life miserable, but only if you let them. They do have a great deal of power, but you are far from powerless, and for your own pride you can not let them dominate you too completely. Because they have real power and you have better things to do with your time, you can not afford to fight them indiscriminantly, but you can win an occasional fight if you remember two simple principles.

1. Professors hate them even more than you do, and we are not powerless. You only have to put up with their incompetence and arrogance for 4 years; we are stuck with them for life, and we will usually take your side against them.
2. Most of them are gutless; they will back down if you fight hard enough, even if they are right. Like all bullies, they really don't want to fight.

So make trouble—but only when the issue involved is important. If you need a transcript to get into graduate school, and the secretary refuses to mail it until after the deadline, threaten her. Tell her that if the transcript is not mailed immediately, you intend to appeal to her boss, your professors, and the editor of the school paper.[7] She will sputter and insist that you should have gotten your request in three months earlier, but she will probably yield. If you are dropped because your grades are slightly below the minimal level, don't waste time with the secretaries, go directly to a professor or dean, preferably one with whom you have some sort of relationship. Even if the rules state that you must be dropped, a professor or dean can have that decision reversed. If you can't get into some class because it is overenrolled, go directly to the professor. He will probably not be too sympathetic because he doesn't want too many students, but, if you can make a reasonable case, he might accept you.

In other words, when the bureaucrats make the decision by the only means they understand—by the rigid application of ridiculous regulations—appeal directly to the professors. Because we care more about education than regulations, we will usually consider each issue on its merits, and, if your case is justified, we will not hesitate to break the rules.[8]

DROPPING OUT

Many students get discouraged, bored, irritated, or just plain "down" and think of dropping out. Some actually decide to withdraw, but many simply ignore their studies and let nature take its course. If they are smart or lucky, they may get a degree without much work, but most students who neglect their studies are flunked out.[9]

Flunking out has much more serious consequences than voluntarily withdrawing. You usually will not be allowed to return to the

[7]The letter to the editor of the school paper is perhaps the most powerful weapon of all. No bureaucrat wants public criticism.

[8]Professors' willingness to break bureaucratic regulations has been deplored by Jacques Barzun, an ex-academic who has become a superbureaucrat. In *The American University* he constantly complains about professors' willingness to subordinate administrative convenience to academic principles. I suggest that you read this book because it shows how insanely rigid the system is, and the ways that professors and students work together against the bureaucrats.

[9]"The majority of students leave college for non-academic reasons. Furthermore, even those drop-outs with college records ascribed to 'academic failure' undoubtedly include many cases in which the underlying problems are psychological, parental, social, or financial. In such cases 'academic failure' may serve the student as a device for leaving school when the problem seems insoluble within college walls." John Summerskill, "Dropouts from College," in Nevitt Sanford (ed.), *College and Character*. New York: Wiley, 1964, p. 190.

same program, and you may not be able to start again in any good school. You will have the failure on your record and waste the time between your psychological withdrawal and the school's decision.

Therefore, if you are so down, uninterested, irritated, or confused that you can't keep up with your studies, have the courage and maturity to make an explicit decision instead of leaving it to the system. Drop out, and do something better with your time, preferably something which helps you to understand what you really want. Then, if you want to continue your education later, you can easily get started again.[10]

Now that we have considered a wide range of issues related to campus life (including the possibility of leaving it), let us move on to the two major decisions about life after college: graduate school and job-hunting.

[10]If you do drop out, make sure that you notify the school and go through all of the required procedures. Otherwise, you may get "F's" for several courses, and these grades can have serious long-term consequences.

GRADUATE SCHOOL

Graduate school is "the sacred cow in
American education."[1]

An astonishing number of students now go on to do graduate work.
Americans, with their penchant for statistics, view this as a healthy
development. We announce to the world, with customary modesty,
"Look how many of our people are getting Master's and Doctor's
degrees."

While some of this increase in graduate enrollment is useful both
to individuals and our society, I think we should recognize that much of
it comes from the inadequacy of the educational system, particularly
the lowered standards for the Bachelor's degree. Bachelor's work is so
easy, and we have awarded so many Bachelors' degrees that it is rapidly
assuming the position held 20 or 30 years ago by the high-school diploma. It signifies a certain minimum competence to potential employers, and gives the holder the right to *begin* professional training.[2]

[1]President Keppel of the Carnegie Corporation, cited by Bernard Berelson,
Graduate Education in the United States. New York: McGraw-Hill, 1960, p. 40.
[2]The most damning evidence of the inadequacy of our undergraduate programs
is that many *graduate* schools now require, and many others should require, that their

260

Economic and population pressures have also contributed to the growth of graduate schools. Because of the vast increase in college enrollments and the insane insistence that all college teachers have the Ph.D., graduate programs have been expanded—and cheapened. It is now *much* easier to get a Ph.D. than it was only ten years ago; departments accept more students; requirements are lower; and financial support is more plentiful.

In addition to needing many Ph.Ds to teach tomorrow's students, the universities need thousands of graduate assistants to teach the increasing number of undergraduate students and to work on research projects. In many large universities more than half of the lower-division courses are taught primarily by graduate students, and most research is done by graduate assistants (although professors take the credit for it).

Graduate school has also become a convenient place for continuing the process of avoiding life which is so much a part of undergraduate programs. If the student doesn't know what he wants to do, and he has reasonably good grades, he can find some graduate school to accept him.

While I deplore this waste of educational resources, I do not blame it on the students. We adults—professors, businessmen, legislators, etc.—have failed to create a system which legitimizes young people's attempts to find themselves, thereby forcing them to try to find themselves in roles and institutions which do not help them very much.

It would be far better for both students and institutions if young people could get the help and support they need to work on these problems instead of facing the intense pressures of graduate studies. In other words, if you hope graduate school will help you to find yourself, you are probably looking in the wrong place.

What, then, can graduate school do for you? And what are the costs? A brief chapter certainly can not answer those questions, but I shall give you some information about the benefits, costs, and kind of life you can expect as a graduate student, make a few suggestions

---

students take a test in basic English literacy. The students who fail that test must take a course in basic grammar and composition. If schools which take only the higher-ranking college graduates must teach a high-school subject, where do we get the nerve to brag about our educational system?

which may help you to cope with certain problems, and provide some references for further study.[3] Before making your decision, you should certainly read some other books.

SHOULD YOU GO?

This entire chapter, by describing graduate students' lives, opportunities and pressures, should help you to answer that question, but a few issues will be discussed or outlined here.

Quality

The best evidence about the quality of any service is the reaction of its consumers, and the reactions to graduate training are overwhelmingly favorable. Of the people who *finished* their Ph.D. training, 88% indicated that they were very satisfied with their training;[4] 90% said that they would do it again, and only 3% said that they would not. Three-fourths would take the same programs, and two-thirds would go to the same institution. This level of satisfaction would be unusually high for any service, but it is astonishing for one which takes several years of very hard work. Employers were even more satisfied. Virtually all of the employers of new Ph.D.s were satisfied with these people's professional training.[5]

New Ph.Ds also indicated that they had better training at the graduate level than at either the high-school or college levels.[6] American graduate training is also regarded as superior or very superior to European and Russian graduate training, even by people who regard our undergraduate programs as markedly inferior. From my own limited experience I would certainly agree with that position. I don't

---

[3]The best and most comprehensive book is by Bernard Berelson *(op. cit.)* Its bibliography includes most of the good work done before 1958. Unfortunately, it focuses almost entirely on programs which lead to the Ph.D. My limited experience causes me to lean in the same direction. Students who are interested in different types of programs can get information and bibliographies from professional associations such as the AMA or the American Institute of Chemical Engineers.

[4]I am sure that the reactions of the people who did not finish would be much less favorable.

[5]Berelson, *op. cit.*, p. 210.

[6]*Ibid.*, p. 210.

think an American Bachelor's degree can compare with a European Bachelor's or Licence, but the quality of our graduate training seems far superior to me, particularly in the sciences and social sciences.[7] I do not have any systematic evidence on the quality or satisfaction with our professional programs, but European doctors and lawyers have told me that American training is superior. We Americans may not be much good at providing a liberal education, but we are the best at providing specialized training.

Benefits

A graduate degree increases your income, opens many doors, and raises your status, particularly if you earn the right to be called "Doctor." Money and status are powerful rewards, but I think that the opened doors and the greater opportunities to choose and to act independently are at least equally important.

Some of these opportunities are the natural, legitimate result of your demonstrated competence in some area, but many of them come from people's childlike belief that someone with lots of initials after his name is a man who does good work. For example, some of you would not have read this book if I were not a Ph.D. The book would have been as good or as bad, as valuable or as useless, if I did not have a title, but the title helps to sell books.

Other sets of initials—M.B.A., L.L.B., C.P.A., M.S.W., and so on —have similar effects upon the general public. A person with a law degree has a much better chance of getting an important position, even if his legal training is essentially irrelevant. In fact, the alumni rosters of most law schools show that many graduates are not practicing lawyers; they are executives, investment counselors, independent businessmen, and so on. They may work in a wide variety of jobs, none of which have much to do with law, but they all let the right people know that they have legal training, and, much more important, a law degree, and a world which can not separate' substance from image says: "You're just the sort of man we want."

Therefore, if you get a graduate degree in almost any field—even

[7]In fact, in the social sciences graduate *training* is virtually nonexistent; a student is just placed on his own and told to write a dissertation.

English or Art History—you increase your chances of getting a good job, in that or almost any other field.

Chances for Completion

While the quality and benefits of graduate training are clear, many of the people who start graduate and professional programs do not enjoy them either because they flunk or drop out. Medical schools have the lowest attrition rates (about 10%), partly because they are so selective. Law schools lose about 40% of the people who start, most of whom leave by the end of the first year. Ph.D. programs have an average attrition rate of 40%, and many people drop out after investing several years. These attrition rates and the costs of dropping out should be considered very seriously when you make your decision.

The Master's Degree

Many students who want some of the benefits of graduate training, but who do not want to make a large commitment, decide to enter a Master's degree program. In a few professional fields such as business, social work, education, and (to a lesser extent) engineering, the Master's is a valuable degree, but in most fields it does *not* make much difference in job opportunities or salaries.

> The major distinction [employers] make in their employing policy is between the Masters and the Doctors, not between the Masters and Bachelors.[8]

If you intend to work in a field in which the doctorate is offered, a Master's degree is probably a waste of time and money, especially if you plan to go on for the doctorate.[9] The Master's degree has little intrinsic or market value, takes a great deal of time, and generally does not help you to get a doctorate. In fact, the Master's has been so down-graded that many schools use it as a "flunk-out degree," which is semiautomatically given to students who can not make it to the Ph.D.

[8]Berelson, *op. cit.*, p. 186.
[9]This rule does not hold true for teaching, social work, business, and engineering. In these and other *professional* fields a Master's degree does have some value.

We give it away because we are much less selective than the good professional schools are. When we realize a student can not do Ph.D.-level work, we have to drop him, but we don't want to send him back to the cold, cruel world with nothing to show for his efforts; so we slap a Master's degree in his left hand, shake his right hand, and kick him out the door.[10]

Although the Master's is a going-away present from many top schools, you usually must work for it in schools which do not offer the Ph.D. Some fourth-rate schools require a year and a half or two years' of hard work for a Master's. Since that same time could be devoted toward getting a Ph.D. and students with Master's degrees normally start from scratch in Ph.D. programs, I advise you to avoid Masters' programs unless your record is so poor that you can not get into a doctoral program.

Full-time versus Part-time

About half of the graduate students in the United States are studying part-time.[11] Part-time students usually live very difficult lives, and many of them do not get their degrees. They work days, go to class nights, study weekends, and have little time or energy for their families. If they are lucky, they earn their Master's degrees after 3 or 5 years, and perhaps a Doctor's in 7 to 10 years, but many of them never make it. The strain is too great for them and their families, and they drop out, usually after investing a substantial amount of time.

Because it is such a miserable life, and because part-time study greatly reduces your chances of finishing your work, I generally advise against it. There are enough fellowships, assistantships, and sources for loans that very few people *must* work.

Furthermore, in terms of return on investment, you will be thousands of dollars ahead if you borrow money and get your degree more rapidly. Your greater earning capacity will more than compensate for your lost income and the interest you must pay on a loan.

---

[10]Some devious students have beaten us at our own game. They have picked up cheap Masters' degrees this way, often from excellent schools. They enter the Ph.D. program, flunk out, and get a Master's as a going-away present! The next time you see a Master's degree from a top school on somebody's wall, don't be so impressed.

[11]Berelson, *op. cit.*, p. 129.

If you are unwilling or unable to study full-time, I suggest that you seriously consider not going. The chances are excellent that you will live a miserable life for months or years, but never get your degree.

If you really can't afford to go full-time now, save your money and go later. It is much better to start late, but make it, than it is to discourage and to exhaust yourself trying to work full-time and to study on the side.

A One-way Street

Before you decide to commit yourself, you should realize that doing so may change your ambition and habits so much that it becomes *psychologically necessary* to complete your graduate work. Graduate schools inculcate a set of habits and values which help you to fit into a particular profession, but, if you should flunk or drop out, these same values and habits can prevent you from being comfortable in other careers.

All over America there are young people whose graduate studies were interrupted, but who have been unable to adjust themselves to that harsh reality. They start again in lower-level schools, study nights at fourth-rate (and perhaps unaccredited) law schools, or try to revise hopeless doctoral dissertations because so much of themselves and their self-respect is committed to earning a set of initials and entering a particular profession.

Many of these people were not that committed when they began graduate school. In fact, some of them went because they had nothing better to do. But graduate school can be so seductive that a student who flunked out because he never really cared can suddenly realize how much it means to him to become a doctor, professor, or lawyer.

Because work loads are so heavy and the other students are so intelligent, indifferent students often flunk or drop out, and they would have been much better off if they had never begun. Therefore, if you do not feel fairly certain that you want to go on to graduate school, *don't go.* Take a year or two off; work or travel; and decide what you want to do—free of the pressures and seduction of the graduate school culture. Don't worry! When you decide what you want to do, the schools will still be accepting students.

Married Men

If you are married, your decision can be particularly difficult, especially if you have children and have worked for a few years. Your present job or future prospects may seem unsatisfying, but you also feel responsible for your family and reluctant to face the insecurity and discomfort of graduate student life. You may also have the same confusion as single men about yourself and your ambitions, and graduate school is an even less satisfactory escape for you than it is for them.

Because each individual case is different, I can not say whether you should go or not, but I do advise you to make an *early decision.* Many men procrastinate: they talk about going, write away for endless catalogues, start savings programs, but never have the nerve to make a firm decision in either direction. Some of them are simply indecisive, but a few use graduate school as a fantasy escape: every time their work or life gets them down they can retreat into this fantasy of a new and better life. Regardless of your reasons for delaying, the longer you wait, the less chance you have of going: your family responsibilities will become greater, and you and your family will become more accustomed and more dependent upon having money, comfort, and security. Therefore, *if you are going, go!* If you are not going, stop thinking about it, and start concentrating on other, more productive things.[12]

Wives

If your husband wants to go to graduate school, but is reluctant to deprive you of comfort and security, I suggest that you encourage him to go. You may be in for a few rough years, but that is much better than a lifetime of being blamed for frustrating his ambitions. He may feel that your reluctance is justified, especially if you have children, but he is almost certain to resent you. We live in a success-conscious

[12]There is some inconsistency between this advice and the earlier comment that it is better to start late than to go part time, but I think that most people who say that they can not afford it are rationalizing to avoid making a full commitment. That is, unless you have unusually heavy family responsibilities or debts, you probably can afford it, but are unwilling to commit yourself, and, if you are not willing to commit yourself, forget it. Graduate school is tough enough for committed students. For indifferent ones it's impossible.

society, and the wife who interferes with her husband's ambitions may pay for it forever. Thousands of women get nagged *eternally* for preventing their husbands from going to school, taking a different job, or starting a new business.

Furthermore, married graduate students live a much more pleasant life than married undergraduates. *Most* graduate students are married, and "of those married, over half had children when they started and almost 3/4 when they finished."[13]

The large number of married students and the presence of children has caused many important changes in graduate students' lives. Dependency allowances, for example, are now a common part of most fellowships. Student housing is now provided by many universities. Students wives often form clubs and other types of social organizations. The married graduate student therefore has a much more pleasant, more socially integrated life than the married undergraduate.

You will not have much money, of course, but neither will your friends, and many of the things you think are so precious are primarily status symbols. Since graduate students do not have any money, they do not compete for materialistic status symbols, and hundreds of couples have found that they can live quite comfortably with inexpensive furniture, an old car, and cheap clothes. In fact, if they are lucky enough to find a congenial group of married students, these years can be the warmest, most honest, and most pleasant of their entire married life.

I certainly do not mean to belittle the economic and time pressures and their possible effects upon your marriage; in fact, you should read the earlier comments on student marriage. But these pressures are probably not so serious as the long-term implications of frustrating your husband's ambitions.

CHOOSING A SCHOOL

Although the general approach to choosing a graduate school is quite similar to that of finding the right undergraduate school, there are

[13]Berelson, *op. cit.*, p. 189. The percentages may be somewhat lower for professional schools, but the general principle is still the same.

some very substantial differences between this decision and the choice of an undergraduate program. The following discussion emphasizes the differences between the prestigious and nonprestigious schools because this dimension is much more important than any other. After you have decided upon the level, you can start working on the other dimensions.

First, the school you attend has much more impact upon your career. Many people from unknown undergraduate schools become prominent, but many professions are so status-conscious and inbred that a degree from a prestige institution is a virtual requirement for the best jobs. For example, no matter how good you are, without a prestige degree you probably can not join a top law firm, or teach in a major university, or practice in a major hospital. Furthermore, people who just barely made it through the top schools trade on their degrees forever. I know several young, semibright businessmen whose only real asset is an M.B.A. from Harvard, but that is all they need.

Second, resources such as libraries, laboratories, and research funds are so much more important at this level that small schools usually can not provide quality training.

Third, the difference between the pressures of the prestigious and nonprestigious schools is even greater than at the undergraduate level. Because the prestige schools have a virtual monopoly on the best jobs, they can get away with anything they want, and students must choose between passive submission and dropping out.

Fourth, at the top schools competitive pressures can be incredibly severe. Only the best students get in, and some of them can't make it through. For example, the mean undergraduate grade point average of my group at Berkeley was about 3.5; more than half of the students had straight A averages in their major field (psychology); and the average Graduate Record Exam ranking was about the 98th percentile. Despite the quality of this group, only about half were able to finish the program. Similar situations exist at virtually all the top schools, making competitive pressures unbelievably severe.

Fifth, top schools support a much higher percentage of their students. Financial problems can keep you out of the lower-level schools, but if you are good enough to get into the top schools, they will probably support you.

To summarize, the benefits of going to a top school are enormous, but they demand a high price in sweat and anxiety. The people who make it through are well rewarded and satisfied. The ones who drop out are often bitter, and many keep trying to compensate for their failure. In other words, going to a top school is a high-stakes risk.

Getting Information

If you want to go to a top school, it is fairly easy to get good information about its real quality and character. The American Council on Education has published several studies of specific departments and graduate schools in general. Many professional associations have done the same. These studies are available at any good university library.

These reports provide an overall assessment of the quality of a program, but little or no information about its specific nature. For specifics you should read some of the professors' publications.[14] The professors' interests are the *primary* determinent of graduate programs; graduate professors teach what they like, not what you want or what is described in the brochures. You should therefore read until you find ideas you would enjoy working on and then go to the men who wrote them.

Although publications are the best guide to the *content* of the program, its character—the way students get treated, the life they lead, the jobs they get, and so on—can best be learned by interviewing recent graduates. If you can't contact one, you may get some information from almost any member of that field who teaches in a top school. Within each field the top schools form a sort of small town in which everybody knows everything about everybody.[15] Professors are extremely clannish and mobile; we know more about the men in our field who work three thousand miles away than we know about a man from another field who works in the next building; we are constantly

[14]For lower-level schools, this information is generally not available because the professors do not publish.

[15]This small town includes only the top ten or twenty schools. For lower-level schools you must use other sources.

meeting each other at lectures, seminars, colloquia, and conventions, and each visit includes a little gossiping session.

While this gossip often includes petty topics such as feuds and politics, it also contains really important information such as personnel transfers and changes in graduate programs. This information is nearly always known to the profession long before it appears in systematic investigations such as the ACE studies, and much of it never gets published.

GETTING ACCEPTED

Unless your record is poor or very distinguished, the decision on your application is based almost entirely upon political and subjective factors. Except at the extremes, grades and admission tests have little or no value in predicting graduate-school success: the correlations between them and grades are small or nonexistent, primarily because the intellectual differences between graduate students are so small. Therefore, if you satisfy the minimum intellectual requirements, the decision will be based upon their estimation of your motivation, sincerity, integrity, and character. Since they will not have any objective information about these qualities, the decision will really depend upon politics and gamesmanship.

The Application

When you fill out that application, remember—they already know your grades and test scores. The application is supposed to give them other information, and this other information is communicated partly by your style. So, be neat. If necessary, have someone type the forms. I know it is nonsense, but you wouldn't wear a dirty shirt to an interview, and a sloppy application makes the same impression.

Even more important than neatness is writing style. Selection committees won't remember everything you say, but they will get an impression of you from the way that you say it. In fact, professors are more interested in your ability to communicate effectively than they are in your preparation in your major field! They know they can teach you their discipline, but they are sick of students who can't write clearly. "The sentiment is strongly against more undergraduate work in one's field."[16]

> Over and over . . . I was told that graduate students today simply can not express themselves with clarity, accuracy, and economy, to say nothing of grace or style.[17]

So let them know that you can communicate effectively! The best way to do this is to answer the essay questions with *well-written*, carefully polished essays. Draft them, revise them, and then copy them onto the application.[18]

Two other brief tips about preparing the application (1) graduate school professors look down their noses at "mere" practitioners; therefore always say that your career objectives are "teaching and research," and never, never, never say that you intend to be a practitioner. (2) If a school offers the Ph.D., either directly or after the Master's, *never* indicate on your application that you intend to stop at the Master's because they will automatically reject you.

Recommendations

Countless investigations have demonstrated that letters of recommendation have little or no objective value as selection devices, but they are weighted heavily by selection committees. Selection committees look for two things in a letter of recommendation, the name, background, and reputation of the man writing it, and his opinion of the student.

Professors are so clannish and provincial that unless the reference is very prestigious, we will almost automatically give more weight to a letter from a known colleague, a graduate of our own institution, or a member of our discipline than to one from a stranger. And we normally ignore letters from nonacademics (lawyers, businessmen, etc.) and holders of educational degrees.[19] It therefore pays to make the acquaintance of at least one professor who is either very presti-

---

[16]Berelson, *op. cit.*, p. 141.
[17]*Ibid.*, p. 140.
[18]You should also mention any writing courses or writing experience that you have had.
[19]In academia, Ed.D. $\neq$ Ph.D.

gious or a graduate of the *department* you wish to enter. Letters from department chairmen are also weighted more heavily, and, because historians ignore physicists and vice versa, get most of your recommendations from members of your discipline.

While your references' background and prestige are weighted heavily, we pay even more attention to their opinions and knowledge about you. *Most* letters of recommendation are ignored because they don't say anything:

> John Jones was a student in my history 1A class and received an A. His work was satisfactory in all respects.

A letter like that, even from a prominent professor, is much less valuable than one—from *any* professor—which indicates that he knows and respects you *as a person*. Remember, they already have your grades. The recommendations are supposed to cover other things, such as your motivation, self-discipline, and writing ability.

Graduate School

An unusual, time-consuming and relatively unknown approach can improve your choice of a graduate school and your chances of acceptance. It is based upon a simple principle: selection committees defer to members of their departments. If any member of a department wants you, your chances are excellent; if a powerful professor wants you, you are in. You must therefore find the way to get the support of at least one member of the department, preferably a powerful one. That support is very easy to get if you remember one rule: the way to a professor's heart is through his research.

If you carefully analyze one or more professors' research, find aspects of it on which you would like to work, and communicate your interst to the professors, they will probably support your application. Nearly all professors are constantly looking for disciples, and they will exert strenuous efforts to bring a potential disciple into their department—if they think he is serious.

You must therefore do more than simply say: "I think your research is great, and I would like to work with you." That will impress a few professors, but most of us are a little smarter than that. You must show us that you have done some real thinking, and that you are prepared to do some real work. The best way to create this impression is to raise some *scholarly* or *scientific* questions or objections about our research, and indicate that you would be interested in working on these questions. The following letter is a bit too general, but it illustrates this principle.

> Dear Professor Jones,
>
>   Your articles on the Russian revolution have interested me greatly, particularly your analysis of Trotsky's personality and motivations. I have read some of the other analyses, including the article by Professor Smith, but believe that your position is much more consistent with the evidence.
>
>   However, as Professor Smith has noted, the evidence about Trotsky's economic policies appears to be inconsistent with your position. I think that a further analysis of the man's actions and correspondence immediately after the revolution might resolve this seeming inconsistency.
>
>   I am applying to your department and wonder whether I could work on this problem under your supervision.
>
> Sincerely,
Charles Thomas

At its worst, this approach can be pure gamesmanship, a cynical manipulation of the professor's vanity. At its best, this analysis and correspondence with individual professors can get you started on a career of scholarship and research. Instead of walking blindly into an institution because you like its general reputation, location, or tuition fees, you can make an intelligent choice based upon the most important information: the nature of the research being conducted at that institution. Analyzing professors' research and corresponding directly with them can therefore help you to clarify your interests, to select the right school, and to get into it.

GRADUATE VERSUS PROFESSIONAL SCHOOL

After distinguishing between graduate and professional schools at several points, it seems appropriate to discuss this distinction more systematically. The basic difference is that professional schools train practitioners—people who intend to work in a profession, such as law, medicine, optometry, and engineering, while graduate schools basically train college teachers and researchers.

Many people argue that this distinction is artificial for several reasons: first, college teaching is a profession, which is not essentially different from other professions. This point is obviously correct, but we do our best to ignore it because it offends our delicate academic sensibilities. We like to think that we are not "mere" practitioners. Second, many professional subjects and specialties are taught in academic departments (e.g., public administration and clinical psychology).

> If such programs are accepted as essentially professional in character though not in label, then not many more than half the doctorates conferred in 1957–1958 were academic.[20]

Third, many people with academic degrees now teach in business, engineering, medical, and other professional schools. Fourth, the Ph.D. is now offered in professional fields such as business and engineering.

While these points are all valid, they indicate that the distinction is becoming blurred, not that it has been obliterated. In the next few pages I shall try to clarify some of the differences between the two types.

Value of the Degree

Until fairly recently there was an enormous gap between the incomes of Ph.D.s and graduates of professional schools. Physicians, dentists, lawyers, and other professionals made twice as much as professors. Professionals still make more money, but the difference has narrowed, and a significant number of Ph.D.s now make huge incomes (over $50,000).[21]

Several factors have increased Ph.D.s' incomes. First, because industry wants us, we are no longer forced to go to universities, and,

[20]Berelson, *op. cit.*, p. 83.
[21]Unfortunately, the following remarks refer primarily to professors at universities and good colleges. Professors in unknown schools (who often do not have the Ph.D.) make much less, an average of less than $10,000 per year.

if we do go into industry we can insist upon industrial-level salaries.[22] At the same time that industry has been taking away potential teachers, rapidly increasing college enrollments has dramatically increased the demand for them. The law of supply and demand has changed professors from helpless petitioners for raises and tenure into aggressive bargainers.[23]

We are also able to supplement our incomes. Not too long ago professors sold shoes and drove trucks during the summer; one of my professors, a distinguished scholar and author of several books, had to work as a guard at Monmouth Park race track. But those days are gone forever, at least at the good schools. Summer support for teaching or research is an almost standard part of most contracts now.

In addition to getting paid decent salaries for the entire year, many professors, particularly in business, engineering, the sciences, and the social sciences, act as consultants to industry and government. A few professors' consulting incomes are actually greater than their salaries.

Therefore, if you would like to go on for a Ph.D., but are afraid of starving, stop worrying. You won't make as much as a good lawyer or physician, but you will have a comfortable income.

On noneconomic dimensions the picture is unclear. Most professionals and professors enjoy their work, and there are no reliable data about which group is more satisfied.

Professors may have a slightly higher status, and they do have more free time and control over their own activities, but they usually work as long hours as professionals.

Professionals generally have more opportunities to do something which is visibly useful; they can have a greater, or at least a more *visible* impact on the world. Professors get a lot of satisfaction from talking to former students or looking at our books, but once in a while most of us think: "Wouldn't it be wonderful to deliver a baby or to build a bridge!"

Both professionals and professors can change places, but it is

[22]Industrial competition has even raised salaries for professors in fields for which there is no industrial demand because universities dislike having excessively large differentials between fields.

[23]Our bargaining position has been weakened recently by the universities' financial problems and a decline in the demand for Ph.D.s, but this decline is temporary (I hope).

much easier for professionals. A lawyer, physician, or dentist can easily become a professor; in fact, many have to fight off invitations, but professors in some fields could not work outside academia.

Since incomes and status are not too dissimilar, you should probably minimize money and status and base your decision upon the subjects and activities you enjoy. If you enjoy studying a subject—whether it is law, medicine, or archeology—study it. Since you can make a good living in any field, you might as well enjoy your speciality.

However, there should be some similarity between the field you study and your basic temperament. A relatively passive thinker who likes to study law can become a law professor, but an activist who enjoys English has a real problem; you can't do very much with an English degree. Therefore, if you are an activist, if you prefer doing to thinking, if full-time research and teaching sound dull to you, pick a program with at least some professional elements (e.g., journalism rather than English, political science rather than history, or chemical engineering rather than chemistry).

Time Till Degree

The time from the Bachelor's to the Ph.D. is much greater (about 8 years) than the time from the Bachelors to an M.D. (4 years) or an L.L.B. (3 years). However, the time spent on full-time study is about the same. Ph.D.s take longer because the students may decide to go on for graduate work much later, often after they have worked for a few years, and because so many of them work part-time while they do their theses. Increased financial support and greater pressures to complete the thesis and other requirements appear to be reducing the time spent on the Ph.D.

Costs

Professional schools are much more expensive. Tuition is as high or higher, and they offer relatively few scholarships, fellowships, or part-time jobs. Graduate schools are much more generous: "Almost all doctoral students get some form of support."[24] This support consists

[24] *Ibid.*, p. 148.

of scholarships and fellowships, which provide tax-free income and require no work, and assistantships, most of which include both a salary and a tuition grant. The difference between the relative costs is more clearly revealed by the fact that many professional students go deeply into debt while graduate students indicated that "since they first began graduate study (except for those just starting), their financial situation has changed for the better for 45% and for the worse for only 21%."[25]

The more scientific a field, the more research support it gets, and the more research assistantships it can provide. Research assistantships are generally more desirable than teaching assistantships because one learns more, and some students even get paid to work on their own theses.[26] The most desirable support is, of course, the fellowships, and they are much more common in the sciences.

Chances for Acceptance

About 50% of the people who apply to medical school get accepted, compared to almost 100% in Ph.D. programs.[27] I have no data on law and other professional schools, but I suspect that they fall between these two extremes.

Nearly all applicants get into some Ph.D. programs because of the exploding need for college teachers, the utter necessity for research and teaching assistants,[28] and the bigger-equals-better mentality of most graduate faculties. Therefore, if you want to get a Ph.D., and have learned how to read and to write, you can probably get accepted some place.

Attrition Rates

Although it is much easier to *get into* Ph.D. programs, it is harder to *finish* them. Medical schools, which select students carefully, flunk out less than 10%, while graduate schools, which accept almost everyone,

---

[25]*Ibid.*, p. 149.
[26]This support is often a mixed blessing. The students get support, but must work on the professor's project.
[27]Berelson, *op. cit.*, p. 133 f.
[28]The system would break down immediately without them.

flunk out *40%*. Law schools also flunk out an average of 40% of their students, but the better law schools, which select their students more carefully, have lower attrition rates, and in all law schools "almost all the attrition . . . occurs in the first year, whereas in graduate school it comes later."[29]

In other words, the graduate schools are much more willing to waste your time than are law and medical schools. Professors need assistants to teach their classes and to do their research, and Ph.D. programs, with their emphasis upon independent study, allow poor students to hide for years. Therefore, if you get into medical school, you will almost certainly get an M.D. If you get into law school, you will either waste one year or get a law degree.[30] If you go to graduate school, you may invest, 2, 3, 4 or even more years and get almost nothing for it.

The Students

For decades people have debated whether professional or graduate students are more intelligent. The data from army intelligence tests indicate that there are no significant differences; both groups are very bright. Therefore, wherever you go, you can anticipate having stimulating companions and difficult competition.

Students in graduate school generally come from lower socioeconomic classes than medical or law students.[31] Financial support for Ph.D. students is probably the major cause, but discriminatory selection policies, particularly for medical schools, also play a role.

Graduate students generally decide to go on for graduate work much later than professional students. Professional students, particularly in medicine and law, usually make their decision early in their college careers, and some make it even before they enter college, while over 55% of the students who went on for the doctorate made their decisions *after* they had left college.[32] Graduate students

[29]Berelson, *op. cit.*, p. 168.

[30]I have no data for other professional schools, but I suspect that they flunk students early or let them finish because: (1) they don't need assistants and (2) programs are "tight" enough so that poor work is immediately obvious.

[31]Berelson, *op. cit.*, p. 134.

[32]*Ibid.*, p. 143. Berelson's data are over 10 years old; I suspect that recent graduates made their decisions sooner; the differences between graduate and professional students may therefore be somewhat smaller now.

are therefore older and are more likely to be married and to have children.

Freedom

Graduate programs offer you much greater freedom, both personal and intellectual. In nearly all professional programs, especially in medicine and law, curricula are extremely restricted. You must take courses a, b, c, d, and e in exactly the order and at exactly the time that they tell you to. Classes can take 15–25 hours per week; attendance is often required; professors require greater deference; teaching is more authoritarian. You will be regarded as a member of a class, and you and the rest of the class must move at the same pace and do the same things.

In graduate school the "class" idea is almost completely ignored. Each student has certain basic requirements, but within very broad limits he can decide when and how he completes them. Classes take only 6–10 hours a week; the rest of the time is for independent reading and research. Professors require deference, of course, but the student-faculty relationship is somewhat more colleagial. First names are fairly common; students are expected and trained to think independently; authority is used less frequently and more subtly.

In other words, a professional student is treated as a *student*, while a graduate student is treated more as a junior colleague.[33]

ADVANCED PREPARATION

Because the first year is very difficult, advance preparation can increase your chances for survival, especially if you plan to go to law school. All graduate students work hard, but law students, knowing that they may be dropped, *really* work—till 2:00, 3:00, and 4:00 in the morning. Even if you don't go to law school, preparation can mean the difference between survival and failure, and it will certainly make that first year less frantic and exhausting.

---

[33]However, this junior colleague status is often a veneer covering an exploitative relationship.

Many students try to prepare, but waste most of their time by not focusing their efforts. They read a few books, but these books may not be important *for their specific program.* It is far better to cover relevant gaps[34] in your undergraduate training or to read books you will need for your first-year courses or examinations. Most departments would be glad to provide a list.

Covering undergraduate gaps is particularly important for Ph.D. students, especially if they are weak in mathematics (including statistics) or foreign languages. In many subjects the student without a solid understanding of basic mathematics is in an almost hopeless position. The sciences and social sciences have become so mathematical that he can not understand what is happening. His professors and classmates talk a foreign language.

This problem is particularly acute in the social sciences because they are generally nonmathematical at the undergraduate level, but quite mathematical thereafter. Students enter psychology, sociology, and economics programs expecting to talk about superegos, social class differences, and the market system, but immediately encounter significance tests, reliability coefficients, and econometric models. Students with poor mathematics backgrounds must therefore do two things at the same time: learn the underlying mathematics and use it to work with these concepts. Some students can cope with this task, but many can not. There are no data on this point, but I feel fairly sure that poor mathematical preparation is the most common reason for flunking out.

Foreign languages are much less valuable today than mathematics (in most fields), but most graduate schools still require them. Students usually dislike studying them, and other demands seem more pressing. The net effect is that tens of thousands of students have had their degrees delayed and thousands have never gotten them. I therefore suggest that you take a cram course during the summer. It can take an enormous load off your back and save you *years* of nagging irritation and repeated examinations.

Any sort of advance preparation greatly increases your chances for survival and makes your life much easier and more pleasant. I can

[34]Relevant gaps are ones which affect your performance in the graduate program. Biochemistry would be relevant for a medical student, but not for a law student.

not exaggerate the stresses of that first year; the work load and competition are so tough that you may be overwhelmed, objectively or psychologically. I therefore guarantee that any time you invest in advance preparation will pay huge dividends in improved chances for survival, lowered anxiety, and increased time for sleep and recreation.

To Stay or Not To Stay

As we noted earlier, graduate schools do *not* flunk out many students in the first few semesters; they let them hang around for 2, 3, 5, or even 10 years without getting a degree. Thousands of students have spent more than five years in doctoral programs, but many will never get their degrees. They and their families live wretched lives, with long hours on low-paying jobs, repeated research proposals or thesis drafts, and occasional encouragement from their well-meaning but extremely inconsiderate professors. It would have been far more considerate to flunk these people out early so that they could begin other careers or start graduate work at lower-level institutions, but a misplaced delicacy and a lack of moral courage have caused many professors to avoid this decision. The net result is that both students' time and educational resources are unnecessarily wasted.

Since your professors may be unwilling to tell you that you have a limited potential in the field you have chosen, I suggest that you take a good, hard look at yourself at the end of your first academic year. Are you intelligent and disciplined enough to complete the program? Can you compete successfully in this profession? Even if your grades are good, even if you are clearly bright and disciplined enough to get the degree, look at your own motivation. Do you really like the sort of work your professors do? Does it excite you enough to want to do it for the rest of your life? If this analysis suggests that you do not have the ability or motivation to be a success in graduate school or the profession to which it leads, get out. It is a lot better to leave now than to waste your life on a graduate school or profession in which you cannot succeed or which you will not enjoy.

THE THESIS

Of all the stumbling blocks between you and a Master's or Ph.D. degree, the thesis is by far the greatest. Tens of thousands of students *never* finish their thesis, and hundreds of thousands of students have wasted countless years on them. A few general principles may help you to cut down the wasted time.[35]

Procrastination

The major reason for delay or failure to complete the thesis is certainly procrastination. Students can find literally thousand of reasons to keep from working on it. These excuses all *look* reasonable, but their primary purpose is to avoid the agony and risks of writing and presenting a thesis. It is so much easier to read another book, or to perform another statistical test, or to conduct another pilot study than it is to write the damned thing. But you will have lots of time later to read books and to do other things. In fact, once you get that degree, you can do almost anything you want. Because all professors know from their own experience how easy it is to procrastinate, our most common advice is simple and very direct: *sit down and do it.*

The Iron Law of Research

The second most common reason for delaying or failing to complete a thesis is ignorance of the Iron Law of Research: *everything takes more time and costs more money than you ever dreamed possible.* We haven't taught you that law because it can only be learned from experience, from the constant frustration of missing deadlines, of running over budgets, of having to do things two and three and five times because you didn't know exactly how to do them. Your professors may have tried to tell you this principle, but, nearly all graduate students ignore our advice.

They set out to write an *opus magnificus,* the final definitive work. The professors, who know how much time and money research really costs, try to tone them down, but most students won't listen to us fuddy-duddies. What do professors—old men whose time has passed —know about great research?

---

[35]One principle is so obvious that it should not have to be mentioned, but some students have suffered by ignoring it. Since a lost thesis or even a chapter is a tragedy, make an extra copy of *everything* and *keep it in a completely separate building* (buildings do burn down, and demonstrators or vandals have repeatedly destroyed years of work).

While I certainly do not want to kill your youthful enthusiasm, I do hope you restrict your thesis to a manageable topic. The thesis is not the end of your career as a researcher, but its *beginning*, the final stage of your apprenticeship in the research craft. An apprenticeship is by definition a time for *learning*, and, if you keep this learning goal paramount in your mind, you will realize that the most important thing is not that it be great—because it will probably not be great anyway[36]—but that you learn how to conduct research. And, unless you are much more intelligent than most of us, you will not learn very much unless you restrict yourself to a manageable topic. If you try to write that final definitive work, you may not complete it, and, even if you do complete it, you will probably learn less than you should.

You may struggle valiantly for years; you may have some brilliant ideas; you may even have a brilliant overall objective and outline, but you almost certainly will end up by dropping some parts of it or by dealing with them superficially. It is, then, far better to pick a topic which you can handle, to handle it well, and to learn the skills you need to write a really great paper after you have mastered the basic techniques of our craft.

Your Advisor

Perhaps the best thing about the American graduate-school system is the advisor-student relationship. While there are legitimate complaints about exploitation and lack of guidance, most American advisors will provide much more help than their European counterparts[37]—if they are approached properly. Your advisor will be most helpful to you, and most willing to be helpful if you ask him to criticize *what you have done.* If you drop your problems in his lap, he will ignore them; he is not willing to do your work for you. But, if you prepare an outline, he will criticize it. If you propose alternatives, he will help you to evaluate them. If you write drafts, he will comment upon them.

His comments and criticisms will be most helpful to you if you

---

[36]Most professors look occasionally at their own theses and wonder how they could have done such poor work. In fact, many of us would not accept such poor work from our own students.

[37]In Europe it is not at all unusual for the chairman of the research committee to have virtually no contact with the candidate before the final draft is submitted.

get him involved *early.* Unfortunately, many students are so afraid of their advisors, or so defensive about looking foolish, that they don't show their advisors anything until after they have made massive investments in it. Then, when their advisor tells them to delete some portion of their research, or to use a different approach, they feel that he is being unfair, a feeling which is often communicated.

Nearly all professors resent being put in this position. Our job is not to rubber-stamp what you have done simply because you have worked very hard; it is to teach you how to conduct research, and we think more of that responsibility than of your need to get a degree. As one professor told me when I complained that I had worked very hard: "Jackasses work very hard, but we don't give them Ph.D.s." Therefore, the all-too-common appeal that one has worked very hard, that he has covered several hundred pages with scribbling, that he has gathered data from several hundred different people, that his wife is sick of graduate student life, etc., fall on deaf ears. You will get your degree much sooner and learn much more if you get our criticisms and advice at every stage in your research. A 10-minute conversation with your advisor can keep you from spending a year wandering down a blind alley.[38]

THE SYSTEM

The preceding comments have focused primarily on the tasks facing you—deciding whether to go, choosing a school, getting accepted, writing a thesis, and so on. Now I shall try to give you a brief picture of some of the unpleasant aspects of the graduate-school system.

The First Semester Blues

After a few weeks of graduate school, many students think that they are not intelligent enough to continue, and some feel so stupid that they wonder how they got their Bachelor's degrees. They experience a graduate-school version of the "freshman jitters." The work seems

---

[38]In addition to its value for learning, frequent consultations with your advisor are also important politically. Even if what you are doing is good, if he doesn't like it, he may not approve it. So play the game; when you finish the thesis, you can do anything you damned please.

overwhelmingly difficult, and their classmates seem to be much more intelligent than they are.

These feelings are caused partly by the increased work load and improved competition; graduate work is hard, and the students are very bright. But these feelings are increased by the students' defensiveness, status-seeking, and gamesmanship. Nearly all the students are scared and confused, but, because they are afraid to admit it, many students put up a front by using jargon and citing authorities that they really do not understand. They *look* sophisticated and frighten other students, causing them to behave in the same way. These attempts to impress each other make students even more confused and frightened.

If, as most other graduate students, you start having doubts about your own ability, don't put up a front. Admit your own ignorance because it is *not* stupidity; in fact, awareness of your ignorance is the first step toward overcoming it. You do not know these terms and authorities, nor do you need to know them *now*. You were accepted because you have the brains to learn them, and, if you have the courage to admit your ignorance, you will make much better use of the time that other people waste trying to impress each other.

The Name of the Game

Fear is the name of the game, and the most important rule is: "Shut up and do as you are told." A graduate student is one of the most helpless creatures on this earth; he must do exactly as he is told because most graduate credits are not transferable, and his work is evaluated on a purely subjective basis. If a professor becomes irritated, either by a challenge to his authority, presentation of a theoretical position he does not like,[39] a refusal to do Mickey Mouse work or to act as an unpaid research assistant, an excessive amount of imagination or independence, or anything else—no matter how petty it is—he can hold up a student's degree.

Thousands of students in this country have not received their

[39]The situation in Europe is *much* worse. Many European professors require their students to sign a contract that they will not publish anything in their own names, and they bury any data which conflict with their own position. One of my Belgian associates even had his dissertation rejected because it stated the well-known fact that Belgian banks hide profits, and his professor was a part-time bank director.

degrees, and they may never receive them, because they have annoyed some professor. Tens of thousands of students have had their degrees delayed or have been required to do additional work to satisfy their professors' whims. An indeterminate, but very large, number are not "allowed to finish because they are needed as teaching assistants for the department or research assistants for the professors."[40]

Because they are so powerless, and because professors take advantage of their powerless position, "Fear is the dominant motif in the life of a graduate student."[41]

THE FEUDAL SYSTEM[42]   In many respects graduate school is a feudal system: the powerless student swears loyalty and obedience to a powerful professor in return for his protection against other powerful professors. The vassal works on the lord's research, does his dirty work, and, if she is a girl, she may even have to sleep with him.[43] In return, the lord fights off criticisms and challenges from other professors, allows the vassal to write up a portion of the lord's research as if it were his own, and arranges his first job.[44]

AN ENDURANCE CONTEST   More than anything else, graduate school is an endurance contest. You do not have to be exceptionally brilliant to get a graduate or professional degree, but you must have stamina, discipline, and the ability to keep your head down, to work like hell, and to do exactly what you are told. Of students who *finished*, 49% said that a major reason for dropping out was a lack of physical

[40]Berelson, *op. cit.*, p. 162. He also notes that 40% of the *graduate deans* agreed that "major professors often exploit doctoral candidates by keeping them as research assistants too long, by subordinating their interest to departmental or the professor's research programs."

[41]Analysis of graduate study in 61 departments of government. Paper written by five graduate students and presented at the 1969 meeting of The American Political Science Association. Quote is from *Newsweek* (Sept. 15, 1969, p. 42), which did not identify the authors.

[42]The term "feudal system" is from a mimeographed paper by Dr. Carl Rogers. Despite his prominence, *The American Psychologist* repeatedly refused to publish his analysis of graduate programs in psychology.

[43]Sexual exploitation is probably less frequent in academia than it is in other places, but I have heard of a few cases.

[44]Academic jobs are usually arranged by one's thesis advisor. Professors in professional schools do not act so directly, but they do determine who works in the best law firms and hospitals. Thousands of very talented men are working well below their levels because they did not get the right professors' support.

or emotional stamina[45] and one student spoke for thousands when he said: "The primary thing I learned in graduate school was how to work 70 hours a week."

OBSTACLE COURSE   In addition to working very hard, a graduate student must be able to jump over *all* the obstacles between him and the degree. Since all the obstacles must be cleared, and there is no bonus for exceptionally good work, the secret of success is to jump the obstacles by the barest possible margin so that energy is saved for the ones ahead. The smart graduate student knows better than to waste his time doing creative work. He recognizes that intrinsic satisfaction and creativity are not nearly so important as the ability to be consistently mediocre, to do exactly what is required.

The intrinsically motivated student who ignores his French, statistics, or other requirements because he enjoys working on his research is going to flunk out—no matter how brilliant or creative he is. For example, one of my group at Berkeley enjoyed his research, worked hard, and was obviously very good at it, but he fell over one of the obstacles, and was dragged off the course—*after publishing 25 articles.*

LACK OF IMAGINATION   Obviously, a lack of imagination is a decided asset. A man with any imagination would realize how ridiculous it is to study two languages he will never use, to write a review of the literature which shows all the understanding and style of a telephone directory, to memorize esoteric statistical formulas which any fool can look up in a book. But the unimaginative man doesn't know all this, nor is he troubled by being little more than a mindless robot responding to external pressures. He does as he is told, keeps his mouth shut and his professors happy, and gets his degree.

THE IDEAL STUDENT   If we looked critically at the system, and were concerned solely with maximizing survival potential, we would pick students who were moderately intelligent, extremely energetic, very disciplined, unimaginative, compulsive neurotics.[46]

---

[45]Berelson, *op. cit.*, p. 168.
[46]Fortunately, most graduate students do not fit that stereotype, but selection procedures and professorial pressures force many to conform to it.

Initiation Rites

Many of the rituals and requirements of graduate schools are essentially hazing, part of our initiation rites. Graduate schools, unlike most other schools, turn out people who are essentially equivalent to their teachers. When you finish, you will be one of us, a professor, lawyer, or physician, and we make you suffer a little bit to join us.

Fraternities, primitive tribes, and the U.S. Senate haze new members, but they admit it honestly. We are too dignified—or perhaps too dishonest—to tell you the truth, but many of the things you have to do (such as taking foreign languages exams or doing dirty work in clinics) are rationalized as important educational experiences. But they are really initiation rites, parts of the academic Bar Mitzvah.

Narrowness

Critics have always complained that graduate and professional programs are too narrow, but they are becoming narrower every day. The professors' narrowness is one casual factor, but the primary cause is the fantastic expansion of knowledge. Knowledge is growing so rapidly that a man simply can not master more than a tiny part of some field.

Many students are therefore bored by their graduate work. They had looked forward to stimulating intellectual activities and atmosphere, but find that they devote nearly all of their time to mastering a narrowly specialized literature and vocabulary. If the narrowness of your graduate training bores you, you should consider a different career. Graduate school is just the first stage in the narrowing process; if you finish it, you will be forced to become *much* more specialized. Therefore, if you don't enjoy this subject enough to devote nearly all of your time to it, find another one.

SOME PROFESSORS TO AVOID

Because you are so powerless, it is even more important to avoid losers[47] now than it was during your undergraduate days. Then a poor professor was just a nuisance, while now he can be a catastrophe.

[47]These remarks refer almost entirely to students in Ph.D. programs.

The Monomaniac

The monomaniac is probably the most common type of loser: everything in the world is seen as examples of one principle or theory, such as the oedipus complex, profit maximization, hunger for power, or semantic confusion. Because of our training, all professors (including this one) are rather monomaniacal. Our training and the demands of our job force us to be narrow, but there is certainly no reason to put up with someone who never departs from the party line.

The Thief

The thief is easy to recognize. He publishes several times a year, the exact number depending upon the abilities of his colleagues and graduate students. If you do 100% of the work on a project, he might give you coauthorship credit, but he is much more likely to give you just a footnote. So *before* you commit yourself to a professor, ask other people how he treats graduate students.

The Distinguished Busy Beaver

These are men that deans fight for, the men with international reputations. They publish regularly, speak all over the country, serve on editorial and advisory boards, and add enormous prestige to the institution. But that is all they add. They are so busy building their reputation and fulfilling their other commitments that they have no time left for students.

At Carnegie-Mellon we had a particularly irresponsible distinguished professor. Students came from all over the world hoping to study with him, but they never even met him. Even *professors* had to make appointments to see him, and his secretary would not give an appointment without an adequate justification. A brief conversation with a student shows how inaccessible he was. The student asked, presumably in jest, "Does professor S really exist?" I answered, "I think so; I've seen him in the hall."

Because these men are so prominent and brilliant, many students ask them to act as their research advisors. If you are exceptionally brilliant and enjoy working almost completely on your own, these men might be ideal. They may not give enough advice or criticism, but the little they give will probably be very good. And, if you do finish your degree, it will be very prestigious, and your advisor can help you to get an excellent job. However, if you are not exceptionally brilliant, if you need guidance and support, pick a man you can talk to.

The Nice Nonentity

The mirror image of the distinguished busy beaver is the nice nonentity. His door is always open; he's always glad to chat or to have coffee; he'd like to help you—but he can't. He doesn't have any power.

Everybody recognizes that he is nice, but not too bright. He probably got tenure several years ago before the school raised its standards, and now he is tolerated, but not respected. He does the departmental dirty work (such as marking foreign language exams and serving on the really annoying committees) and teaches his classes, but no one takes him seriously or trusts him with any real responsibility.

If he acts as your research advisor, he may not be able to prevent the other professors from rejecting your thesis. Even if you get your degree, he can't help you to get a good job.

Since both extremes of approachability and power are bad for students, I generally advise students to work with men who are recognized as competent, but are not so self-important that they ignore their students.[48]

ENJOYMENT

After criticizing the system so harshly, I feel obliged to point out that many students enjoy graduate school. They like the work, respect the atmosphere of dedication and commitment, and value their relationships with professors and other students.

These relationships, which are based upon both personal and career considerations, are probably the best part of graduate school. In graduate school students share more experiences, frustrations, and

---

[48]Of course, if you are lucky enough to find a distinguished researcher who is also accessible, work with him, but such men are very rare. In my entire career I have only met about four of them (Professors Haire, Sarbin, Kelley, and Cooper).

values than they do at any other time, and the relationships which
emerge are often very warm and satisfying. In fact, most of us look
back from time to time, forget the anxiety and exhaustion, and think
fondly of the friendships.

SUMMARY

If you complete graduate school, you will get good training and increase your income, status, and opportunities. You may also develop
personal relationships which you will value for the rest of your life. In
return for these benefits, the system will extract a high price in work
and stress, including the legitimate fear of not making it. If you go to
a top school, both the benefits and the costs will be much higher.

Because graduate school is so demanding, I suggest that you go
only if you are willing to make a complete commitment. The demands
are too high for the indifferent, uncommitted student: you can't get
the benefits without paying the price.

So think it over carefully and look at the men in that profession.
Do you have enough desire for that kind of work and life to commit
yourself, *willingly and wholeheartedly,* to several years of hard work?
If you don't have that desire and commitment, save your time. If you
do have it, *go.*

JOB HUNTING

At last it is pay-off time. Thanks to the system, you didn't get much of an education, but you are finally getting your degree and the job opportunities that come with it. Unfortunately, because we have not done an adequate job of preparing you for the job market, you probably do not know what job you want or how you can get it.

We did not prepare you for many reasons, but one is especially important. First and most important, the universities have not tried to develop your self-understanding or ability to assert your independence. In fact, they have deliberately worked toward keeping you docile and dependent so that you can be processed by their machinery and marketed to the large corporations. The corporations generally want people who are not too independent, and the universities regard the corporations' demands as more legitimate than their students' needs.

In fact, some professors have even regarded these demands as a moral imperative. I have tried many times to teach courses on company politics, career strategy, bargaining, and other ways to assert independence. Some professors have felt these courses were necessary and justified, but others have told me that doing so is *unethical*, that business schools should focus *only* on those topics which increase productivity and profits, that we should work only for the corporations, not for our students.

Productivity and profits are certainly legitimate goals, but they are not the only legitimate ones, nor does making the maximum contribution to them necessarily increase your personal satisfaction. Since you are primarily interested in your own satisfaction; this chapter will focus entirely on ways for you to find the right job, to get it, and to bargain for the best possible deal.[1]

THE TASKS

Job hunting can be one of your most important educational experiences. Interviewing, plant trips, analysis of offers, and discussions with other job hunters can help you to understand who you are, what you want, where you are going, and what the world is really like.

These activities have been so valuable and involving for so many students that some professors and administrators complain that students spend more time on them than they do in class. One student's reply to this complaint should be hung in every professor's office: "I spend more time there because I learn more in interviews than I do in class."

An intelligent approach to job hunting should therefore try to take the maximum advantage of its educational possibilities. Interviewing many different *kinds* of companies, systematically analyzing these opportunities, systematically analyzing your own feelings about these opportunities, and openly discussing your feelings and opportunities with other people can help you with both learning tasks: *understanding your own career goals and understanding the opportunities you really have to reach these goals.*

---

[1] Most of this chapter deals with the first job after graduation because the immediate practical considerations usually prevent you from using summer jobs as learning experiences or preparation for your ultimate career. You should, however, try to apply these general principles and use the interview tactics when you look for summer jobs.

It will, of course, be years before you can completely understand your goals and opportunities, but you can make a good beginning during this period. Once you have a fair understanding, you can start your third task: *developing a tentative career plan.*

Your plans must be tentative because your understanding is so incomplete. But you do need a plan. Without one you are adrift, moved by external forces, instead of controlling your own life and career. Drifting will probably cause you to end up in the wrong place, and the drifting process creates feelings of anxiety and alienation.

In the process of developing your understanding and career plans you have probably gotten some offers, but you may have to develop more offers and bargain with the companies which have made previous offers to accomplish the fourth task: *getting the best possible offers.*

You need several good offers for three reasons: (1) they help you with your educational task; (2) they increase your bargaining power; (3) they allow you to make a real decision. Many students can't make a real decision because they have only one offer that appeals to them. With two or more attractive offers you are forced to make a more careful analysis, and this analysis helps you with the learning tasks. Then, after you have made this analysis, you can accomplish the fifth task: *making a decision that fits your style and long-term career plans.*

As the preceding paragraphs clearly indicate, these five tasks are interdependent. You must work on all of them and shift back and forth from one to the other. Analysis, planning, bargaining, and interviewing are not easy. They take time and create anxiety. It is much simpler to choose the job that pays the most money or offers the "best opportunities for advancement."

But this decision is much too important to be made hurriedly. In fact, for many people it is the second most important decision of their entire lives.[2] It opens some doors and closes others. It starts you moving in one direction, and that direction may not be right for you. Each week I encounter the personal tragedy of men who have started in the wrong direction and are now locked into the wrong jobs.

They may be only 35 or 40 years old, but they have responsibilities they cannot ignore and salaries and pension rights they cannot

---

[2]The most important decision is whom you marry, a decision which is also often made without proper analysis (as our high divorce rate clearly indicates).

give up. They must therefore resign themselves to unsatisfactory careers—a terrible fate for a man who cares about his work. If you make this decision hurriedly, you may realize in 15 or 20 years that it was a mistake which led inevitably to a series of other mistakes. I therefore urge you to treat this decision with the respect it deserves and to do all the analysis and planning that it requires.

CAREER STRATEGY

In other words, your first job should fit into coherent and comprehensive plans for your life and career. The techniques for making and implementing these plans are described in my book *Executive Career Strategy*.[3] The following pages outline this strategy and the questionnaires in the appendix can help you to apply it. Given your limited information about yourself and the world, this plan must be rather tentative, but the following suggestions and the questionnaires in the appendix should help to make it more realistic and useful.

Analyze Your Career Goals

The very first step in your career strategy must be carefully analyzing your own career goals. You obviously must decide what you want from your career before you can take any intelligent action toward getting it. Unfortunately, the data on the turnover of new college graduates indicate very clearly that many of them do not understand what they wanted or what their companies offered when they took their first job. Within 5 years more than half change jobs, and by the time they are 30 or 35 many change jobs several times.

It is certainly not easy to analyze your goals. It takes a great deal of skill and courage to look at yourself objectively. Ideally, your college years should help you to develop this courage and skill, but the educational system, with its emphasis on coercion and dependence, actually makes it harder for some people to understand themselves or to think independently. We have been telling you what you are and what you must do for so long that you may not know how to act independently or to look at yourself objectively. The schools and

---

[1]Published by the American Management Association.

American society in general have told you what goals you *should* have —you should want to get ahead, make money (or the educational equivalent, good grades), try for the top, and so on—and many students are unable to decide what goals they *do* have. For some people money, position, and other indices of conventional success are important, but they are not important for everyone. Furthermore, they are not enough for anyone. Everyone needs more than money or success, even the compulsive neurotic who thinks that these things can satisfy him. You must therefore resist the pressures and decide how important other things are to you. For example, how much freedom do you need? Do you want to have a regular or irregular schedule? What kind of work do you want to do? What sort of people do you like? What sort of values do you have?

This is not the first time I have suggested asking yourself these questions, but self-analysis is particularly important at this point in your life. You are making a decision which will dramatically affect your future. The following suggestions therefore focus on methods for performing these analyses, and the questionnaires in the appendix provide an orderly procedure.

Because you have had relatively little contact with the real world, the analysis of your goals should be tied into the analyses of your assets, liabilities, and opportunities. You should interview a few companies, analyze their opportunities, see how you feel about them, and use this information to help you to understand yourself. This understanding of yourself gives you further insight into the opportunities various companies really offer.

You should also relate your career goals to the psychological needs which you are trying to satisfy. The American aversion to introspection causes most people to think in terms of concrete goals rather than psychological needs. People say that they want to be corporate presidents, to earn $25,000 per year, or to have a secure job, not that they want to satisfy their needs for status, power, security, or comfort. This tendency to think in terms of goals rather than needs causes many men to waste their lives. They spend years striving for some goal, only to learn that it does not satisfy them. Some men sacrifice their marriages, children and friends to reach the top of the pyramid, but find that they don't enjoy it. The money, power, and status do not compensate for the pressure and loneliness. As one very wealthy and powerful man put it: "The thing I most regret about my life is that I never knew there was a life to live until it was too late."

This kind of tragedy occurs every day, and it is the inevitable result of thinking in terms of concrete goals rather than needs. There is no such thing as a need to be a corporate president or to earn $25,000 a year or to accumulate a million dollars. These things are not ends in themselves; they are means for satisfing your real needs.

In an ideal world jobs would satisfy all types of needs, but in the world we live in each job satisfies some needs and frustrates others. High paying jobs are usually insecure. Jobs which offer power and prestige usually interfere with family life. It is therefore crucially important to understand which needs are important to you and to select jobs which will satisfy these needs. If you do not, you may spend your life chasing rainbows.

Furthermore, if you interview companies which do not recruit on campus, you will learn much more about yourself and the world and develop a broader range of options. Interviewing only the ones that do campus recruiting means, in effect, that you are letting the companies and placement office make that basic decision for you. *They* would be deciding what companies you will consider and what you will learn about the business world. If you do not approach other companies, you will not learn much or have a broad enough range of options because the recruiters are quite similar to each other. They use the same advertising agencies to prepare their literature, and offer you about the same opportunities. It takes some effort to approach other companies, but the effort is well spent. (The section on interview tactics will discuss ways to approach these companies.)

Psychological counseling and T-groups can play a valuable part in your goal analysis by providing insights that you can't get on your own and in developing your ability and courage to be honest with yourself. If you have not already tried counseling or T-groups, it might be useful to do so now.

The Goal Analysis Questionnaire in Appendix 4 is no substitute for counseling or T-groups, but it can help you to clarify your goals and needs and to relate them to your career plans. Furthermore, even if you do get outside help, it may be of some use because the approach is more structured and organized than the one you would use without it. I therefore suggest that you complete it, preferably after you have worked with a counselor or T-group.

Analyze Your Assets and Liabilities

The opportunities to satisfy your career goals will depend on the job you get and the assets and liabilities you bring to that job. No accountant would try to plan a company's future without a thorough analysis of its balance sheet, and a personal balance sheet will help you to plan your own career.

Three obstacles can hinder making this analysis: measurement problems, your own reluctance toward analyzing yourself, and other people's resistance to giving you the information you need. You can measure a company's assets and liabilities fairly accurately, and they can be compared to each other by stating them in terms of an unambigious standard: dollars. But you can't put an exact value on your judgment, social skills, originality, or any other characteristics, nor can we compare an asset such as originality to a liability such as low energy. You can only make a subjective judgment on how you compare with other people on each dimension.

This judgment may be very distorted because most of us have rather false images of ourselves, and *we want to preserve these false images.* We don't want to look too hard at ourselves because it makes us uncomfortable.

In addition to the discomfort it causes, we don't analyze ourselves because we do not see any immediate pay-off. Not doing so may hurt us in the long run, but we are unwilling to pay the immediate cost in discomfort for the future and unmeasurable benefits self-analysis provides.

Even if you should be willing to analyze yourself, you would still need information from other people, and they don't want to give it to you. They feel as uncomfortable as you do about giving honest information. T-groups and other groups in which honest and open communication are stressed can be invaluable here. They can help you to get a clearer picture of yourself and see how other people perceive you.

You may also get some useful information from psychological tests. Tests provide a great deal of information, and they do so quickly and reliably. If your university offers testing and counseling, you should take advantage of it, and you might even want to go to a commercial testing organization. Unfortunately, most people accept only those scores that agree with their preexisting beliefs about themselves and reject the information that is really new to them.

The *Personal Balance Sheet* in Appendix 5 can be a supplement or a substitute for psychological testing. It cannot provide any new information, but it can help you to organize the information you now vaguely understand and relate this information to your career plans. Furthermore, if you discuss your Personal Balance Sheet with someone else, you may actually get some new information. People are less reluctant to provide information when you go to them and ask specific questions about specific dimensions.

The basic principle of the Personal Balance Sheet is quite simple: you rate yourself on several characteristics, divide these characteristics into assets and liabilities, and make plans which take the best advantage of your assets and minimize the effects of your liabilities.

Analyze Your Opportunities

Normally the word "opportunity" refers primarily or entirely to your chances for advancement, but here it refers to the chances to reach your goals, regardless of what these goals may be. If you want money, a chance to move into top management, and the other conventional measures of success, "opportunity" refers to your chances of getting them. If you want a low-pressure job, or one with satisfying work, regular hours, a good location, travel, or likeable associates, "opportunity" refers to your chances for reaching these goals.

I suggest you analyze your real opportunities as cold-bloodedly as possible. This analysis may be difficult because you have so little experience, and most companies are quite dishonest about the opportunities they really offer. Their brochures about "your unlimited potential with _____" provide as much and as honest information as a cigarette advertisement, and recruiters deliberately create false expectations to attract people.

Lying is costly to everyone because companies lose money on people who leave in the first few years, but the competition for college graduates is so intense that they really have little choice. They have to lie because everyone else is lying and creating completely unrealistic expectations. The students (especially engineers and M.B.A.s) are wooed so ardently that they expect much more than the firms can possibly deliver. When they learn what the company and the world are really like, many change jobs or become cynical and apathetic.

Expectations about salaries offer an excellent example of this process. Most students are very interested in the salaries they will get, both to start and over the long run, but they rarely understand even the salary opportunities offered by a company. Since money is much easier to measure than type of work, relationships with superiors, and any other aspect of a job, expectations about these other things must be even more distorted.

The basic principle that you must understand is that your first salary will be set by the market, but your later salaries will be set by policies, customs, and traditions. At this moment several companies are bidding for your services, and they must offer about the same salary. But, unless you go to graduate school or become rather prominent, there will never again be an open market for your services, and your salary will depend almost entirely on company and industry policy.

A public utility, steel company, and an aerospace firm may offer you the same starting salary, but (other things being equal) you will end up making much less in a utility than in a steel company, and much less in steel than in aerospace. You may be offered similar starting salaries to work in production, finance, marketing, and personnel, but personnel offers more limited opportunities and lower long-term salaries than other fields, and finance and marketing usually offer much greater opportunities than production. These principles are fully explained in the chapter on executive compensation in *The Executive Life.*[4]

Most of you also have the false impression that large companies offer greater financial rewards than small and medium ones. They do offer larger starting salaries because they can afford to pay you more than you produce, but they offer you much lower chances than small or medium businesses of ever accumulating a lot of money.

M.B.A.s are an atypical example, but the data on them are so

[4]By the editors of *Fortune* magazine, Garden City, N. Y.: Doubleday, 1956.

complete and recent that we will use them as an example. A recent survey[5] shows that: "In every industry small business executives have a greater possibility of achieving a high net worth position." This survey also suggested that small and medium businesses satisfy other needs more than big business does: "Most MBAs now in a small firm would choose another small firm if they had the opportunity to start over, while less than half of those in big business would re-choose, big business. . . . It is the medium sized firm which offers the greatest opportunities and challenges for the MBA." These data indicate how important it is to interview the smaller companies which do not recruit on campus and to look at the long-term opportunities instead of just the starting salary.

Regardless of whom you interview, you must gather information from more sources than the men who are trying to hire you. They are selling, and you need more complete and objective information than they will provide. It takes time and hard work to dig out this information, but, if you know how to do it, it is not too difficult. If your parents have a stockbroker, he can be of great help you; knowledge is his stock in trade, and he can tell you a great deal and direct you to other sources of information. Even if you do not have a broker, you can get information about most large companies from the research departments of the large brokerage houses. They will provide this information because they hope to get your account. Newspaper files, Dun & Bradstreet, consulting firms, trade journals, people who have left the firm, and men in related companies can also tell you a great deal. A particularly valuable resource that most students never use is alumni of their school who work for the same company. It takes time to scan the alumni office files, and no one likes to call strangers, but most alumni would be glad to help you.[6]

All sources of information, including the recruiters, can be helpful if you know what questions to ask and how to ask them. The *Opportunity Analysis Questionnaire* and the *Offer Comparison Form* in Appendix 6 and 7 and the suggestions in the section on interview tactics can help you to obtain the information you need and to use it to make the right decisions.

---

[5] *Generation*, vol. 1, no. 4,
[6] Most people just love to give advice, even to strangers.

The *Opportunity Analysis Questionnaire* moves progressively downward from industry, to company, to major unit (such as department or division), to specific jobs. Most people begin at the other end with specific jobs, but doing so can obscure the forces involved in a larger context. These forces are not easy to understand, and they may seem less important than the opportunities offered by a particular job, but their influence is decisive. If an industry is growing, most of the people in it will prosper. If it is contracting, most of them will suffer. If it is dependent upon government contracts or other uncontrollable forces, the people in it will do well at some periods and poorly at others.

When we look at them abstractly, these points seem too obvious to discuss, but thousands of people have harmed their careers by ignoring them. Again and again I have heard that same old story: "Things were going beautifully. I had three promotions in five years. I had almost tripled my income. Then, all of a sudden, the government cut back on defence spending (or money got tight, or the competition got too tough, or foreign manufacturers flooded the market, and so on). Now I am out of a job (or going nowhere, or waiting to be phased out). Nobody seems to need my experience, and I am starting to get desperate."

Whether an apparently promising career was ruined by government cut backs, or tight money, or excessive competition, or similar factors, the man feels the same. "It is not my fault. I did good work —just look at my record. But now my record is not worth anything. There are dozens of men like me, and nobody wants us."

These tragedies are the inevitable result of focusing only on the job or the company. A proper understanding of the forces affecting our economy and the implications of these forces for different industries and companies could prevent these problems. So *start* your analysis at the industry level and work your way down. Analyze the opportunities offered by the industry, company, and department before you worry about issues such as whether your boss will be a nice guy. Bosses come and go; economic forces are more permanent.

The questions asked in the *Opportunity Analysis Questionnaire* will provide so much data that you can become confused or unable to comparing offers from different companies. Each offer will have good and bad points. The *Offer Comparison Form* in the appendix provides a simple procedure for making your final decision.

Plan Your Career

Although these analyses can be time-consuming and even annoying, they make it possible for you to do something that very few men ever do: to plan your career, to decide where you are going and how you are going to get there. Since many men never plan their careers, they may take the wrong job, or stay in it long after they should have quit, or change jobs prematurely or for irrational reasons, and they rarely have an overall concept of where they are going and how they are going to get there. They therefore do not control their own lives and careers, nor do they satisfy all their goals. You can avoid this experience by making these analyses and then planning your career.

The first step in planning your career is obviously setting a concrete long-term objective. Where do you want to end up ultimately? What kind of position and company best fit your goals, assets, and liabilities?

Once the long-term objective is set, you should establish intermediate-term goals. What jobs will you have to take, what connections will you need to reach your ultimate objective? Once you have set these long-term and intermediate objectives, you can set up a plan for obtaining the connections and training you need and getting into the stepping-stone jobs.

Finally, your first job should clearly fit into this plan for your entire career. It should be picked not only for its salary or "opportunities for advancement," but for the chances it provides for the training and connections you need to reach your long-term goal. The job which is superficially attractive because it has a high salary, or offers the opportunity for immediate advancement, or is located in a desirable place, may be a mistake from the standpoint of your long-term career.

Note that the planning strategy advocated here is exactly the opposite of the strategy followed by most people (if it can be called a strategy). Most people do not plan farther ahead than their next job (if they plan their career at all). They take a job because it looks attractive, and then they see what they can do with it. I advocate looking as far into the future as you can and deciding where you want to end up and what steps lead to it. In that way your life and career fit into some intelligent plan, and you are in control of your own life.

Analyze Your Progress

Most people will regard the creation of a career plan as the final step in a career strategy. Unfortunately, because you have so little information and things change so rapidly, you cannot expect to make a career plan now which will hold true for an indefinite period. A job which was originally seen as a stepping stone to bigger things may turn out to be a dead end. A firm which looked as if it was going places may run into financial difficulties. You might not make as much progress as you expected toward your goals. You must therefore keep a periodic record of your progress and see whether your goals, strategies, or both have to be changed.

INTERVIEW TACTICS

In the interview itself you have three tasks: you want to get the best possible offer, find out whether you want the job, and learn as much as possible about yourself and the business world. If you handle the interview properly, you can accomplish all three tasks, but very few students know how to handle interviews.

Your problem is aggravated because the interviewer has a significant edge on you. He is a pro and you are not. He has probably studied the principles of interviewing, and he has practiced them again and again, while you are inexperienced and do not even know the basic principles. He also has a psychological advantage because he is older and in a higher status position.

To even things up and accomplish your tasks you will have to *study, to practice,* and *to prepare.* You must learn the principles of interviewing, practice the necessary skills, and prepare for each interview, or else the interview will be a general and meaningless discussion of "your great future with our company." The following sections will describe these basic principles, but you have to practice using them. So that you can learn the game, your first interviews should therefore be with companies in which you have no interest. You can increase the learning value of these early interviews by conducting a post mortem after each interview, preferably with someone who has been through the same process.

Phases in Recruiting

The recruiting process usually has two phases: the campus interview and the plant trip. The campus interview is a general screening, while the plant trip is a more specific discussion of your abilities and a particular job.

Campus interviews used to be conducted by special college recruiters who are part of the personnel department. Since many of these men were not very knowledgeable in the fields for which they were recruiting, students got a rather negative impression of their companies. To preserve their images and to increase their chances of getting good people, many companies now send alumni to visit their own schools. These men usually know the field in which they are recruiting, but they may not have much information about the specific jobs they are offering. Your discussions with them will therefore be rather general and focus on your abilities and personality and their general program for young men in your field. You can try to get some "feel" for the company and its policies from the campus recruiter, but you will usually be unable to get much specific information about the job. Your primary task in this phase is therefore to convince the recruiter that you are good enough to invite to their plant or office.

On the plant trip you can get the information you really need, but you must be very careful that the important messages do not get drowned in the "noise." You may be so impressed by the fancy hotels and first-class restaurants and plane tickets that you lose sight of the longer-term aspects of the job.

Many corporations deliberately confuse you with the first-class treatment. You have been poor for so long, and enjoy living it up so much that the wining and dining routine can turn your head. You may even get the false impression that you will be living that way after you take the job. Some students have even taken lower salaries simply because the company treated them more lavishly, and they inferred that they would be treated well in the future. Lavish treatment is excellent economics for the company, but very poor economics for the student. The company spends a few extra dollars on a one-shot basis and gets away with lower salaries indefinitely. I therefore urge you to enjoy the trips, but to keep your attention firmly on the longer-term picture.

To understand this longer-term picture you must ask questions and listen carefully to the answers, but you must also keep your eyes open and ask some silent questions: what are the real goals and values of the organization, and how do they conflict with their stated ones? How do people act toward each other? How are promotions really made? How often and to what areas will you have to relocate? Where have people gone from this particular job? The *Opportunity Analysis Questionnaire* lists other information you need, and the following sections describe several techniques for getting this information.

Approaching the Nonrecruiters

It is quite tempting to confine your attention to the campus recruiters. You just have to walk over to the placement department; you know you will be treated politely; they have shown an interest in you by coming to campus; and they seem to offer unlimited opportunities and high starting salaries.

On the other hand, the companies which do not recruit on campus may pay lower starting salaries, and you have no idea how they will respond to you. Some will invite you to fly out to talk to them. Others will say "drop in if you get into the area." And most will either reject or ignore your application.

Approaching the nonrecruiters will cost you money, time, and discomfort, but it will provide you with a broader range of information and options. Furthermore, if the surveys are correct, they will offer you a chance for a more lucrative and satisfying career.

You can approach the nonrecruiters in two different ways, and you should probably use both. You can send out a résumé to a large number of companies which might be interested in you, and you could send individual letters, with or without a résumé, to companies in which you are particularly interested.

If you broadcast a résumé, you should prepare a rough draft and then take it to a professional résumé service. They will edit it to make it more attractive and useful and then type or mimeograph it. You can then use several different sources to find the companies you want to approach.

The best overall source of information is the Dun & Bradstreet publications. They can be found in any large library and are indexed by size of company, geographical area, and industry. Moody's and various other investment and business advisory services have similar publications, but the Dun & Bradstreet books are a little easier to use. If you are interested in working in a particular city, the Chamber of Commerce can provide you with a complete list of businesses in that area. Their publications are often indexed by industry. The U.S. Chamber of Commerce can also provide you with industry lists. If you want to work in a particular industry, its trade association can give you the names and addresses of all its members; it may also tell you a little bit about each company. The *College Placement Annual* lists the companies which are interested in recruiting college students (indexed by major field of study and geographical area), and many of these companies do not recruit on your campus. These companies are generally large, but some smaller companies which can only afford to recruit in their own area are also listed.

If you have majored in a clearly defined field such as engineering or accounting, professional associations are a particularly good source of leads. In fact, you may be able to write directly to them and have them route your résumé to interested companies. Your librarian can provide names and addresses of these associations. A few specialized publications also act as clearing houses for people and companies (for example, *Generation* magazine).

The placement office can also provide you with a great deal of information, and you should take full advantage of its facilities. Not too many years ago students came to them primarily for advice, but now campus recruiting has largely taken over. Nevertheless, these people still have a feel for the market and can direct you to many companies which cannot or will not recruit on campus. You may have a little trouble getting the help you need from the placement director because many of them feel that their job is to keep the recruiters happy and the campus interviews flowing, but you should at least try a few people in the placement office before you set out on your own.

If you are willing to put in even more time, you can study the want ads in *The Wall Street Journal* and *The New York Times*. If you live in certain areas, your edition of *The Times* may not include all the ads, but you can write directly to the newspaper for a complete edition. If you do respond to an advertisement, you should send a résumé and an *individually* prepared, typed letter which indicates *how* your ability, training, and other characteristics fit the needs stated in the advertisement. The section on "Making the Match" develops this principle more fully and shows you how to apply it.

If you want something out-of-the-ordinary and are willing to risk some money, you can put an ad in *The Wall Street Journal, The New York Times,* or some local paper. You should spell out clearly what you are looking for and indicate why your background is appropriate. Unless you have some special talent or training, your advertisement will probably not yield very many replies, but it is a legitimate "businessman's risk." Advertising in the *NYT* and *WSJ* costs about $50 per column inch; local papers are less expensive.

Several books can help you to approach companies and handle interviews with recruiters and non-recruiters. Only one is written for students, *Job Strategy* by Allan Rood (McGraw-Hill). The *Executive Job Market* by Auren Uris (McGraw-Hill) gives an excellent overall description of the market and ways to approach it. *Executive Jobs Unlimited* by Carl Boll (Macmillan) describes an outstanding method for approaching companies and handling interviews. Most public libraries have at least one of these books.

Preparation

The key to successful interviewing is preparation. If you walk in without any idea of what you are going to say, if you do not know anything about the company, if you are unclear about why you want to work for it, the interview will probably be a failure. The interviewer will control it, and you will walk out without impressing him or getting the information you need.

The more preparation you do before the interview, the better your chances of getting a good offer, and the less you have to dig for information when you try to evaluate your offers and to make your decision. With proper preparation you can ask intelligent questions[7] and have a real conversation. This conversation will provide you with the information you need to make an intelligent decision, and it will also solve the "visibility problem."

You have a visibility problem because interviewers see so many students that they cannot remember who is who. Some of my students have gotten letters thanking them for trips thay have not yet made or referring to conversations they have never had because the recruiters got their names mixed up. Others have gotten offers for jobs which were clearly inappropriate because people remembered that they were bright and likeable, but not what they were interested in. You can solve this problem and stand out from the crowd by preparing several specific questions and comments which show that you have done your homework. So few students do this that you will make a lasting impression on the interviewers.

Some of this homework is very easy. Simply reading the company's recruiting literature and preparing two or three specific questions *before* you sit down with campus recruiters will make a highly favorable impression. Before you go on a plant trip you can read the annual report and other material obtainable from the public relations department, and this material will suggest several questions and comments. Further information can be gathered from all of the sources mentioned earlier in the section on "Opportunity Analysis" (stockbrokers, trade associations, Chambers of Commerce, etc.). If you use these sources before the interview rather than after it, you will ask the right questions, stand out from the crowd, get better offers, and be able to make an informed, intelligent decision.

First Impression

You have heard that first impressions are important, but only recently have we found out how important they are. Psychological research indicates that the first few *seconds* determine what we think of people. The first impression creates a *"set,"* and all later information is interpreted to fit that set. For example, Professor Harold Kelley had two

---

[7]Some students are afraid that asking questions will create the wrong impression, but intelligent questions asked in a respectful manner show the interviewer that you have done your homework and take the interview seriously. They therefore increase his respect and interest.

groups of students hear an almost identical introduction to a guest lecturer. The only difference between the two introductions was the word "warm" versus the word "cold." Then both groups sat in the same auditorium and heard the same lecture. Despite the fact that they were exposed to this man for a full hour, and there was only a one-word difference in the introduction, the two groups had quite different perceptions of the lecturer and they behaved differently toward him. The group with the "warm" introduction rated him consistently more favorably. They saw him as more considerate, more informal, more sociable, more popular, more humorous, and more humane. They also participated more in discussions with him than the group that got the "cold" introduction.

If a *one-word* difference in an introduction can have that much impact, it is obvious that the first few seconds of the interview—your clothes, walk, voice, handshake, posture—are crucial. If you can create the impression of businesslike self-confidence, you are well on your way toward a successful interview.

If you approach a nonrecruiter, or send written materials to the recruiter before you see him, his impression of you begins before he ever meets you. Your written materials, voice on the phone, and conversations with his secretary can get things started on the right or the wrong bases. In fact, many men ask their secretaries: "How does he look?" before they start talking to you. Her comment can have more impact upon his impression and decision than anything you do.

What's His Problem?

The most basic principle of all selling is that people will not buy something unless doing so solves a problem. If you want him to buy you, you have to find out what his problem is and show him that you can solve it.

Your qualifications and experience are therefore important only insofar as they help him solve his problem. Many of the things you have done and learned have no relevance to his problem, and he is not really interested in hearing about them. Learning what his problem is lets you know whether you want the job, and it helps you to get it. If he wants you to solve a problem which does not interest you, then you know that you don't want the job. If his problem is one that you could enjoy working on, then you might want the job. The proper focus for the interview is therefore not on your background, but on his problem.

Make the Match

You must go one step further. You must make the match between his problem and your qualifications. Most job hunters do not make the match. They simply provide information about themselves and leave the matching process to the interviewer. But he probably does not know how to interpret your experience or to relate it to his problem. Hence, after you leave, he sits at his desk, looking at your qualifications, wondering whether they fit his needs.

You should therefore go back and forth between your qualifications and his problem, learning what his problem is and showing him *how* your training and experience will solve it. Make the interview into a tennis game, not a golf match—a genuine give and take conversation, not parallel monologues.

It is really simple to create a genuine conversation. The basic principle is: *if he asks you for information, give him some, and throw the ball back to him.* He will then have to give you some information, and he will throw the ball back to you. For example, after the pleasantries are over nearly all interviewers ask some specific questions or ask the man to: "Tell me about yourself." The interviewee then gives a long story which may or may not be relevant to the interviewer's needs. It is much better to tell him some of the basic things about yourself and then say: "How does that fit your needs?" He will then say something, and his response will indicate what direction you should go in the future. You can then be more specific about your relevant qualifications, and ignore discussing the ones in which he has no interest.

The best kind of interview is one in which the attention is directed away from your qualifications in a formal sense and to the problem he is trying to solve. Many of my older clients have been able to get into interviews in which they essentially served as consultants for some organizational problem of the interviewer. They told him how they would solve or approach the problem the interviewer had. Many of them have gotten jobs as a result of this consultant's role without ever discussing the usual material—age, degrees, courses taken, references, etc. They *showed* the man that they could solve his problem. As a new college graduate, you may not be able to act as a consultant, but it certainly pays to show him *how* you would approach and solve the problem he is concerned with.

You should make the match at all stages in the job-hunting process. Instead of sending a résumé in response to an advertisement, write a short letter which shows, point by point, *how* your experience matches the specific requirements listed in the advertisement. The same general approach works on the telephone.

Build a Personal Relationship

Focusing on his problems and having a give-and-take conversation also helps you to build a good personal relationship. He is probably tired of the typical interviews, and an intelligent, well-prepared approach will create a favorable impression. However, it takes more than task-oriented conversation to build a good relationship.

The basic principle of interpersonal attraction is that people like people who are similar to themselves. Democrats like Democrats; rich people like rich people; sportsmen like sportsmen, etc. You do not want to get away from his problem until he indicates that he'd like to know more about you as a person, but when he does so, try to have a give-and-take conversation with him about the other aspects of your life. If you are interested in hunting, ask him about the hunting near the plant. If you're a golfer, a fisher, a swimmer, etc., let him know it—and ask him if he participates in the same sports. The more bonds of similarity you can build between you, the more he will like you, and, because we overvalue the people we like, the more competent he will think you are.

Bargaining

Bargaining is a touchy topic. Almost everyone feels uncomfortable and incompetent about it; some people feel so uncomfortable that they stand on their dignity and "refuse to bargain." But the principles are easy to understand, and intelligent bargaining can increase a salary offer by 5 to 10% and improve other aspects of the job as well.

The first and most important principle is to avoid giving salary requirements until *after* he wants you. All salesmen quote the price only after a man wants the merchandise, and there is a little sense in losing the sale or selling too cheap by discussing salary prematurely. You should leave that space blank on the application or write "to be negotiated."

The second principle is that bargaining has always been based on power, not morality, and power depends on the number of alternatives available to each party. Your needs are therefore irrelevant. His offer will be based on his situation, the value he places on your services, and the alternatives he thinks you have available to you, not your financial problems.

Fortunately, you are in an excellent bargaining position now because you have a market for your services. If you don't take advantage of your situation, you will lose thousands of dollars. Taking a low offer now will keep your salary low for an indefinite period of time because the business world works on a very simple principle: *you are worth what you get paid.* If you switch jobs, they will switch you at that salary or only slightly above it. Your future raises will be a percentage of your salary. Therefore, bargain for every dollar you can get, because each one of those dollars is worth $10 or $15 or $30.

The bargaining process need not be acrimonious. In fact, the most important part of it is showing that you can solve his problem. Then, once he wants you, you must clearly communicate that you have other offers. The more offers you have, the more highly he will evaluate you (you must be good if other people want you). He will also know that he has to make a more attractive offer to get you.

A particularly lucrative technique is to get offers from companies in which you are not interested, but which pay high salaries. You can then use this high salary offer to extract concessions from the desired employer.

Some students try to bluff or lie about the salary offers they have. A few get away with it, but it is very difficult unless you are an extremely skilled liar. Remember, he is a professional, and he has had dozens of people try that on him. I therefore suggest that you play it straight.

Bargaining should not refer only to salary. There are many other aspects of the job which are not necessarily fixed, and you can bargain about any of them. You can bargain for location, job title, reporting relationships, training programs, tuition, and many other things. Furthermore, many companies are more willing to bargain about these things than they are about salaries.

Most bargaining should be done indirectly because directness may appear rude or unprofessional and create resentment. It should also take place *before* he makes a concrete offer because he will be more rigid after he makes one. You therefore want to create a great deal of desire on his part, and the impression that he has to make a high offer to get you. Then let him make an offer!

Unfortunately, not many people have the nerve to wait him out. They get trapped into indicating what they will take. However, since *you will never get more than you asked for* and asking for too much can cost you the job, it is far better to indicate your other alternatives and say you will naturally take the offer that sounds best to you. He will probably ask the question in several different ways, and you may feel quite uncomfortable, but you will usually come out ahead by waiting for him to make an offer. This can take almost iron nerve, because many interviewers are highly skilled at getting you to commit yourself, but you have just got to hang tough.

Present Yourself Honestly

Despite everything I have said about bargaining, first impressions, etc., I firmly believe that you should try to come across as what you are. You do want to make a good first impression, but, before he makes you an offer, you want him to know who you are. If he doesn't like you as you are, if he thinks you wouldn't fit in, you are much better off not getting an offer from him.

You don't need a job. There are so many companies after college graduates that you are certain of getting a job, but you want it to be the right job. It has to be right not only for your abilities but for your personality. And interviewers know much better than you whether your personality fits their organization. If you present a false front, you may get an offer you wouldn't get if they knew who you were, but how long can you pretend? To paraphrase the hair coloring ad: if I have one life to lead, let me live it as myself.

THE DECISION

If you have performed all these analyses, and used the suggested interview tactics, you should not have too much trouble making an intelligent decision. You simply make a systematic comparison of all of your offers. In order to include all the dimensions of a job that are important to you, you need an orderly procedure because nearly everyone focuses on only a few aspects of a job and ignores others. For example, you might overemphasize the importance of salary or type of work and ignore location, promotion policies, or educational opportunities.

These ignored aspects may turn out to be much more important than you expected and make you dissatisfied with your choice. The *Offer Comparison Form* in Appendix 7 is designed to improve your decision by isolating the important dimensions of each offer and comparing them on all dimensions.

READINGS

C. R. Boll, *Executive Jobs Unlimited*, New York: Macmillan, 1965. An excellent method for approaching the market, but one focused on needs of older people.

A. Z. Carr, *Business as a Game*, New York: New American Library, 1968. An interesting, useful book. Chapter 13 is the best source on bluffing in business.

Allan Rood, *Job Strategy*, New York: McGraw-Hill, 1961. The best book for your situation.

Alan Schoonmaker, *Executive Career Strategy*, New York: American Management Assocation. A much more complete version of the system outlined here. It is written for older men.

Auren Uris, *The Executive Job Market*, New York: McGraw-Hill, 1965. A general analysis of the market for more established people. Useful background if you want to approach nonrecruiters.

A FINAL WORD

Enough has been said. We have analyzed the system and discussed issues which ranged from your early college career to your life after graduation. I have nothing more to say, but I would like to reemphasize a few critical points.

First, things don't change very much or very rapidly. The system will be essentially the same when you graduate as it was when you began. You will grow up a little, but your basic personality was set a long time ago. The person you marry will not change either.

The American rhetoric ignores the facts and demands change—in our institutions, our spouses, our friends, ourselves. We have been conditioned to be dissatisfied, to strive constantly to make things bigger and better. This commitment to change has made us wealthy, but it has also made us neurotic and miserable.

You will be a far happier, more successful human being if you learn to live with reality, instead of wasting your time trying to change the unchangeable.

These remarks do not mean that you must passively comply with all the demands of our present educational and social systems, nor do they mean that *no* changes are possible. They just mean that the forces against change are so powerful that rapid, revolutionary changes cannot occur.

My generation understands this principle; we may even understand it too well. We have seen so many abortive attempts to change the system that we have become old, cynical, tired, and conventional. We have decided that any attempt to change the system is bound to fail and have resigned ourselves to being dominated by trivia. Instead of changing essentials, we make bigger houses or faster cars or more colorful cereal boxes. Instead of trying to do something worthwhile with our lives, we concentrate on creature comforts. We have traded our dreams for a house in the suburbs and a comfortable life.

You must therefore bear the burden of progress. You must go beyond us to create a world and an educational system which are better than the ones we gave you, and to create these systems you must develop a fine sense of balance. You must retain the vision and enthusiasm you have now, but learn how to live and to cope with the system we have now. If you do not, the system will destroy you as it has destroyed us, and 30 years from now your children will be as disgusted with you as you are with us.

APPENDIX 1:
A NOTE TO PARENTS

If you are like most students' parents, you are angry, frightened, and confused. What is going on with demonstrations, LSD, premarital sex, and all those other things you read about? And what about your child? Is he going to grow a beard, or try marijuana, or violate our sexual rules?

Probably.

But it won't kill him, and it probably won't even hurt him very much. Young people have always gone beyond their parents, but most of them survive. So, if you want to preserve your sanity and peace of mind, Rule 1 is: *don't worry too much.*

Many parents have objected to this advice; they have even been outraged at my "callous attitude". "What do you mean, don't worry? Do you realize what they can do to my little girl? Do you know what sort of things are happening on campus?" Then they tell me all about the things that I experience every day, and say that they intend to protect their children.

But they cannot protect their children, and every attempt to do so drives them farther apart. The children are trying to break out of the nest. They are groping for their identities in a harsh and confusing world, and they need understanding and support, not more rules and pressures.

They need a home base, a place where they are safe and free from pressure, where they can rest between ventures and try to make sense out of what has happened to them. They are, in a way, similar to my three-year-old girl. She wants to explore the world and to try new things, but every once in a while she gets scared and wants to sit on my lap. If I just hold her and try to understand her, the fears soon go away and off she goes to try something new. But, if I let my own anxiety get in the way, if I try to preach to her or control her directly, she jumps off my lap and runs—not toward new adventures, but *away from me.*

Many of the problems you read about are caused by the same sort of running away, a rejection of you and adult society in general. The pressure is so great that many young people try to find themselves not by exploring themselves and the world, but by deliberately breaking the rules. They need to be free, and the only freedom they can see is rebellion. Since deliberate defiance is not nearly so helpful to them as pleasurable exploration, you must try to create a relationship in which they feel safe and comfortable enough to be themselves, to admit their fears and confusions, to look honestly at themselves and the world, and to learn from their experiences.

As one very wise father put it: "I know my daughter will try marijuana, whatever I say. I just hope she trusts me enough to tell me about it." He realized that the important thing is not whether or not she tried marijuana, but the relationship they had between them, and that relationship depended on trust and his willingness to listen. Rule 2 is, therefore, if you want to help your children to find themselves: *don't lecture, listen.*[1]

Surprisingly, if we do not lecture, if we respect and listen to

---

[1]Dr. Haim Ginott's bestseller *Between Parent and Teenager* (New York: Macmillan, 1969) shows how to apply this principle to many different situations. I wholeheartedly recommend this book.

them, they start respecting and listening to us. Many parents who have tried listening to their children have been amazed to find that the same children who have rejected all of their advice, who would never listen to them, suddenly reach the very decisions they had tried to force upon them. If your daughter goes out with a boy you dislike, she will probably resist your criticisms of him and violate your prohibitions against seeing him. But, if you respect her judgement and let her make up her own mind, she may well see that he is not right for her and drop him. The boy you are trying to pressure into going to college may resist all of your arguments, but, if you let him work for a year, learn what the world is like, and respect his right and ability to make up his own mind, he will probably decide he needs a college education. Your children have innately good judgement, which they will generally exercise if you take the pressure off. Rule 3 is therefore: *respect your children's ability and right to make their own decisions.*

They will make mistakes, of course, and some of these mistakes may even have serious consequences. They may go to the wrong school, or choose the wrong major, or date the wrong person. Mistakes are inevitable, and, even if you make all of the decisions, you might make as many mistakes. But, if you make the decisions, they cannot learn from the mistakes, while, if they make them and are given a chance to think about them, without lectures and "I told you so's," they will learn from their mistakes and become better people because of them. Rule 4 is therefore: *let your children make and learn from their own mistakes.*

Listening to your children and giving them a chance to be honest with you also helps them to become more honest with themselves. Their cockiness is really defensiveness. They are whistling in the dark because they are very frightened and confused. If you listen and respect them, they will be less afraid, more honest with themselves, and more able to deal with their fears and confusion.

Unfortunately, it is very hard to help them to drop their defenses because we are so defensive ourselves. We know we are a major cause of their problems, but we do not want to admit it. We try to preserve our self-images as good parents and citizens by ignoring or denying our own weaknesses. We tell our children not to lie, but we cheat on our income taxes. We tell them to be compassionate, but we keep the blacks locked up in the ghettos. We talk about democracy, but we undermine its institutions. We tell them that the society should be improved, but we insist that they play it safe to get good jobs. Children resent our hypocrisy, and this resentment becomes another barrier between us. Rule 5 is therefore (if you want to keep your children's respect): *be honest with them and yourself.*

It is not easy to be honest, especially when they are attacking us, but it is essential. Confronted as they are by the contradictions between our words and our actions, what else can they do but conclude that we are hypocrites? And to young people, with their vision and enthusiasm, hypocrisy is a terrible thing. They have taken our principles seriously and are shocked to learn that we have not. Their efforts to change society and the educational system may seem like infantile rebellion to you, but they are often motivated by the noblest of impulses—a desire for justice, concern for the underprivileged, and insistence on honesty. We must do more than listen. Rule 6 is therefore: *we must also respect and encourage their efforts to make this a better world.* [2]

Perhaps the hypocrisy they resent most is our insistence that we are trying to help them when we are really using them for our own purposes. They resent professors pretending that their research improves teaching or helps the students. They are outraged by politicians who talk about their opportunity to defend the national honor. They want to choose a college and courses that satisfy their own needs, not ones that let their parents brag at cocktail parties. In a word, they want what they want, not "all the things I didn't have as a child." And they cringe when they think of what they have to do to satisfy our needs for status, social acceptance, and "family responsibilities." They are selfish, of course, but using them or making them feel guilty will not make them any less selfish, and it will drive them further away. Rule 7 is therefore: *let your children's decisions be based on their own needs, not yours.*

None of these rules is easy to follow, and no one can follow all of them, all of the time. Our own needs, fears, and weaknesses keep us from being as good parents as we would like to be. But we must not expect to be supermen or critisize ourselves too severely when we

---

[2]We must respect them, even when their outrage, exuberance, or methods frighten us.

fail as parents. Rule 8 is therefore: *accept yourself for what you are, a human being who is doing his best.*

In the preceding paragraphs I have listed several rules, but they are obviously not applicable to all situations. Parenthood is not a science, but an art—*the art of letting go,* an art which most of us never master. We hold on too long and too tightly, then let go too abruptly. We insist on controlling our children; then, when they resist, we get angry and say: "All right, do it your way, but don't cry on my shoulder if it doesn't work out." If we want to be successful parents, ones who help their children through the difficult transition from child to adult, we must avoid the two extremes and the vacillations between them which so many of us practice.

We must recognize that adolescents are neither children nor adults, but a little of each. They must find themselves and define their relationship with the world, tasks which we cannot do for them. We can only help them by understanding them and the pressures they face, by giving them the support they need to face themselves and these pressures, and by letting them leave us at their own pace.

In the first chapter I noted that it is not easy to be a student today, but you and I both know that it is not easy to be a parent either. We know that we have our own fears and anxiety, and we often need understanding. But our children rarely give it to us. They are too self-centered to know how they affect us, even when they break our hearts. It has always been this way, and always will be. Raising a child is a one-way street, and it is especially that way now, when the pressures they face are so powerful and contradictory. They need so much that they cannot give us much in return. They have to work on so many problems that they cannot understand the problems they create for us. They do not know how mixed and how natural our feelings are: we are proud that they are growing up, but also want to keep them small and close to us.

Parents in all eras and in all countries have had this conflict, but for us it is much more severe. Our children will not grow up and live in the same town or even the same world as we do. The world is changing rapidly: their goals, attitudes, and habits will be different from ours; and the distances are becoming greater. Our children will go away to college, work in other states, perhaps even live in other countries. We would like to keep them close to us, but we know that they will leave some day.

The only solution to this problem is to find other satisfactions in our lives, to develop lives of our own. Many parents (especially mothers) never do that. They live for their children and wake up one day to find the children gone, the house and their lives empty and deserted. Some recover from the shock: they join clubs, go back to school, travel, or take extra jobs; others brood, whine, collapse in front of the TV, or keep trying to interfere in their children's lives.

Because they have so little in their lives, their reactions to their children are exaggerated and irrational. They cannot let go because the children are all they have. The most important rule of parenthood is therefore: *develop your own strength, interests, and resources. Then you can live and enjoy your own life and let your children do the same.*

APPENDIX 2: MARITAL READINESS GUIDE

This form is not an adequate substitute for personal or premarital counseling, but it may help you to think clearly about some of the factors which are related to marital success. It may be useful to refer to the relevant parts of the text when you answer the questions in each section. Naturally, the more objectively you answer these questions, the more you will gain.

MOTIVES

Why do you want to marry now?

Are you often very unhappy?

Do you regard marriage as an escape from personal problems or unhappiness?

AGE

If you are less than 20, why do you believe that your marriage will have a better chance than most teen-agers' marriages?

If you were an outsider, would you agree with the answer to the preceding question?

TIME

How long have you known each other?

How well do you know each other?

How long did you know each other before you became engaged?

If the answers to the preceding questions suggest that you have been acting hastily, what does your haste tell you about yourself and your readiness for marriage?

INERTIA

Do you seem to be drifting toward marriage?

Was your decision to become engaged based upon a careful analysis?

Have you dated only a few people?

Do you know much about the opposite sex and the way you get along with different kinds of people?

SEX

Is sex the primary motive which is driving you toward marriage?

YOUR CHOICE

Is he the sort of person with whom you have a good chance for a happy marriage?

Do your parents, friends, and other relatively objective people feel that you are right for each other?

Is there a great difference in your ages?

If so, what does this difference tell you about yourself?

Does one person dominate the relationship?

If so, what does this domination tell you about yourself?

Are you very different from each other?

If the above information indicates that you have chosen the wrong person, what does it tell you about yourself?

INDEPENDENCE

Do you hate to be alone?

Are you unable to act effectively when the other person is away?

Are you afraid he will leave you?

Are you very jealous?

Do you worry excessively when he is ill or traveling?

Are you very dominant or submissive toward him?

Do you constantly test his love or demand proofs of it?

SELF-RESPECT

Do you like yourself *as you are?*

Do you often present a false front?

Do other people have the same impression of your personality that you have?

If not, why not?

Do you compare yourself critically with some ideal you have set for yourself?

Are you always trying to change yourself?

Are the things you are trying to change trivial or basic parts of your personality (e.g., reading speed versus basic values)?

SITUATIONAL PRESSURES

Can you afford to get married?

Can you devote enough time to put your marriage on a firm foundation?

Would marriage interfere with your long-term plans (such as going to graduate school or starting a business)?

If yes, what is your most likely reaction to this interference?

Is either set of parents likely to interfere?

How will you both feel if the wife has to act as the major source of income?

How will you react to becoming isolated from other students and student affairs?

Will the wife have to stop or to interrupt her education?

THE CRUCIAL QUESTION

Review all of the preceding information, then answer this question. If you were an outsider, looking at data from another person, would you say that he was ready for marriage?

APPENDIX 3:
MATE ANALYSES GUIDE

This form is not an adequate substitute for premarital counseling, but it may help you to think about some of the factors which are related to marital success.

You may use it to evaluate a prospective mate, or both of you can answer these questions independently and then compare notes. Either procedure may help you to avoid an unhappy marriage, and comparing notes may also clarify some misunderstandings and prepare both of you for the problems you will face. It may be useful to refer to the relevant parts of the text as you answer the questions in each section. Naturally, the more objectively you answer these questions, the more you will gain.

RAW MATERIAL

Do you like the other person *as he is?*

Could you enjoy living with him *as he is?*

Are you always trying to change his personality?

Are the things you dislike about him easy to change (e.g., table manners) or relatively permanent parts of his personality (e.g., basic values and goals)?

CHANGING YOURSELF

Do you think he accepts you *as you are?*

Is he constantly trying to change your personality?

Do you try to change your personality to fit his needs or demands?

Are the things that you and he dislike about you easy or hard to change?

FAMILY

Do you like each other's families?

If not, why not?

Do you feel comfortable with each other's families?

If not, why not?

How similar is each of you to his family?

Do your families approve of your relationship?

If not, why not?

What are your family's basic attitudes toward life and marriage?

Your mate's family's attitudes?

Possible problems?

SOCIOECONOMIC CLASS

Yours

Mate's

Impact on each?

Possible problems?

RELIGION

Yours

Mate's

Impact on each?

Possible problems?

ETHNIC BACKGROUND

Yours

Mate's

Impact on each?

If there is a difference, have you thought *carefully* about the problems you will face?

Possible problems?

OTHER BACKGROUND FACTORS

What sort of home did you have?

Your mate's home?

Possible problems?

In what sort of area did you live (small town, city, etc.)?

Your mate?

Possible problems?

What educational level do you expect to attain?

Your mate's?

Possible problems?

VALUES

What are your most important values?

Your mate's?

What value conflicts do you have?

Possible problems?

CONCEPTION OF MARRIAGE

What is your viewpoint (including number and spacing of children)?

Your mate's?

Possible problems?

LIFE GOALS

What are your major life goals? (Not necessarily the specific profession, just the general social and economic position.)

Your mate's?

Possible problems?

TALENTS

Can your mate compete successfully in the league you plan to enter?

Can you compete in his league?

Possible problems?

INTERESTS

What interests do you share?

How important are they to each of you?

What interests do you have which are not shared?

Are there many things you enjoy doing together?

Are they the sort of things you can do after marriage?

Possible problems?

NEEDS

What are your strongest needs?

Your mate's?

How well do they fit?

Possible problems?

POWER

Is there a large difference between your commitments to each other?

Does either partner dominate the relationship?

How are disagreements normally settled, by compromise or by one person's giving in?

Does the same person usually yield?

Possible problems?

PLEASURE

How well do you get along now?

Do you communicate well with each other?

Do you confide in each other?

What problems do you have now?

Are you both satisfied with the amount and type of affection you give each other?

How well do you expect to get along after marriage?

How well do you expect to communicate after marriage?

Do you expect to confide in each other after marriage?

What problems do you expect after marriage?

Do you expect to be satisfied with the amount and type of affection after marriage?

If there is a difference between "now" and "after," explain the difference.

OTHER INFORMATION

Do you often wish that you weren't engaged?

Have you broken up before and then gone back together?

How many times?

Possible problems?

List any other information or problems you regard as relevant.

THE CRUCIAL QUESTION

Review all the preceding information; then answer this question: If you were an outsider, looking at data from another couple, would you recommend marriage?

APPENDIX 4:
THE GOAL ANALYSIS
QUESTIONNAIRE

This questionnaire deals primarily with goals and needs in an ideal sense. What do you really want? Not what can you reasonably expect to get? Other questionnaires deal with limitations. To simplify matters, ignore limitations and focus only on what you want.

Many of these questions are hard to answer, and a few may even irritate you. They force you to think about topics you generally ignore, and they go beyond the standard cliches about money, advancement, and responsibility. They ask what needs you are really trying to satisfy, and you usually do not think in terms of needs. However, as we noted earlier, not thinking about needs virtually guarantees that you will not satisfy them.

I. NEEDS

Most of the following questions have two parts: the first asks what concrete goal you want such as amount of income or type of work.

The second asks what needs are involved. The concrete questions are asked first because most people cannot analyze their needs abstractly. The questions about needs are asked to clarify your real motives. A list of needs is included here to help you answer these questions. Look through it from time to time to refresh your memory.

1. Physiological
2. Economic Security
3. Social Acceptance
   (a. from superiors
   b. from associates
   c. from subordnates)
4. Status
   (a. from general public
   b. from associates and friends)
5. Good family life
6. To live in a nice location
7. To learn

8. To use my abilities
9. Independence
10. Time for myself
11. To achieve
12. To benefit society
13. Power
    (a. direct control over people and resources
    b. influence on overall policy)
14. To define or to prove myself
15. High income

II. OVERALL CAREER GOALS

1. a. If you could have *any* job you wanted, what job would you take? _____
   b. Why? What needs would that job satisfy? _____
   _____

2. a. How important is earning a lot of money to you? ____
   b. Why? What needs does it satisfy? _____
   _____

3. a. How much income per year do you *need* to live at the standard of living you desire?
   1. Now _____   2. In 5 years _____
   3. In 10 years   4. Ultimately _____
   b. How much income do you want?
   1. Now ____   2. In 5 years _____
   3. In 10 years   4. Ultimately _____

c. If there is a difference between what you *need* and *want*, *why* is there a difference? What needs would this "unnecessary" money satisfy? _____

_____

_____

4. a. How much income does *your wife want* you to earn?
   1. Now _____   2. In 5 years _____
   3. In 10 years   4. Ultimately _____
   b. If there is a difference between your wants and hers, *why* is there a difference? How are her needs different from yours? _____

_____

_____

   c. What are the probable effects of this difference? _____

_____

5. a. How much capital do you want to accumulate? _____
   b. What would you do with it? _____
   c. What needs would it satisfy? _____
   d. How important is it to you to accumulate this capital?

_____

6. a. What kind of work do you really want to do? Ignore income and status differences and be as explicit and as specific as possible. _____

_____

_____

   b. What needs does this kind of work satisfy? _____

_____

7. a. Do you really want to do executive work (not lead an executive's life)? That is, do you really want to accomplish things by motivating, directing and controlling other people, or would you prefer a job in which you advised people or worked on your own? _____
   b. Why? What needs would executive work satisfy? _____

_____

_____

8. a. If you really want to do executive work, *at what level* would you like to work? Ignore income differences and focus your attention on the duties, responsibilities, pres-

sures, etc. of different levels. (e.g. Top Management, middle management)   _____

   b. Why? What needs are satisfied by working at that level?

_____

 9. a. In what size firm would you prefer to work (in assets)?
    1. Over a billion   4. 1 – 10 million
    2. 100 million – billion   5. Under one million
    3. 10 – 100 million   6. Your own business of any
                                  size

   b. Why? What needs are involved?   _____

10. a. In what industry would you like to work?   _____
   b. Why? What needs are involved?   _____
11. a. For what company would you like to work?   _____
   b. Why?   _____
12. a. What kind of company would you prefer to work for?

   b. Why? What needs would that kind of company satisfy?

_____

13. a. Would you rather work for a "tough" or "democratic" firm?   _____
   b. Why? What needs are involved?   _____

14. a. Would you rather work in a "flexible" or "bureaucratic" firm?   _____
   b. Why? What needs are involved?   _____

15. a. Would you rather work for a "tough" or "democratic" boss?   _____
   b. Why? What needs are involved?   _____

16. a. Would you rather work in a company where most decisions are made by individuals or committees?   _____
   b. Why? What needs are involved?   _____

17. a. What kind of work would you like to do *now?*   _____

b. Why? What needs would it satisfy? _____
_____

18. a. Would you rather have a secure job or one in which you could "sink or swim?" _____
    b. Why? What needs are involved? _____
    _____

19. a. Would you rather work independently in an unstructured situation or have clear guidelines from above? _____
    b. Why? What needs are involved? _____
    _____

20. a. Would you prefer a high or low pressure job? _____
    b. Why? What needs are involved? _____
    _____

21. a. Where do you and your wife want to live and work?
    _____
    b. Why? What needs are involved? _____
    c. How important is it to both of you? _____

22. a. How much time do you want for yourself? _____
    b. How important is it to you? _____

23.   How important is on the job variety to you? _____
    _____

24. a. How important is it to you to feel that you are achieving something? _____
    b. What sorts of things give you that feeling? _____
    _____

25. a. How important is it to you to feel that you are contributing to society? _____
    b. What sorts of things give you that feeling? _____
    _____

26. a. How important is it to you to have power? _____
    b. What kind of power? _____

27.   How sure are you of your own identity? _____

28. a. What have you most liked about the jobs you have had?
    _____
    b. What needs are involved? _____
    _____

29. a. What have you most disliked? _____
    b. What needs are involved? _____

30. a. What do you want out of your next job (in your current or another firm)? _____

    b. What needs are involved? _____

_____

III. SACRIFICES AND THE PRICE OF SUCCESS

1. a. Are some of your needs being frustrated because of your job or career ambitions? _____
   b. What are they? _____
   c. Why aren't you satisfying them? _____
   d. How important are they to you? _____
   e. When do you expect to satisfy them? _____
   f. Why will you be able to satisfy them then, when you can't now? _____

   _____

   _____

2. a. Are you willing to risk your health to get ahead? ____
   b. What does your answer say about your needs? _____

3. a. Are you willing to risk disrupting or damaging your family life? _____
   b. What does your answer say about your needs? _____

4. a. Are you willing and able to "play politics" to get ahead?

   _____

   b. Is your wife willing to do so? _____
   c. Can you maintain your self-respect if you do so? ____
   d. Can she maintain her respect for you if you do so? __
   e. What do the answers to these questions say about your needs? _____

   _____

5. a. Are you willing and able to "cut corners" (to act in unethical, semi-legal, or illegal ways) to get ahead? _____
   b. Is your wife willing to do so? _____
   c. Can you maintain your self-respect if you do so? ____
   d. Can she maintain her respect for you if you do so? __
   e. What do the answers to these questions say about your needs? _____

   _____

6. a. Are you willing and able to drop old friends as you move upward? _____

b. Is your wife? _____

c. What do the answers to these questions say about your needs? _____

7. a. Are you willing and able to change your living style and pattern as you move upward? _____

b. Is your wife? _____

c. What do the answers to these questions say about your needs? _____

_____

8. a. How many hours per week do *you want* to work? ____

b. How many does your *wife want* you to work? _____

c. How many hours a week will you *have to* work to reach your goals? _____

d. Do you *prefer* a regular schedule of hours or an irregular one? _____

e. Does your wife *prefer* a regular or irregular schedule?

_____

f. Will you *have to* work a regular or irregular schedule to reach your goals? _____

9. a. Are you willing and able to relocate whenever and wherever your firm directs? _____

b. Are you willing to relocate for promotions or raises?

_____

c. Is your wife? _____

d. What do the answers to these questions say about your needs? _____

_____

10. a. Are you willing to spend a substantial amount of time away from home on company travel? _____

b. Does your wife mind your being away from home? __

c. What do the answers to these questions say about your needs? _____

_____

11. a. Are you willing and able to engage in necessary business socializing? _____

b. Is your wife? _____

c. What do the answers to these questions say about your needs? _____

_____

12. a. Are you willing and able to "butter up" important people to advance your career? _____

b. Is your wife? _____

c. What do the answers to these questions say about your needs? _____

_____

IV. NEEDS, GOALS, AND PLANS

Re-read all of your previous answers and think carefully about them. Then carefully answer the following questions:

1. Look at the list of needs at the beginning of the questionnaire. Rank them in the order of their importance to you. Needs which have more than one part (such as status) can be broken down if you feel differently about each part. For example, if social acceptance from your associates is much more important than social acceptance from your subordinates, rank them separately._____

1.	_____	13.	_____
2.	_____	14.	_____
3.	_____	15.	_____
4.	_____	16.	_____
5.	_____	17.	_____
6.	_____	18.	_____
7.	_____	19.	_____
8.	_____	20.	_____
9.	_____	21.	_____
10.	_____	22.	_____
11.	_____	23.	_____
12.	_____	24.	_____

2. There are many factors to be considered for any career choice (e.g. duties, title, income, superiors, location, firm, travel). On a blank sheet of paper list all of the factors which

you feel are important to you (and to your wife if you sincerely intend to allow her wishes to influence your decisions). Then arrange them in order of their importance to you on that sheet. When you have completed putting them in order, write them in the spaces below. (1. = most important, etc.)

1. _____	6. _____	11. _____
2. _____	7. _____	12. _____
3. _____	8. _____	13. _____
4. _____	9. _____	14. _____
5. _____	10. _____	15. _____

3.   If these are your priorities, how can you best meet them? That is, what do you really want to do with your career?

a. Now: _____

b. In 5 years: _____

c. In 10 years: _____

d. Ultimately: _____

APPENDIX 5:
YOUR PERSONAL
BALANCE SHEET

Directions

1. Rate yourself on each characteristic. All ratings should compare you to people in the same position as you, not to the general public. You aren't competing with them any more.

   −2 means much poorer
   −1 means poorer
    0 means equal
    1 means better
    2 means much better

2. Then enter the characteristic and ratings on PBS-1. Minus ratings go in the Liabilities column. Plus ratings go in the Assets column. Zero ratings can be left out or put in either the Assets or Liabilities column depending on your opinion of whether being average here

will hurt or help your career. PBS-1 then gives you an overall picture of your assets and liabilities.
3. Then go to PBS-2.
   A. List your Assets and ways to take advantage of them.
   B. List your Fixed Liabilities and ways to compensate for them. Fixed Liabilities are characteristics which you cannot change such as your IQ or energy level.
   C. List your Changeable Liabilities and ways you can make these changes. Changeable liabilities are characteristics you can change such as your education or experience.
4. Discuss your PBS with two people, a friend and an older person. Get their opinion of your personal ratings and plans. Write their comments on PBS-3.

CHARACTERISTICS AND RATINGS

Characteristic	*Rating*
1. Technical competence	___
2. Administrative knowledge and ability	___
3. Marketing knowledge and ability	___
4. Supervisory skill	___
5. Oral communication skill	___
6. Written communication skill	___
7. Ambition	___
8. Energy level	___
9. Originality	___
10. Sociability	___
11. Broad perspective	___
12. Sense of humor	___
13. Desire to excel	___
14. Business judgment	___
15. Cooperativeness	___
16. Ability to budget time wisely	___
17. Formal education	___

18. Special training
    (identify)   _____   —
19. Ability to organize other
    people   —
20. Other characteristics
    (list and rate)

    _____   —
    _____   —
    _____   —
    _____   —
    _____   —
    _____   —

PBS-1

Date_____

Assets

Liabilities

PBS-2

I. Assets

List your assets and indicate briefly how you can use them most effectively.

Asset   Use

_____   _____
_____   _____
_____   _____
_____   _____
_____   _____
_____   _____
_____   _____
_____   _____
_____   _____
_____   _____
_____   _____
_____   _____
_____   _____
_____   _____
_____   _____
_____   _____
_____   _____
_____   _____
_____   _____
_____   _____
_____   _____
_____   _____
_____   _____
_____   _____
_____   _____
_____   _____
_____   _____

PBS-2

II. Fixed Liabilities

List the liabilities you can't change and indicate briefly how you can compensate for them. For example, a man who is weak at detail work can get a good assistant and delegate most of it.

Fixed Liability   Compensation

_____   _____
_____   _____
_____   _____
_____   _____
_____   _____
_____   _____
_____   _____
_____   _____
_____   _____
_____   _____
_____   _____
_____   _____
_____   _____
_____   _____
_____   _____
_____   _____
_____   _____
_____   _____
_____   _____
_____   _____
_____   _____
_____   _____
_____   _____
_____   _____

PBS-2

III. Changeable Liabilities

List the liabilities you can do something about and indicate briefly what you intend to do. For example, communication skills can be improved by courses.

Changeable Liability   Corrective Action

_____   _____
_____   _____
_____   _____
_____   _____
_____   _____
_____   _____
_____   _____
_____   _____
_____   _____
_____   _____
_____   _____
_____   _____
_____   _____
_____   _____
_____   _____
_____   _____
_____   _____
_____   _____
_____   _____
_____   _____
_____   _____
_____   _____

PBS-3

Comments from a friend and an older person.

This part of the process should provide you with a more objective view of yourself and your plans.

The important thing is not to complete a form; it is to have an open and frank discussion. PBS-3 is simply to help you to record the main points made in that discussion and should therefore be completed during or after these discussions. Make special note of any disagreements with your ratings or suggestions for action.

Comments by older person

Comments by friend

APPENDIX 6:
THE OPPORTUNITY
ANALYSIS QUESTIONNAIRE

The questions raised here are far from easy, especially the ones about the effects of certain factors on your career. You may be unable to answer some of these questions, and you may even get annoyed at the repetition of "How does this affect your career?" Your annoyance is understandable; it is irritating to be asked a question you cannot answer, especially such a vague one. But this vague question is essential. It helps you to relate facts about industries and companies to your career, and thinking this way clarifies your real opportunities. So answer as many questions as you can, even if you have to consult other sources. *Executive Career Strategy* explains the career implications of many of these issues and lists many other sources.

When you get tired and irritated, put it down for a while. Opportunity analysis takes a long time and a complete analysis cannot be rushed.

This questionnaire does not directly compare different situations.

If you are considering more than one situation, you should answer these questions for each one, but leave out the key questions. Just use blank paper and number your answers. After you have completed the questionnaire for each situation, turn to the *Offer Comparison Form* in the next appendix. It describes a procedure for comparing situations and provides a form to simplify the comparison process.

I. OPPORTUNITIES IN THIS INDUSTRY

1. a. Name of industry _____
   b. How profitable is this industry compared to other industries? _____
   _____
   c. How does this affect your career? _____

2. a. How rapidly has this industry grown in past ten years? (If possible, in annual per cent increase in both profits and sales.) _____
   _____
   b. How does this affect your career? _____
   _____

3. a. How does the past growth rate in this industry compare to the growth rate of the rest of the economy? _____
   b. How does this affect your career? _____

4. a. What rate of future growth can this industry expect? (Answer in percentage of sales growth per year if possible.)
   _____
   b. Why do you expect this rate of growth? What will cause this growth? _____
   _____
   c. How does this affect your career? _____
   _____

5. a. How do the future growth prospects of this industry compare to those of the rest of the economy? _____
   b. Why are the growth prospects different? _____
   _____

   c. How does this affect your career? _____
_____

6. a. How well does this industry pay compared to other indus-
      tries? _____

   b. How does this affect your career? _____
_____

7. a. How many firms dominate this industry? _____
   b. How does this affect your career? _____
_____

8. a. What other industries would value experience in this in-
      dustry? _____

   b. Why? _____
_____

9. a. How dependent is this industry upon government policies
      and actions, especially defense-related contracts? _____

   b. How does this affect your career? _____
_____

10. a. What would be the effect upon this industry of a great
       decrease in military or governmental spending? _____
    b. How probable is such a decrease? _____
    c. When would it probably occur? _____
    d. How does this affect your career? _____
_____

11. a. How dependent is this industry on the economic cycle?
_____
_____

    b. What part of the cycle is it in now? _____
    c. How does this affect your career? _____
_____

12. a. What is the prestige of this industry compared to other
       industries? _____
    b. How does this affect your career? _____
_____

13. a. Is this industry centered in one region? _____
    b. What region? _____

    c. Do you care to live there? _____

    d. How does this affect your career? _____

    _____

14. a. Do you value the products or services provided by this industry? _____

    _____

    b. How does this affect your career? _____

    _____

Review the answers to your previous questions, think carefully about them and then answer the following questions.

15. a. Which goals will you probably reach in this industry?

    _____

    b. Why? _____

    c. Which goals will you probably be unable to reach? __

    _____

    d. Why? _____

    e. How will this affect your career? _____

    _____

16. a. Is this the right industry for you? _____

    b. Why? _____

    _____

17. a. If this is not the right industry, which ones would be better? _____

    _____

    b. Why? _____

II. OPPORTUNITIES IN THE COMPANY

1. a. Name of company _____

    b. How profitable is this company compared to its industry?

    _____

    c. How does this affect your career? _____

    _____

2. a. What is the financial position of this firm? _____

    b. How does this affect your career? _____

    _____

3. a. At what rate has this firm increased its profits and sales for

the past ten years? (Answer in percentage increase per year if possible.) _____

b. How does the growth compare to the rest of the industry's growth? _____

_____

c. What are the causes for this difference? _____

_____

d. How does this affect your career? _____

_____

4. a. At what rate will this firm increase its sales in the future? (Answer in percentage points per year if possible.) ____

_____

b. Why do you expect this rate of growth? What will cause it? _____

c. How does this affect your career? _____

_____

5. a. Does this firm sell to only a few customers? _____
   b. Are these customers' needs growing, declining, or remaining constant? _____
   c. Are these customers developing other suppliers or can they easily do so? _____
   d. Is the firm developing new markets? _____
   e. How does this affect your career? _____

_____

6. a. Is this firm dependent upon the sales of one or a small group of products or services? _____
   b. How does this affect your career? _____

_____

7. a. Is this firm diversifying? _____
   b. How (by mergers, by developing new products, or by some other strategy?) _____
   c. If it is diversifying, is it diversifying into areas in which your skills and background will be valued? _____
   d. Can experience with this company open doors to several industries? _____
   e. How does this affect your career? _____

_____

8. a. How many new products has this firm introduced in the past ten years? _____

   b. How many new products does it intend to introduce in the near future? _____

   c. How does its development of new products compare, both quantitatively and qualitatively, to that of similar sized companies in the same industry? _____

   d. How does this affect your career? _____

9. a. What is the position of this firm in the industry? ___

   b. How many firms would value experience or training in this firm? _____

   c. Which firms? _____

   d. How does this affect your career? _____

10. a. What is the prestige of this firm? _____

    b. How does this affect your career? _____

11. a. Where is the home office located? _____

    b. How does this affect your career? _____

12. a. To what degree is this firm dependent upon government actions and policies, especially defense-related contracts? _____

    b. How does this affect your career? _____

13. a. To what degree is this firm dependent upon the economic cycle? _____

    b. How does this affect your career? _____

14. a. Do you value the products or services it provides? ___

    b. How does this affect your career? _____

Review your answers to the previous questions, think carefully, and then answer the following questions.

15. a. Which goals will you probably reach in this company?
    _____
    b. Why?   _____
    c. Which goals will you probably be unable to reach?   __
    _____
    d. Why?   _____
    e. How will this affect your career?   _____
    _____
16. a. Is this the right company for you?   _____
    b. Why?   _____
17. a. If this is not the right company for you, which companies would be better? _____
    b. Why?   _____

III. OPPORTUNITIES IN THIS MAJOR UNIT

Name of unit   _____
1. a. Is this unit a profit center?   _____
   b. How does this affect your career?   _____
   _____
2. a. Is it part of another unit which is a profit center?   ____
   (If so, it may be a good idea to answer these questions for both units.)
3. a. If it is a profit center, does it have a good profitability record? _____
   b. How does this affect your career?   _____
   _____
4. a. What is this unit's purpose?   _____
   b. Are the problems it is trying to solve important to top management?   _____
   _____
   c. How does this affect your career?   _____
   _____
5.   What is the relationship of this unit to parent company?
    _____
    _____

6. a. What is this unit's reputation with top management? __

   b. How does this affect your career? _____

7. a. How independent is the management of this unit? ____
   b. How does this affect your career? _____

8. a. Can you move upward from this unit to the parent company? _____
   b. Are these promotions desirable? _____
   c. Where else can you move? _____
   d. How does this affect your career? _____

9. a. Into what jobs and units have men from this unit been promoted or transferred? _____
   b. Do these jobs and units appeal to you? _____
   c. Where do you expect to go from this unit? _____
   d. If you expect to go to a place which the others have not gone, why do you expect to go there? _____

10. a. Is the road to the top of this unit blocked? _____
    b. How and why is it blocked? _____
    c. How does this affect your career? _____

11. a. To what degree are your skills and background valued in this unit? _____
    b. How does this affect your career? _____

12. a. Where is the top management of this unit located? __
    b. How does this affect your career? _____

13. a. How dependent is this unit on government actions or policies, especially defense-related contracts? _____
    b. How does this affect your career? _____

14. a. How dependent is this unit on the business cycle? ____

    b. How does this affect your career? _____

15. a. Do you value the products or services provided by this unit? _____

_____

   b. How does this affect your career? _____

_____

Review your answers to the previous questions, think carefully, and then answer the following questions:

16. a. What goals will you probably reach in this unit? _____

   b. Why? _____

   c. Which goals will you probably be unable to reach in this unit? _____

_____

   d. Why? _____

   e. How does this affect your career? _____

_____

17. a. Is this the right unit for you? _____

   b. Why? _____

18. a. If this is not the right unit for you, what unit would be better? _____

   b. Why? _____

_____

   c. Can you transfer to it? _____

   d. How? _____

IV. OPPORTUNITIES OFFERED BY THE JOB

(Some of these questions should stimulate questions during the interview; you have no other way to answer them).

1. a. How much do you like this job (in general)? _____
   b. Why? _____
2. a. How much do you like the pay? _____
   b. Why? _____
3.   How does your pay compare to other people reporting to the same boss? _____
4. a. How much do you like the fringe benefits? _____
   b. Why? _____

5. a. How much do you like the hours and schedule? _____
   b. Why? _____

6. a. Do the hours and schedule allow you enough time with your family? _____

   _____
   b. Does this bother you? _____

7. a. How much do you like the amount of company travel?

   _____
   b. Why? _____

8. a. How much do you like the superiors? _____
   b. Why? _____

9. a. How much do you like the associates? _____
   b. Why? _____

10. a. How much do you like the duties and responsibilities?

    _____
    b. Why? _____

11. a. What are the best things about it? _____

    _____
    b. Other things you really like? _____

    _____

12. a. What are the worst things about it? _____

    _____
    b. Other things you don't like? _____

    _____

13. a. How many people who have had this job have gone on to bigger things? _____
    b. Who are they? _____
    c. How high have they gone? _____
    d. How did they advance? _____
    e. How does this affect your career? _____

    _____

14. a. How many people who have had this job have moved to other jobs which you would rather have, but which are not considered significantly higher than your present job?
    b. Who are they? _____
    c. Where have they gone? _____
    d. What does this mean for your career? _____

    _____

15. a. How many people who are important to your future *can* you contact if you utilize all the possibilities of this job?

_____

_____

   b. Who are they?   _____

   c. What does this mean for your career?   _____

_____

Review your answers to the previous questions, think carefully, and then answer the following questions:

16. a. How good is this job in itself (that is, ignoring the possibilities for advancement to other positions)?   _____

_____

   b. Why?   _____

17. a. How good is it as a stepping stone to jobs you want?

_____

   b. What are these jobs?   _____

   c. How good are your chances of getting them?   _____

18. a. What goals will you probably reach on this job?   _____

_____

   b. Why?   _____

   c. Which goals will you probably be unable to reach in this job?   _____

_____

   d. Why?   _____

   e. How does this affect your career?   _____

_____

19. a. Is this the right job for you?   _____

   b. Why?   _____

20. a. If not, what job would be better?   _____

   b. Why?   _____

APPENDIX 7:
OFFER COMPARISON
FORM

This form is simply a guide to help you to compare your offers on many dimensions. Your decision is difficult because so many factors are involved and you cannot directly compare different factors. You cannot say how many dollars in salary equal more interesting work, nor can you compare a good location with a bad boss.

This form attempts to reduce this problem by converting comparisons between companies on each factor into ranks, then multiplying these ranks by the weight you feel each dimension deserves. You then add up the weighted ranks to get the over-all dominant alternative.

You may find, however, that this procedure yields a result which conflicts with your own "gut feelings." It indicates that one job is best, while you prefer another.

This conflict provides an opportunity to learn something about yourself or your opportunities. You have either failed to include something that is important to you, or have made an incorrect ranking, or assigned the wrong weight to some dimension. You should therefore analyze the comparison process to see where things went wrong. Then, as you change weights or ranks or add other dimensions, you learn more about what the offers really mean and what you really want.

DIRECTIONS

1. Put the name of the company in place. To keep things simple, compare only offers which you are seriously considering.

2. Go to the Goal Analysis Questionnaire, question IV, 2, (the factors to be considered for any career choice). Write down the factors in the same order in which you have ranked them. Their ranks equal their weights. However, if you feel that these rankings are not the weights you want to give to different factors, make whatever changes you wish. Remember, because the basic procedure uses ranks, the *smaller* the number, the *greater* the weight. Insert the ranks or other weights in the "Weights" column.

3. Rank each company on each dimension.

4. For each company, and each factor, multiply the rank times the weight.

5. Add up the weighted ranks. The lowest score is the best offer. However, if one score is very close to the lowest score, it might be wise to re-do the entire procedure using only these two offers.

6. If the "best offer" agrees with your "gut feeling", your problem is over. If it does not agree, analyze your feelings and the comparison process. You do not want to throw out your intuition, but you also do not want to rely upon it completely. The idea is to understand your own feelings and to make your decisions conscious and explicit. To do this add dimensions or change ranks or

weights until the offer with the lowest score seems right to you. Then look at the entire process to see where and why you made an earlier mistake. This analysis can greatly improve your understanding of yourself and the situation.

DECISION COMPARISON FORM

Name of Companies

Rank	Factors	Weight	Rank	RxW	Rank	RxW	Rank	RxW	Rank	RxW	Rank	RxW	Rank	RxW
1.	___	___	___	___	___	___	___	___	___	___	___	___	___	___
2.	___	___	___	___	___	___	___	___	___	___	___	___	___	___
3.	___	___	___	___	___	___	___	___	___	___	___	___	___	___
4.	___	___	___	___	___	___	___	___	___	___	___	___	___	___
5.	___	___	___	___	___	___	___	___	___	___	___	___	___	___
6.	___	___	___	___	___	___	___	___	___	___	___	___	___	___
7.	___	___	___	___	___	___	___	___	___	___	___	___	___	___
8.	___	___	___	___	___	___	___	___	___	___	___	___	___	___
9.	___	___	___	___	___	___	___	___	___	___	___	___	___	___
10.	___	___	___	___	___	___	___	___	___	___	___	___	___	___
11.	___	___	___	___	___	___	___	___	___	___	___	___	___	___
12.	___	___	___	___	___	___	___	___	___	___	___	___	___	___
13.	___	___	___	___	___	___	___	___	___	___	___	___	___	___
14.	___	___	___	___	___	___	___	___	___	___	___	___	___	___
15.	___	___	___	___	___	___	___	___	___	___	___	___	___	___
Total RxW				___		___		___		___		___		___

INDEX